"This book on the perennial and fateful paradox of cognitive dissonance is a philosophical *tour de force*. It skillfully lays out the general structure of the problems of 'self-deception', integrating philosophical analysis with relevant work in the social sciences. This makes the author's own critique especially illuminating. It deserves to become a standard work."

—*David Pugmire, University of Southampton, UK*

"This is a superb book, ideal for anyone looking for an accessible and systematic introduction to the philosophy and psychology of self-deception. It is well organised, beautifully written, and does a wonderful job of addressing the key issues surrounding this puzzling phenomenon."

—*Ema Sullivan-Bissett, University of Birmingham, UK*

SELF-DECEPTION

Self-deception poses longstanding and fascinating paradoxes. Philosophers have questioned whether, and how, self-deception is even possible; evolutionary theorists have debated whether it is adaptive. For Sigmund Freud self-deception was a fundamental key to understanding the unconscious, and from *The Bible* to *The Great Gatsby* literature abounds with characters renowned for their self-deception. But what exactly is self-deception? Why is it so puzzling? How is it performed? And is it harmful?

In this thorough and clearly written introduction to the philosophy and psychology of self-deception, Eric Funkhouser examines and assesses these questions and more:

- Clarification of the conceptual background and "Basic Problem" of self-deception, including Freud and Davidson and the important debate between intentionalists and motivationalists
- Deflationary accounts that appeal to cognitive and motivational biases, with emphasis on how motives and emotions drive self-deception
- Intentional self-deception and the "divided mind," including the role of the unconscious in recent psychological research
- Challenges that self-deception poses for philosophy of mind and psychology, especially for our understanding of intention, belief, and deception
- Biology and moral psychology of self-deception: Is self-deception functional or beneficial? Are the self-deceived to be held accountable?

Combining philosophical analysis with the latest psychological research, and including features such as chapter summaries, annotated recommended reading and a glossary, *Self-Deception* is an excellent resource for students of philosophy of mind and psychology, moral psychology and ethics, as well as those in related fields such as psychology and cognitive science.

Eric Funkhouser is a Professor in the Philosophy Department at the University of Arkansas, USA. He is the author of *The Logical Structure of Kinds* (2014).

NEW PROBLEMS OF PHILOSOPHY

Series Editor: José Luis Bermúdez

"*New Problems of Philosophy* is developing a most impressive line-up of topical volumes aimed at graduate and upper-level undergraduate students in philosophy and at others with interests in cutting edge philosophical work. Series authors are players in their respective fields and notably adept at synthesizing and explaining intricate topics fairly and comprehensively."

—*John Heil, Monash University, Australia, and Washington University in St. Louis, USA*

"This is an outstanding collection of volumes. The topics are well chosen and the authors are outstanding. They will be fine texts in a wide range of courses."

—*Stephen Stich, Rutgers University, USA*

The New Problems of Philosophy series provides accessible and engaging surveys of the most important problems in contemporary philosophy. Each book examines either a topic or theme that has emerged on the philosophical landscape in recent years, or a longstanding problem refreshed in light of recent work in philosophy and related disciplines. Clearly explaining the nature of the problem at hand and assessing attempts to answer it, books in the series are excellent starting points for undergraduate and graduate students wishing to study a single topic in depth. They will also be essential reading for professional philosophers. Additional features include chapter summaries, further reading and a glossary of technical terms.

The Metaphysics of Identity
André Gallois

Consciousness
Rocco J. Gennaro

Abstract Entities
Sam Cowling

Embodied Cognition, Second Edition
Lawrence Shapiro

Self-Deception
Eric Funkhouser

For more information about this series, please visit: https://www.routledge.com/New-Problems-of-Philosophy/book-series/NPOP

SELF-DECEPTION

Eric Funkhouser

LONDON AND NEW YORK

First published 2019
by Routledge
2 Park Square, Milton Park, Abingdon, Oxon OX14 4RN

and by Routledge
52 Vanderbilt Avenue, New York, NY 10017

Routledge is an imprint of the Taylor & Francis Group, an informa business

© 2019 Eric Funkhouser

The right of Eric Funkhouser to be identified as author of this work has been asserted by him in accordance with sections 77 and 78 of the Copyright, Designs and Patents Act 1988.

All rights reserved. No part of this book may be reprinted or reproduced or utilised in any form or by any electronic, mechanical, or other means, now known or hereafter invented, including photocopying and recording, or in any information storage or retrieval system, without permission in writing from the publishers.

Trademark notice: Product or corporate names may be trademarks or registered trademarks, and are used only for identification and explanation without intent to infringe.

British Library Cataloguing-in-Publication Data
A catalogue record for this book is available from the British Library

Library of Congress Cataloging-in-Publication Data
Names: Funkhouser, Eric, author.
Title: Self-deception / Eric Funkhouser.
Description: Abingdon, Oxon ; New York, NY : Routledge, 2019. | Series: New problems of philosophy | Includes bibliographical references and index.
Identifiers: LCCN 2019006148 | ISBN 9781138506114 (hardback : alk. paper) | ISBN 9781138506121 (pbk. : alk. paper) | ISBN 9781315146782 (ebook)
Subjects: LCSH: Self-deception.
Classification: LCC BD439 .F86 2019 | DDC 128—dc23
LC record available at https://lccn.loc.gov/2019006148

ISBN: 978-1-138-50611-4 (hbk)
ISBN: 978-1-138-50612-1 (pbk)
ISBN: 978-1-315-14678-2 (ebk)

Typeset in Joanna and Scala Sans
by codeMantra

 Printed in the United Kingdom by Henry Ling Limited

To Erika, for showing me new possibilities

CONTENTS

Acknowledgements	xi

1   Introduction   1

1.1	Self-deception: common, yet puzzling	3
1.2	Psychological tendencies	8
1.3	Why study self-deception?	16

2   The Basic Problem and a conceptual map   25

2.1	The Basic Problem	26
	2.1.1 Static problems	31
	2.1.2 Dynamic problems	34
2.2	A classic picture: Freud and Davidson	40
2.3	A minimal conception: motivated irrationality	50
	2.3.1 Intentionalism and motivationalism	54
	2.3.2 Degrees of deception	60
2.4	What is the content of the motive? What is the proximate goal?	64
2.5	What is the end state?	71
2.6	Conceptual map	73
2.7	Nearby phenomena	77

3   Deflationary accounts   85

3.1	Motivated bias accounts: eliminating intention	86
3.2	Mele's account	88
3.3	Psychological details	93
	3.3.1 Biases, hot and cold	94
	3.3.2 Hypothesis framing and confirmation biases	95
	3.3.3 Belief thresholds and errors	96

X CONTENTS

3.4	Issues with psychological measures	102
3.5	Objections	110
	3.5.1 Negative self-deception	110
	3.5.2 The selectivity problem	112
	3.5.3 Is this even deception?	114
	3.5.4 Tension is necessary	119
3.6	Anxiety-based deflationary accounts	129

4 Intentionalism and divided mind accounts   **135**

4.1	Intentionalism: the general case	137
	4.1.1 What are intentions?	137
	4.1.2 The case for intentions	140
	4.1.3 Connection to divided minds	144
4.2	Divided mind accounts	147
	4.2.1 Conscious and unconscious	147
	4.2.2 Distinct functional units	158
4.3	Temporally divided selves	163
4.4	Other intentionalist and dual belief views	166

5 Revisionary accounts: belief and purpose   **171**

5.1	Revising belief	172
	5.1.1 Subdoxastic attitudes	173
	5.1.2 Partial or indeterminate belief	176
	5.1.3 Thought, acceptance, imagination, and pretense	178
	5.1.4 Suspicion, anxiety, and fear	185
5.2	Biological accounts: non-psychological purposiveness	186
5.3	Signaling accounts	193
	5.3.1 Self-signaling	193
	5.3.2 Other-signaling	195
5.4	Social influences on self-deception	197

6 Responsibility for self-deception   **203**

6.1	The ethics of belief	203
6.2	Self-knowledge	210
6.3	Rationality and responsibility	216
6.4	Does context matter?	222

7 Functions and cost-benefit analysis   **227**

7.1	The costs of false belief	228
7.2	Psychological benefits	231
7.3	Social benefits	236
7.4	Biological benefits	243

8 Conclusion   **248**

8.1	Future directions	249
8.2	Warning	253

Glossary	254
Bibliography	258
Index	271

ACKNOWLEDGEMENTS

My philosophical interest and research on self-deception began over 20 years ago, when I was a graduate student at Syracuse University. As with my first book, it started with a paper in a seminar taught by Tamar Gendler. That is when I first came to appreciate the philosophical problems of self-deception, as well as develop my own positive views. I especially remember prolonged and passionate discussions with my then fellow graduate student Steffen Borge, who was always adamant that there is no such thing as *genuine* self-deception. I, in contrast, thought it was *obvious* that self-deception occurs. I also believed that one of the jobs of philosophy is to teach people how to resist the human tendency to escape reality and indulge fantasies. But, as I hope this book shows, I recognize that the terrain of self-deception is by no means well-marked. (I hope this work goes some way toward marking off this terrain – pointing out the "natural" divisions, landmarks, precipices, and other obstacles.) And I now see positive value in at least some types of self-deception.

Over the last 15 years I have written a series of articles on self-deception, discovering that piecemeal treatments are the norm and that theorists have quite different understandings of what it even means to be self-deceived. These writers also disagree about what makes self-deception so interesting or problematic. But all are apparently equally confident that their understanding of the phenomenon is correct. In light of this, I came to appreciate the need for a systematic, broad treatment of the possible philosophical and psychological responses to the various problems of self-deception so that we could at least have a common starting point. I was very pleased, then, when Tony Bruce first approached and invited me to write a book – originally on the more specific relationship between self-deception and the unconscious – for Routledge. The original proposal was much narrower than what we find here, and I am grateful that series editor José Bermudez recommended this broader approach on the wider range of "new problems" of self-deception. I owe a great debt to the reviewers of my book proposal, and then especially to the three very thorough and insightful referees who reported on the completed manuscript. My thanks also to Helen Baxter for her judicious assistance with copyediting.

Finally, I would like to thank the University of Arkansas for the institutional support it has provided me on this project. My chair, Ed Minar, graciously arranged for me to teach our spring 2018 capstone course for philosophy majors on the topic of self-deception, which allowed me to present much of this material to a target audience. I benefited from those exchanges, as well as from several discussions with my colleague Trip Glazer and graduate student Robert Ragsdale. I also have great appreciation for the Fulbright College Humanities Summer Stipend that I received in the summer of 2018 to support the writing of this book.

1

INTRODUCTION

1.1 **Self-deception: common, yet puzzling**
1.2 **Psychological tendencies**
1.3 **Why study self-deception?**

Many of us tend to think that the work we do has special importance, if only because we want to believe this. So perhaps it is a bit of self-deceit on my part, but I believe that the topic of *self-deception* – roughly, failing to believe what the evidence indicates you should believe (and perhaps even believing contrary to it), because you are motivated or make an effort to do so – should have special importance within philosophy. As I understand the philosophical enterprise, at its core philosophy involves *reflecting* on our beliefs, wants, and values and then *rationally* scrutinizing and adjusting what we find. It is the love of wisdom. Self-deception is a real threat to the philosophical enterprise – and perhaps a real threat to leading a good human life, as well – because it is a failure of both reflection and rationality. The self-deceived are not appropriately examining their beliefs and making rational adjustments.

On the positive side, the phenomenon of self-deception introduces a host of philosophical and psychological problems for us to study toward the end of gaining a better understanding of the human mind, rationality, and our

2 INTRODUCTION

well-being. Philosophy benefits from having problems to solve and difficult questions to answer. How can a mind suppress the truth? How can wanting to believe something contribute to making it happen? What does all this say about the structure of the mind, the nature of belief, and the extent to which we are – and must be – rational? Are we best served by always pursuing the truth or loving wisdom, anyway?

Self-deception is not merely of theoretical interest; it is deeply important for practical life. If we have a predilection toward self-deception, then this tendency can be exploited by ill-intentioned advertisers, political propagandists, as well as friends and lovers. A beer company can indulge a man's self-deceptive fantasy about his appeal to the opposite sex; a political website offers you "fake news" that confirms your own biases and prejudices; an alluring romantic prospect leads you to self-deceive regarding the kind of relationship and family life you would enjoy. Self-deception can certainly be dangerous in itself to the extent that it takes us away from the truth yet still guides our actions. It can also be dangerous by making us more vulnerable to manipulation by others.

This opening chapter provides an informal introduction to some of the problems of self-deception and the psychological tendencies that incline us to self-deceive. The chapter closes by explaining some of the theoretical and practical reasons why one might be interested in studying self-deception in the first place. Beginning in Chapter 2, we will treat these problems with greater technical rigor. Chapter 2 more rigorously charts the terrain of self-deception: its basic problems, its driving motives, and its purported end states. Chapters 3–5 present and evaluate the most prominent and promising positive accounts of self-deception that have been offered to address these problems and questions. These are accounts that appeal to motivational biases, divide the mind, or introduce nuanced purposes and states of mind. In Chapters 6 and 7, we will consider the person's responsibility for their self-deception, as well as engage in a bit of cost-benefit reckoning to see how dangerous self-deception is or if it could even be advantageous.

Our focus throughout will be primarily on the *philosophical* problems of self-deception, using the various methods of philosophy. These include: *investigating critical concepts* such as belief, deception, and self; *exploring the limits of rationality*, especially as this relates to posessessing contradictory beliefs, engaging in projects aimed at misleading the self, and the influences of non-rational factors on belief; *distinguishing different degrees of human agency*, especially in our capacity as epistemic agents; breaking down the process

INTRODUCTION 3

of self-deception into its logical parts and charting (and assessing) the possibilities in psychological space. These are all familiar philosophical topics and tools. That being said, we will also turn to psychology and even biology as we search for answers to our questions about why and how self-deception occurs. The approach taken here aspires to have philosophical investigation work in concert with empirical investigation.

§1.1 Self-deception: common, yet puzzling

This book approaches the topic of self-deception from many angles: What is it? How is it possible? How do we execute it? What purposes does it serve? Is it beneficial or harmful? Is it laudable or condemnable?

Self-deception is normally viewed as a negative, something to be criticized and looked down on. It even seems a bit perverse that we deceive ourselves, nevertheless it is so common that there likely is some pleasure or benefit to it. But what is the thrill or the reason for which we trick ourselves? It is obvious how we humans, as well as other animals, could benefit from lying to or tricking *others*: We can exploit them. Lying is a malicious weapon belonging to the same general category as theft and assault, each of which can have positive strategic value if one can get away with it. Of course, these things are immoral; but Mother Nature does not care. It seems that lying to your-*self*, however, would be no more beneficial than stealing from or assaulting yourself. How foolish! (Or maybe not! In §5.2 and §7.3, we will evaluate the biological advantages and costs of self-deception when we turn to Robert Trivers's famous theory that we self-deceive in order to better deceive others.)

Neither is it clear that it is even possible to execute. If we take the word at face value, it would seem that self-deception is the deception of the self by the self (for the self?). In some sense, it is lying to or tricking yourself about some truth. We know how easy it can be to deceive someone *else*: You come home late and lie to your mother, claiming that you were doing something other than going out drinking with your friends. The deception succeeds because your mother is not aware of the facts – the outrageous bar tab and the various concoctions imbibed. Neither is she aware of your intention to mislead. But how could you possibly succeed at lying to *yourself* about that? You know the truth and are well-acquainted with the evidence. Hiding the truth from yourself seems like a hopeless task, akin to tickling yourself. It cannot work because, unlike your mother, you know *exactly* what you are up to. But yet in self-deception, somehow the left hand does not know what the right hand is doing.

INTRODUCTION

Suppose that, unlike your mother who is simply in the dark, your father *is* self-deceived about your behavior. He knows more than your mother does, yet he is unwilling to face the truth. Father blames your partying ways on your peer group – they are to blame for your self-destructive behavior. Yet if he were not your father he would see that, if anything, *you* are the bad influence in the group. His desire to think well of you clouds his judgment, motivating his self-deception and causing him to lose objectivity. If you were somebody else's son, he would think quite differently. But, as it is, he focuses only on your friends' flaws, blocking out (forgetting, avoiding, downplaying) what he knows to be your poor choices. He knows the truth in at least some sense – he is not completely detached from reality – yet in many regards it is as if he does not know. His mind avoids certain thoughts and facts, yet he knows *exactly* what to avoid. He says that he trusts you, yet he makes sure not to leave money lying around. Here we see telltale marks of self-deception: irrationality, division, and contradiction. Left hand, right hand.

As we will see beginning in Chapter 2, one of the central roblems of self-deception is demonstrating *how all this is even possible*. This is a peculiarly philosophical task: showing how something that we know to be actual is even possible![1] Nevertheless, this kind of task arises in various domains and across philosophical history. Zeno of Elea famously gave us paradoxes – stories like the one about Achilles and the tortoise – which purport to show that motion is impossible. Zeno apparently thought that these stories actually demonstrated the impossibility of motion, but for most of us they issue a challenge to show how motion is possible while granting that, of course, it occurs. Many philosophers have also wondered how free will can possibly exist (in either a deterministic or indeterministic world) or how consciousness could arise from matter. Of course, some do deny that these things are truly possible, but for many others these questions challenge us to demonstrate *how* they could be possible even though we assume their actuality. Answering such paradoxes often sheds deep insight on the nature of the phenomenon – it *corrects* or *expands* our understanding.

Many, but by no means all, of the problems of self-deception are philosophical. Self-deception offends against two classical philosophical ideals in particular: the pursuit of truth and self-knowledge. First, the very word "philosophy" comes from the Greek word for "love of wisdom." Philosophers are widely supposed to value the pursuit of knowledge and truth. Yet self-deceivers are driven in the opposite direction, wanting ignorance or falsehood instead. The self-deceived fail to confront reality. Second, philosophers tend to value reflection and *self*-knowledge in particular. Plato had Socrates speak favorably of the Oracle at Delphi's injunction to "Know thyself!" This same oracle also famously proclaimed that no one is wiser than Socrates. Plato depicted Socrates as interpreting this claim, at his trial, in a way that fits nicely with valuing self-knowledge. Socrates's great wisdom, in contrast with what he found when questioning the supposedly wise men of Athens, consisted in knowing the limitations of his own knowledge:

> I am wiser than this man; it is likely that neither of us knows anything worthwhile, but he thinks he knows something when he does not, whereas when I do not know, neither do I think I know; so I am likely to be wiser than he to this small extent, that I do not think I know what I do not know. (Plato, 1997: *Apology* 21d)

Self-deceivers are not simply unaware that they have false beliefs; worse yet, they go out of their way to preserve this ignorance. (As we will discuss later, it seems impossible to be aware that you are self-deceived and maintain that state in full awareness.) Contrary to these philosophical ideals, the self-deceived seem to value or pursue falsehood and self-ignorance.

As with many philosophical topics, it is good to stock the mind with several examples. Literature is a particularly good source of detailed case studies into the human condition, and self-deception is certainly a core and univeral feature of humanity. Self-deception is a common, yet typically complex, psychological phenomenon that often generates a state of conflict or tension in response to a less than ideal world. It is no surprise, then, that it features prominently in many great works of world literature. Sometimes the self-deception is described as a simple process that has immediate effect. In Ernest Hemingway's *The Old Man and the Sea*, the protagonist Santiago aims to convince himself that, despite his advanced age and the long battle he has already waged against the great fish, he still has the strength to bring it into his boat:

> I am not good for many more turns. Yes you are, he told himself. You're good for ever. (Hemingway, 1952/2003: 92)

Santiago has a short-term goal – persevering at an arduous physical task – and he appears to accomplish it merely by reassuring himself, albeit with irrational optimism. Self-deception at the drop of a hat.

INTRODUCTION

But self-deception often requires more work than that. In the 17th Century, Blaise Pascal considered someone who takes a mathematical approach to the question of whether to believe in God. Calculating the expected payoffs for belief and disbelief, this person should "wager" that it is safer to believe in God (with the chance of eternal reward and the risk of merely wasting one's time) than it is to not believe (with the risk of eternal damnation and the scant gain of being able to sleep in on Sunday mornings). Yet she cannot succeed at believing this simply at will, as she can raise her arm at will. She needs to take an indirect route instead:

> Follow the way by which they began, by behaving just as if they believed, taking holy water, having masses said, etc. That will make you believe quite naturally, and according to your animal reactions. (Pascal, 1995: 156)

In short, Pascal recommended "fake it until you make it" – belief will eventually follow practice. Self-deception often demands quite systematic lifestyle choices. Think of the great efforts that James Gatz had to go to in order to convince himself that he was something more than a Midwestern boy of modest means; he was the Great Gatsby.

Literature and the world of letters more generally show us that self-deception can have broad scope, both in terms of its psychological implementation and its agenda. I remember visiting the Clinton Presidential Library and being struck by one book in particular taken from the bookshelf of Bill Clinton's youth: Ernest Becker's *The Denial of Death*. In that book, Becker argued that greatness requires living under a "vital lie," denying our own mortality by throwing ourselves into projects that can outlive our meager biological lives:

> The great boon of repression is that it makes it possible to live decisively in an overwhelmingly miraculous and incomprehensible world, a world so full of beauty, majesty, and terror that if animals perceived it all they would be paralyzed to act. (Becker, 1973/1997: 50)

Repression and lies at the heart of a meaningful life! It is not hard to imagine how this line of thought resonated with the ambitious mind of a future President. After his presidency, Clinton wrote:

> According to Becker, as we grow up, at some point we become aware of death, then the fact that people we know and love die, then the fact that

someday we, too, will die. Most of us do what we can to avoid it. Meanwhile, in ways we understand only dimly if at all, we embrace identities and the illusion of self-sufficiency. We pursue activities, both positive and negative, that we hope will lift us beyond the chains of ordinary existence and perhaps endure after we are gone. All this we do in a desperate push against the certainty that death is our ultimate destiny. Some of us seek power and wealth, others romantic love, sex, or some other indulgence. Some want to be great, others to do good and be good. Whether we succeed or fail, we are still going to die. The only solace, of course, is to believe that since we are created, there must be a Creator, one to whom we matter and will in some way return ... I've spent a lifetime trying to do that. Becker's book helped convince me it was an effort worth making. (Clinton, 2004: 235)

Clinton read the book on his honeymoon.

But do not think that self-deception is always driven by optimism or goodwill. In literature, as in life, the self-deceived are not always deceived in a favorable direction. Fyodor Dostoevsky was particularly adept at crafting characters who displayed psychological complexity with a negative orientation. For example, the narrator in Notes from the Underground rationalizes his inactivity and misery. He sees himself as superior to the "men of action," but simultaneously he is filled with self-loathing. His methods are perverse:

I thought up adventures for myself, I concocted a life for myself so that at least I could live somehow. How many times did it happen that – well, for example, that I took offence just like that, for no reason, deliberately! and after all, I used to know very well that I'd taken offence for no reason at all, that I was making a show of myself; but you carry on to such an extent that by the end, it's true, you really are offended. Somehow all my life I've been so attracted by this sort of game-playing that by the end I was no longer in control of myself. (Dostoevsky, 2008: 18–19)

We are likely to see the Underground Man's strategy for the pathetic defense mechanism that it is. He is not alone. Who knows why Dr. Seuss's the Grinch ended up as he did? The Wizard of Oz? Or Mr. Potter from It's a Wonderful Life? How many real life failures similarly attempt to comfort themselves with self-deceptive withdrawal, negativity, and externalization of blame?

§1.2 Psychological tendencies

Self-deception is driven by psychological and biological facts about human nature that transcend cultural variation; they are universal. Experimental cognitive and social psychology has confirmed what writers and amateur psychologists have long suspected: people tend to think better of themselves, their family, their friends, and the other groups to which they belong than an objective assessment of the evidence would warrant. People tend to be *biased* in various ways that either count as self-deception in their own right or which provide motives for it. Most of these biases are self-serving in some regard, and they show people as favoring beliefs skewed away from the real and toward the ideal, self-serving, or simply convenient. The following well-studied categories of such biases are especially relevant to self-deception:

> *Self-enhancement biases.* People tend to overestimate their positively valenced traits along a broad swath of dimensions. We disproportionately report being "better than average" along traits as diverse as: leadership, athleticism, sociability, material wealth, humanity, invulnerability, professional success, romantic success, happiness, and even our immunity to such biases. (Sedikides and Alicke, 2012: 307–308) For example, participants in experimental settings tended to select photographs of themselves that were morphed 20% with an ideally attractive face rather than selecting their true photograph. We see our faces as more attractive than they are, and as a result we literally fail to identify ourselves as we truly are. Significantly, this skewed self-perception is not completely delusional – e.g., in that study, it did not extend to 50% blends.[2]

> *In-group biases.* One's sense of self can also expand so as to include those with whom we identify: our kin, our close friends, and even arbitrary "in-groups." Indeed, we have a similar positivity bias in assessing those people whom we see as belonging to the same group as us (Tajfel and Turner, 2004). So, we should expect self-deception not only for our personal traits, but also regarding our children, religion, nation, etc.

> *Self-serving attribution biases.* In another unsurprising result, psychological research has shown that people tend to interpret events in a way that is self-serving. This effect is cross-cultural, although highly variable (Mezulis et al., 2004), suggesting that it is either part of our genetic endowment or has been independently discovered (individually or culturally) to be a

beneficial strategy or comforting mindset. Specifically, we tend to claim more responsibility for positive outcomes and externalize responsibility for negative outcomes. These biases also extend to our larger in-groups. (Hewstone, 1990)

In one of its most well-known forms, this general tendency manifests itself in what is known as *the fundamental attribution error* (Ross, 1977). When another person acts negatively, we tend to assign responsibility to that person's character traits rather than to external factors. But when we act negatively, we tend to put blame on external factors rather than attributing it to our poor character. (And, the converse holds for positive acts.) For example, if someone fails to reply to my email, I judge them to be an inconsiderate jerk. But if *I* fail to reply to someone's email, it is merely because I was distracted with other matters. This is clearly self-serving. Given these tendencies, we should expect self-deception aimed at mitigating our responsibility for various negative outcomes in our lives – e.g., I was not a professional success because nobody gave me a chance or they were out to get me, not because I was lazy or self-centered.

It is somewhat sad to note that those who are (moderately) depressed tend to have more accurate views when it comes to both self-assessment (Taylor and Brown, 1988: 196) and attribution (Mezulis et al., 2004).

Status quo biases. People tend to be conservative in the most general sense. They tend to think that it is better to just keep doing things the way that we currently do them – *status quo bias* (Samuelson and Zeckhauser, 1988) – and that what exists is better than what does not exist – *existence bias* (Eidelman, Crandall, and Pattershall, 2009). In short, we are motivated to conserve things as they are. So, we should expect self-deception when we consider and evaluate proposals for significant personal, institutional, economic, or political change.

Optimism. Looking toward the future, we also tend to overestimate the number of good outcomes that will befall us and underestimate the number of future bad outcomes. Again, this extends across a wide range of event types. It covers our estimates of things that merely could *happen to* us – like getting in a car accident or being diagnosed with cancer – and things that we can *actively control* to a significant extent (e.g., career success). This optimism bias covers predictions concerning the near future as well as events in the distant future – 50 years and beyond. (Sharot, 2011) So, we should also expect somewhat frequent self-deception regarding the future – e.g., the likelihood that our marriage will be a happy one, that our children will be particularly accomplished, or that our careers will be especially noteworthy.

Illusions of control. We also overestimate the extent to which we have control over outcomes. As Ellen Langer (1975) first showed, people often think they can influence outcomes when they have no causal connection to them (it is a matter of chance) and even when this fact should be clearly known. These overestimations are especially pronounced when elements associated with skill – such as competition – are present. This illusion explains self-deception about gambling behavior, as well as stock market successes and superstitious beliefs about the paranormal. It is important that people feel that they have control over their environment, and it is understandable that people would want to take credit especially for positive outcomes in their lives. So, we should expect self-deception concerning our abilities to control our environment and future.

These first six biases explain why we would self-deceive. They present us with motives: We want to think well of our traits, our group, our actions, our future, the present situation, and our autonomy. But we should also consider belief-forming tendencies that can partially explain how we achieve self-deception, even if these tendencies do not themselves provide us with a motive to self-deceive. Although the division between motives and means is not always clear-cut, let's consider three more biases that are frequently drawn on as means to achieve self-deception.

Memory biases. There are several memory biases that can affect our ability to selectively recall information or even modify (outright fabricating, in some cases) the information that we "recall." Such biases can be activated by the motives driving self-deception, in which case they are called "hot biases." We tend to selectively recall memories that are self-serving, and this is clearly a helpful means if our goal is to have a positive self-assessment or attribution. Specifically, we selectively remember our past decisions and the alternatives available to us at that time in a way that favors our past choices (*choice-supportive bias*). Mather, Shafir, and Johnson (2000) conducted studies in which participants were forced to choose among potential job candidates, blind dates, and roommates in narratives known to be fictional. The narratives described a balance of positive and negative attributes for each option. But after a decision had been made, participants were much more likely to correctly remember the positive attributes belonging to their selected choice as opposed to remembering the positive attributes for the option they did not select (and conversely for negative attributes). Memory biases such as these can be employed in the service of all sorts of self-deception regarding life choices. In the Mather et al. studies, the effect was significant even though the participants did not have a vested interest in the only hypothetical choices they made. It is likely that memory biases are much more pronounced for our real world decisions, as we have a much greater emotional investment in them (e.g., career or marriage choices).

There are many other memory biases beyond the choice-supportive bias, such as those for egocentricity, mood congruence, positivity, etc. All these biases could be employed in a manner that is either strategically or *de facto* deceptive by producing biased evidence in support of a favored belief. In addition to providing means to enable self-deception about various matters, memory biases can provide motives for systematic self-deception concerning our pasts – like the optimism bias, but in the other direction. Memory biases can also contribute to the confirmation bias, discussed next.

Confirmation bias. We are not only biased when we rack our memories, but also when we turn to the world to search for new evidence and assess it. We tend to seek, attend to, and interpret evidence in a skewed manner, such that it unduly supports what we antecedently believe (and want to continue believing), what we hope to believe, or what we simply have been primed to believe. The confirmation bias is when this bias occurs unintentionally, as opposed to the intentional acquisition of evidence or arguments by a lawyer paid to advocate for one side or by a political propagandist. As Nickerson (1998) helpfully details, this bias can take many forms. In one of its most well-known forms, the Wason selection task (a commonly used test for logical reasoning) experiments suggest that ordinary and even intelligent people give undue weight to illusory confirmations and do not adequately search for falsifying evidence. (Wason, 1968)

The confirmation bias might be most obvious when we have a motive to so believe (hot bias). But it can also emerge when we lack a motive to believe, as when we simply selectively attend to evidence supporting what we already believe without having any desire or incentive to do so (or in cases like the Wason selection task).[3] This would be a "cold bias." So, one should not make the mistake of thinking that every occurrence of a bias is thereby self-deceptive. We will discuss this point in much greater detail later.

Belief perseverance bias. Beliefs also possess inertia, meaning that they are resistant to change even when the evidence makes it rational to do so. This bias is similar to, although also importantly different from, the status quo bias. Whereas the status quo bias concerns our preferences for the world, the belief perseverance bias concerns our (implicit) preferences for our thoughts: we want our beliefs to remain the same. A partial explanation for this could be that we are often unwilling to admit that we are wrong, or that it is otherwise psychologically disturbing to admit uncertainty or fallibility.

While a desire not to be wrong or uncertain could explain many instances of this bias, the connections to self-deception grow even stronger when we turn to the most commonly studied categories of belief perseverance. Namely, we commonly manifest biased perseverance when it comes to self-impressions, social impressions, and our folk theories of the world (Anderson, 2007). This is understandable – we want a stable and coherent sense of ourselves and our place in the world. So, we should not be surprised to find the self-deceptive perseverance of beliefs that favor one's standing self-conception or theories of the world. Not only do we want the world to stay the same, we want our thoughts to stay the same as well.

These nine biases provide some of the major motives and means for self-deception. While this is by no means an exhaustive list, it is a good start and covers many cases. Throughout this book, we will revisit the issue of cognitive and motivational biases, adding more to the list and going into further detail concerning the psychological mechanisms as we draw on them in detailing the various theories of self-deception. Over the past several decades this literature has grown to be enormous. The explosion can be traced to the highly influential work of psychologists, including Amos Tversky and Daniel Kahneman, that started in the late 1960s in what became known as the "heuristics and biases" literature. The human mind is a patchwork of different *heuristics* – rules of thumb – that work fairly well for estimating, judging, concluding, discerning causal relations, and the like in the natural environments from which we evolved. We employ rationally imprecise, but ecologically strong, heuristics because Mother Nature is stingy and resources are limited – we do not have unlimited computing power or time. In our everyday lives, we do not estimate probabilities in

INTRODUCTION   13

a mathematically rigorous manner, but we use rules of thumb that tend to yield "satisficing" results. The term "satisficing" comes from Herbert Simon, and it basically means "good enough" – which is exactly what tends to survive and reproduce in natural environments. Simon was an early cognitive scientist who did pioneering work on decision making and problem solving in both human and AI systems as far back as the 1940s. Simon emphasized our "bounded rationality" and the reality of evolutionary pressures – pressures that led to cognitive shortcuts such as those later discovered by Tversky and Kahneman (Simon, 1982). And how did they discover the precise heuristics that we employ? By and large, they discerned the heuristics by discovering our patterns of errors. While these heuristics were effective for the ecological niches in which we evolved, they are prone to systematic errors in different environments or for problems different from those for which they were designed.

There are many cognitive heuristics to turn to for examples (e.g., availability, representativeness), and the anchoring-and-adjustment heuristic for estimating quantities will serve our purposes well.[4] When using this heuristic, we "anchor" on an initial value – perhaps as an educated guess, but it could also be an arbitrarily chosen starting point or a value suggested by others. We then modify or "adjust" our estimate, deviating from our original anchor. I first guess that the car is worth $30,000, say. After being told that it is worth more than that, I adjust and estimate that it is worth $32,000. This sounds sensible enough. The problem is that the anchor can unduly influence our subsequent estimates, biasing us such that we fail to deviate as far from our original starting point as we should. This is especially problematic when our first estimate is uninformed or, worse yet, suggested by a malevolent negotiator. Kahneman (2011: Chapter 11) describes two highly insightful experiments that show the domain generality of this bias. In one study, a giant wheel with segments numbered from 0 to 100 was spun. But the wheel was rigged such that it would land on only 10 or 65, equally divided between two experimental groups. Participants were then asked if the percentage of African countries in the UN is larger or smaller than the number "randomly" spun. More significantly, they were then asked to estimate the true percentage of African countries in the UN. The shocking result was that the average answer for the two groups was so significantly different: 25% for the former group, 45% for the latter! The participants obviously knew that the "random" number spun had no bearing on the correct answer, but it somehow affected their answers nonetheless. They could not shake the anchor. Many subsequent studies have confirmed this tendency across a variety of domains. Kahneman (2011: 123–124) describes a similar study, in which half of the participants were asked if the tallest redwood tree is over 1200 feet, and the other half was asked if it is over 180 feet. When they then gave their guesses as to the true height of the tallest redwood, their average answers were 844 and 282 feet respectively. No wonder car dealerships always display an inflated sticker price!

In our initial discussion of some of the psychological tendencies relevant to self-deception, we have already invoked a significant distinction – that between cold and hot biases. This distinction warrants further analysis, and it will reappear throughout our discussion of self-deception. "Hot" biases are called such because they are often driven by emotions or desires – passions – that commonly connote heat. Because I am filled with the emotional heat of love, I am biased in evaluating my girlfriend. Or because I am filled with the heat of desire, I am biased in evaluating the merits of a hamburger. Counterfactuals can be invoked to show that these are hot biases. If I did not love my girlfriend or desire a hamburger, I would evaluate each quite differently. This seems to show that my ability to reason is not in itself defective (Kunda, 1990). Rather, its functionality is distorted or impaired by my emotions or desires. It is sometimes said that reasoning competency is not impaired when a hot bias is present; rather, only reasoning performance is impaired. Such biases contrast with the purely cognitive, non-motivational, "cold" biases. The biases that emerge from heuristics such as anchoring-and-adjustment, availability, representativeness, and so on are domain general and do not depend on desires, emotions, or similar motives. They are cold.

I will distinguish the two categories of biases as follows:

> *Hot bias.* A systematic deviation from the standards of ideal reasoning (logical, causal, probabilistic, etc.) that occurs because the person has a desire, emotion, motivation, or incentive that causes her to reason in a biased manner on some topic.

> *Cold bias.* A systematic deviation from the standards of ideal reasoning (logical, causal, probabilistic, etc.) that exists merely as an acceptable imperfection given trade-offs elsewhere, as a functionally desirable distortion, or otherwise as a by-product. No desire, emotion, motivation, or incentive accounts for the deviation. These biases tend to be domain general.

There are a few salient differences between these categories of bias to keep in mind. Foremost, hot biases are cases of motivated reasoning and cold biases are not. This motivation is normally understood as manifesting itself as a psychological state,[5] but I intend for it to include any kind of incentive or motivation to believe in a certain way, even if that incentive or motivation does not manifest itself in the person's psychology. For example, an animal might display hot, biased reasoning (or at least behavior) concerning its offspring, even if there is no psychological state that we would identify as a desire or emotion that is driving the bias. One might want to call this "functional" desire or motivation, a somewhat familiar move in the literature on animal cognition. Given the motivation behind hot biases, they are strategic or at least targeted. As such, they apply to specific topics. Cold biases, because they are not driven by a particular motivation, are not targeted. As such, cold biases tend to be domain general, holding regardless of the subject matter (e.g., applying to reasoning about redwood trees and African nations). That said, it is at least possible for there to be cold biases that emerge only when reasoning about certain topics, even though that deviation is not driven by a motive or incentive to so believe. Finally, because hot biases exist in virtue of a motive or incentive, the bias would not exist without that motivation. Indeed, it may be possible to eliminate hot biases by removing the "heat."

Many different facts about the structure of the mind and human thought will end up being significant for understanding the whys and hows of self-deception. We will talk about conscious and unconscious processes quite a bit later, but a somewhat related distinction should be flagged now as it relates to the heuristics and biases literature. In recent decades psychologists have distinguished between what they call System 1 and System 2 processing, or dual process psychology more generally (Sloman, 1996; Stanovich and West, 2000). System 1 processing is the kind of thought that is automatic, fast, and effortless – like, recognizing the anger in someone's face or figuring out that a baseball is zooming right toward your head. You cannot help but think these things, and the thoughts appear quickly without any discernible effort on your part. In contrast, solving a calculus problem or deciding on a college are deliberate, comparatively slow, and effortful acts. These are the hallmarks of System 2 processing. (See Kahneman (2011) for an authoritative, yet highly accessible, characterization of this distinction.) While we are inclined to identify most of our mental life – indeed, our very self – with System 2 functioning, a theme of recent cognitive psychology is that the bulk of our thought is largely autonomous (and often unconscious) System 1 processing.

As System 1 processing is automatic, it requires neither reflection nor deliberation. I have claimed that self-deception is a failure of reflection and deliberation, and as such System 2 failures – be they omissions or malfunctions – are to be expected. Reflection, doubt, and rational scrutiny – the bread and butter of philosophy, and some of the critical elements (if only in their absence) of self-deception as well – all reside with System 2. If self-deception is also intentional, then it would seem to map onto an effortful System 2 process. As we will see, the extent to which self-deception is intentional or otherwise deliberate is hotly disputed. It may be that System 1 tendencies can be exploited and perhaps even habituated in the service of self-deception as well.

§1.3 Why study self-deception?

This book is primarily a philosophical investigation of self-deception, although we should be skeptical of any sharp line dividing philosophical investigations from psychological or other forms of inquiry. It is sometimes thought that philosophy employs a purely *a priori* (pure reason) or "armchair" methodology, whereas the sciences use empirical methods (observation and experimentation). But more and more, this division is seen to be too crude as well as unfaithful to productive practice in both philosophy and the sciences. Much philosophy is informed by scientific practice, and some philosophers even generate and argue for empirical hypotheses. On the other hand, some science depends on *a priori* assumptions or speculations, as well as chains of *a priori* reasoning. *A priori* reasoning also plays a prommient role in securing a conceptual foundation for the sciences, and it can be used to derive conceptual and rational connections among their various claims.

As the previous section suggests, the philosophical and psychological investigations of self-deception will often overlap. Some of the issues that arise will appear to be largely conceptual or otherwise *a priori*: What does it mean to be deceptive? How irrational can someone be and still count as a believer? This seems like philosophical terrain. But we philosophers should be cautious, as the empirical sciences can inform or revise what we once thought were conceptual or *a priori* truths. Perhaps we think, from our armchairs, that deception requires an intention or desire to mislead. But then evolutionary biology comes along and shows us a perfectly legitimate sense in which deception can emerge without any psychological intentions to deceive. Or perhaps our *a priori* speculations concerning interpretation demand that we assume a robust degree of rational consistency when we attribute beliefs. Then psychological

INTRODUCTION   17

pathologies and actual interpretative practices come along to correct what we once thought were *a priori* necessities.

The sciences can often benefit from a philosophical approach that challenges longstanding assumptions and offers novel proposals for future research. So, a philosophical investigation of self-deception should not limit us to armchair speculation. Indeed, we will see that this has been a strong theme from the last couple decades of philosophical work on self-deception. We should readily concede that there are reasons to be interested in self-deception that extend well beyond philosophy, and one of my aims is to illustrate the practical significance of self-deception in various "real world" contexts, oftentimes with relatively high costs or benefits. Also, as much as possible we should see if the empirical sciences can resolve or at least contribute to understanding our philosophical problems of self-deception. We should search for psychological tests that can help resolve the various philosophical debates – e.g., by imposing cognitive load on study participants to test whether they are exerting effort to deceive themselves.

These caveats in place, let's first begin with the major *philosophical* reasons for interest in self-deception:

1   *Rationality and truth as norms.* Reason and rationality are central to the methodology of philosophy. Philosophers are interested in rational support, and we search for arguments, theories, and other means to rationally justify and unify our conception of the world. As Socrates said even when considering whether to escape his death sentence: "Not only now but at all times I am the kind of man who listens to nothing within me but the argument that on reflection seems best to me" (Plato, 1997, Crito: 46b). David Hume, a great skeptic with a notoriously mixed view of reason, nevertheless proclaimed: "A wise man, therefore, proportions his belief to the evidence" (Hume, 1777/1975: 110).

Self-deception offends against this philosophical ideal of rational guidance. Oftentimes the self-deceived do not believe according to the best argument, neither do they proportion their belief to the evidence. Indeed, deception is necessary only because the evidence does not straightforwardly support the preferred belief. A father deceives himself about his daughter's academic accomplishments only because there is much evidence of her poor academic performance (e.g., bad grades, disappointing reports from teachers, little time devoted to studying). If the evidence were positive instead, the father would just straightforwardly believe on the basis of it. It is only because the facts are negative – against what he wants to believe – that the father needs to work at achieving belief, and deception is the means by which he does so. Philosophers can be interested in self-deception, then, to the extent that it violates our standards of rationality.

But it is not just that self-deception violates the *objective* standards of rationality. Even more disturbing, in the act of self-deceiving the person is violating *his own standards* of rationality. Some think that just as we deceive others by leading them to believe something we know (or simply think) to be false or unjustifed, we self-deceive by leading ourselves into believing something that we know to be false or unjustified. This raises problems for us to address later. How can we realistically be so gullible as to both recognize the rational force of evidence and not recognize the rational force of that same evidence? And is it even possible to ignore the evidence that we in some sense respect, such that we believe out of indifference or spite of it? The problems here are not just that self-deception is irrational – like any old cognitive bias might be – but that it is an irrationality that the self-deceiving subject himself in some sense recognizes. Otherwise, he would not engage in self-deception at all, let alone the very specific evidence-manipulating machinations that self-deceivers sometimes execute. Philosophers are often very interested in these cases that test the boundaries of human irrationality.

2 *Philosophy of mind.* Philosophers are also interested in understanding the general structure of the mind, and some think that self-deception demands a special type of cognitive architecture. A particularly common approach to self-deception has been to divide the mind into distinct parts – say, the conscious mind and the unconscious mind (but there are other ways to partition it as well). This makes self-deception much more like interpersonal deception: One part of the mind contains knowledge, intentions and the like that another part lacks. In this way, a person can coherently and plausibly deceive themselves.

But self-deception touches on much more than just the structure of the mind. It touches on cognitive biases, memory biases, unconscious processes, the nature of belief, intentions, motives, and much more. These are all psychological phenomena, to be sure, but this is also terrain for empirically oriented philosophers of mind. Philosophers can both clarify concepts and make proto-psychological speculations in these areas.

INTRODUCTION   19

3 *Self-knowledge.* As we have already noted, self-knowledge is of particular interest to philosophers.[6] It is often thought that we have special access to our own thoughts, say by direct introspection. It was once more common to think of the mind as exclusively conscious and transparent to itself (in the sense that you can "see through" to your own thoughts), but we now know that that is far from the case. Self-deception might demand a particularly strong form of mental opacity, in which the mind does not fully know its own intentions or beliefs. What makes this an especially interesting failure of self-knowledge, however, is that it is motivated. One might think that self-deception could not possibly succeed unless there were a failure of self-knowledge, as keeping someone in the dark is exactly what deception is all about.

Besides these purely philosophical reasons, we can also be drawn to study self-deception out of interest in its functions, psychological implementation, consequences, and applications. What is self-deception for, how do we do it, how does it affect us, and where do we find it? One might think that these are all empirical issues that are beyond the reach of philosophy, but again we should resist strongly separating philosophical and scientific questions. Philosophers are particularly good at finding reasons and explanations, so we philosophers should consider these questions and participate in generating answers to them. These additional reasons for interest include:

4 *The psychological study of reasoning and belief construction.* We already saw that philosophers are interested in self-deception because it tests the conceptual limits of irrationality and belief, and it bears on normative claims about how to reason and believe. Additionally, it is a fascinating entry point into how we actually reason and come to form, maintain, and revise our beliefs. We might be interested in self-deception because we are interested in the heuristics, procedures, algorithms, and whatnot that shape our mental lives as a matter of contingent fact. Philosophers value reflection, but, in practice, we might wonder about the extent to which it guides belief construction. Philosophers have also recognized that there are many *rational* ways to form, maintain, and revise our beliefs in light of new experiences and evidence. Dogmatists and conspiracy theorists can both be very rational in that they hold onto their beliefs by making the necessary adjustments elsewhere – e.g., they uphold their belief that no one ever walked on the moon by discrediting the video evidence (have you seen how strangely the flag behaves?), offering a motive for the United States government to

20   INTRODUCTION

mislead the world on this point, and so on. As philosopher W.V.O. Quine (1951) has famously argued, *any* belief can be rationally held so long as you are willing to make the necessary adjustments elsewhere. Out of these many possible rational ways of adjusting belief in light of experience, what tendencies do people tend to favor and to what extent is the malleability of belief exploited by self-deceivers?

5   *The psychological study of unconscious processes.* In the last 100 years, reference to the unconscious has become part of the average person's psychological toolkit for understanding both themselves and others. People are especially likely to speak of the unconscious when it comes to explaining cases that we would classify as self-deceptive. The father unconsciously knows the truth about his son's partying ways, we might say. Or, an insecure male might consciously think that he is quite the ladies' man, but unconsciously he knows otherwise (which is why he acts so nervously). If everyday folk psychological theorizing is to be trusted, self-deception has much to reveal to us regarding the power and nature of the unconscious.

The unconscious went through a period of academic disrepute after the wild speculations of Freudian psychoanalysis were replaced with more empirically grounded, experimental psychology. But in recent years the unconscious has seen a resurgence (controversial though it remains) within academic psychology. For both psychologists and philosophers there remain pressing questions about the attributes of the unconscious and even how to define it. Some theories of self-deception demand robust unconscious powers – powers that may or may not obtain. Can the unconscious *intentionally* produce action or thought? Can it *reason*? Can it *manipulate* the conscious mind?

6   *Self-deception and psychological well-being.* Self-deception often seems driven by a desire to manipulate one's state of mind, resulting in changes in mood, self-esteem, and motivation. It is arguable that self-deception can make you happier, boost your ego, and motivate you to persevere at a task longer than you would otherwise. Are these beneficial changes, however, especially when weighed against the potential harms of having a less accurate representation of reality? We could be interested in these quite practical psychological benefits, as well as the more philosophical question of whether they are worth the epistemic sacrifice. Of course, we must investigate whether certain kinds of self-deception truly yield these benefits in the first place. For that matter, we must also

INTRODUCTION 21

investigate whether the deviations from rational belief are truly costly. A philosophically and empirically informed account of "the good life" could help us adjudicate the matter.

7 *Physical effects of self-deception.* Self-deception can have physical as well as psychological effects. Perhaps you have noticed that you have trouble sleeping when you are hiding from reality or that you are more likely to get sick when under the mental stress that self-deception can induce. Sleep and immunological problems are among the more salient risks of self-deception. On the positive side, self-deceptive optimism could potentially boost health (say, as mediated by improved affect). Considering these benefits takes us a bit further from philosophy, but they are certainly considerations to take seriously in evaluating the overall utility of self-deception. And as with the boundaries between philosophy and psychology, we should not expect that there will be a bright line separating psychological and physiological phenomena.

8 *Self-deception and social functioning.* Our self-deception can influence how others treat us, whether or not they recognize that we are self-deceived. If others are not aware of our self-deception, they might acquire the same beliefs from us, unaware of the fact that they are ill founded. This could be to our advantage, especially if these are self-enhancing or otherwise self-serving beliefs. Alternatively, others could recognize our self-deception and think less of us: We are careless and ignorant, they conclude. Our worldviews and belief-forming practices significantly affect our likeability and trustworthiness. We will carefully examine one theory of self-deception, developed by evolutionary biologist Robert Trivers, that gives special weight to social effects like these.

9 *Our susceptibility to economic, journalistic, political, and other forms of informational exploitation.* It is possible for other people or groups to exploit our tendency to self-deceive, prodding us toward self-deception or even imposing it on us. Advertisers, authors, propagandists, wooers, employers, our children, and countless others have the ability to sense what we *want to believe* and provide us with just enough of the right suggestions to get us to do the rest of the work ourselves. Perhaps we can play defense against these offensive strategies by studying self-deception and learning how to guard against their tactics. (We will discuss such forms of what I will call *collective, enabled,* and *baited* self-deception in §5.4.)

10 *Our ability to use self-deception as a tool to manipulate others.* Finally, and perhaps somewhat cynically, we can learn how to use self-deception as

an offensive tactic against others. This could be either our own self-deception or, as just discussed, we could lead others to their own self-deception for our benefit. More disturbing yet, maybe we will see that we have already been wielding self-deception as a social weapon without even realizing it.

Summary

- While self-deception is common, it is also philosophically and psychologically puzzling. How can we deceive ourselves, and why would we do this?
- There are various heuristics and biases that self-deceivers can exploit or succumb to. These biases can provide both motives and means for self-deception. The distinction between hot (motivated) and cold (unmotivated) biases will also prove important in marking off real self-deception.
- There are several philosophical and extra-philosophical reasons to be interested in self-deception. For philosophers, self-deception is especially problematic because it goes against the ideals of truth and self-knowledge.

Recommended reading

The *Stanford Encyclopedia of Philosophy* entry on self-deception by Ian Deweese-Boyd is an excellent, shorter introduction to the philosophical issues surrounding self-deception: https://plato.stanford.edu/entries/self-deception/

There are also a few good anthologies, especially Brian McLaughlin and Amelie Oksenberg Rorty's *Perspectives on Self-Deception*.

You might consider how some classic works of literature depict self-deception. There are many works to consider, including: *Othello*, *Madame Bovary*, *Pride and Prejudice*, *Notes from the Underground*, *Crime and Punishment*, *The Great Gatsby*, *Invisible Man* (Ellison), and *Lolita*.

For a good, general introduction to the heuristics and biases literature, see Daniel Kahneman's *Thinking, Fast and Slow*. For those wanting to delve further, Nisbett and Ross (1980), Kahneman, Slovic, and Tversky (1982), Kahneman and Tversky (2000), and Gilovich, Griffin, Kahneman (2002) contain many research articles reporting on the laboratory studies that test for the various biases and heuristics, although some of this work might be a bit dated now.

Lisa Bortolotti's book *Irrationality* serves as an excellent introduction to philosophical treatments of irrationality in general. Her empirically informed discussion gives special attention to the connections between irrationality and mental health, the role of the emotions in a rational life, and the extent to which rationality is conducive to overall well-being.

W.K. Clifford's "The Ethics of Belief" offers a classic statement of the philosophical ideal of rationally acquired belief, extending it to all matters and for all people. For an excellent discussion of the historical and contemporary issues relating to self-knowledge, especially from an epistemic perspective, see Brie Gertler's *Self-Knowledge*.

Notes

1   Most academic philosophers and psychologists think that self-deception occurs, but not all do. David Kipp (1980) and Steffen Borge (2003) outright deny the very possibility of self-deception. Of course, they acknowledge that there is an interesting psychological phenomenon that we call "self-deception." But they think that description of it is a misnomer. Kipp (1980: 315) argued that so-called self-deceivers put on a show for others, pretending that the world is as they desire it to be. In particular, there is a desire to appear "existentially successful." But this is not a *literal* self-deception, a condition supposedly made impossible by the unity of consciousness. For Borge, so-called self-deception is simple ignorance of how emotions bias one's beliefs. Neither philosopher believes that the so-called self-deceived have contradictory beliefs or otherwise succeed at deceiving themselves.

2   Epley and Whitchurch (2008). This study is also discussed in von Hippel and Trivers (2011).

3   The Wason selection task has been a hugely influential construct for testing logical reasoning. In a typical example, participants are presented with four cards presented with one side facing up. They are truthfully told that each card has a letter on one side and a number on the other. Suppose that the four cards show "D," "3," "B," and "7." They are then asked which of these four cards *must* be turned over in order to test the rule "If there is a D on one side of any card, then there is a 3 on its other side" (Wason, 1968: 275) The correct answer is that "D" and "7" must be turned over. This is because the "D" card could have something besides a "3" on the other side, and the "7" card could have a "D" on the other side. Either possibility

24 INTRODUCTION

would show that the rule we are testing is false. But participants rarely provide this correct answer. They tend to think that the "3" card should be tested and overlook the significance of the "7" card. This is just one example. Subsequent applications of the Wason selection task have shown how different ways of framing the problem and different subject matters affect performance.

4 See Tversky and Kahneman (1974) for the original discussion of this heuristic and its biases.

5 For example, Kunda describes the motivation driving motivated reasoning as "any wish, desire, or preference that concerns the outcome of a given reasoning task, and I do not attempt to address the thorny issue of just how such motives are represented" (Kunda, 1990: 480).

6 For an excellent introduction to the philosophical problems of self-knowledge, see Brie Gertler's book *Self-Knowledge* in the Routledge New Problems of Philosophy series.

2

THE BASIC PROBLEM AND A CONCEPTUAL MAP

2.1 **The Basic Problem**
2.2 **A classic picture: Freud and Davidson**
2.3 **A minimal conception: motivated irrationality**
2.4 **What is the content of the motive? What is the proximate goal?**
2.5 **What is the end state?**
2.6 **Conceptual map**
2.7 **Nearby phenomena**

The first chapter informally presented some of the problems of self-deception, but the present chapter will provide a much more rigorous account. This is followed by an introduction to some of the major moves, both historically and theoretically, in response to these problems. The chapter concludes with sections that raise further diagnostic questions or decision points for characterizing self-deception. This will get us well on our way to developing a conceptual map for charting theories of self-deception and the psychological space of motivated irrationality.

§2.1 The Basic Problem

On its face, self-deception is the deception of the self by the self.[1] As innocuous as this simple and straightforward characterization might seem, it quickly leads us into both philosophical and psychological problems. We will begin this chapter by considering the "Basic Problem" of self-deception:

> The Basic Problem: The Basic Problem of self-deception is to show the compatibility and actuality of three key elements of self-deception: 1) real deceptive measures taken against, 2) a single self, and 3) with some success at this deceptive enterprise.

As we will see, there are actually several more specific problems that fall under the Basic Problem. This section also introduces you to some of these more specific problems, including what are known as the *static problems* and *dynamic problems*.[2]

Trouble emerges when we start with the more familiar examples of *interpersonal deception* and try to conceive of self-deception in a similar manner. There are no deep philosophical puzzles over the very possibility of interpersonal deception, as the Deceiver and Victim are distinct individuals with their independent psychologies. As they are wholly distinct, they can easily have contradictory thoughts, conflicting motives, and lack awareness of one another's mental states. In addition to interpersonal deception in the human world, we can also find deception in the biological world (interorganism deception), such as with the patterned wings of a butterfly that is a Batesian mimic or the inviting "dew drops" of sundew plants. But for now let's stick with human cases of deception that involve psychological states – beliefs, intentions, motives, and the like.

Let's again turn to literature to get a particularly convincing and vivid example: Shakespeare's masterful description of Iago's deception of Othello. Iago wishes to deceive Othello about Desdemona's fidelity, so he takes very specific, rational, and sometimes complex measures to get Othello to believe that his wife has committed adultery with Cassio. Iago draws Othello's attention to the fact that Desdemona has been deceptive in the past (toward her father), he encourages Desdemona to advocate for Cassio in order to arouse Othello's suspicions, he fabricates outright a story about Cassio calling out Desdemona's name in his sleep and behaving affectionately, and he plants Desdemona's handkerchief in Cassio's room. Sadly, Othello is all too easily manipulated, and the deception succeeds. Othello is himself predisposed to be deceived about his wife's fidelity, having been primed by Desdemona's own father with his early warning: "Look to her, Moor, if thou hast eyes to see: She has deceived her father, and may thee" (Shakespeare, 2006, 1.3: 290–291). (Since Othello's own jealousy and wild imagination, once triggered, can largely drive the deception on their own, Iago might be baiting Othello into deceiving himself. We will discuss the concept of *baited self-deception* in §5.4.) Othello's false belief in Desdemona's infidelity leads him to smother her in her bed. In the tragic ending, the deception is finally revealed to Othello. He quickly loses his false belief, feels tremendous regret, and ends up taking his own life as well.

What are the key elements of this story that make this a case of deception? Iago's motives and intentions to deceive – he wants to mislead Othello and intends to make this happen – are clearly critical and essential. Iago also knows the truth about Desdemona's fidelity, so he knows that he is going to have to take deliberate and rational steps in order to mislead Othello. Iago carries out the deception by intentionally drawing Othello's attention to misleading truths, staging misleading "evidence," and fabricating other evidence outright. Let's generalize these observations and mark what is typical of deception:

> *Interpersonal model*: In paradigm examples of interpersonal deception, the Deceiver *knows or at least believes* the truth all along and is *motivated or intends* to produce a false belief in the Victim. The Deceiver takes *deceptive measures* against the Victim to achieve this goal, as they apparently think that the Victim *would not simply consent to be misled or reach the false belief* on their own. Finally, the Victim comes to *believe* the falsehood.

Now let us suppose that self-deception is the special case fitting this model in which the Deceiver and the Victim are one and the same person. To dramatize this, imagine that instead of targeting Othello, Iago has the same intention and takes the very same deceptive measures against himself – simply replace Othello with Iago. Three specific problems, each of which falls under the more general Basic Problem, emerge straightaway if we model self-deception on interpersonal deception:

> *Belief Problem*: The self-deceived both believes the truth and believes the falsehood. Try imagining Iago believing both that Desdemona is faithful and that she is unfaithful.

> *Motivation/Intention Problem*: The self-deceived is motivated to mislead himself and intends to do so; yet he simultaneously is unwilling and does

not consent to be misled. Try imagining Iago intending to deceive himself about Desdemona's fidelity, while also not consenting to be misled.

Deception Problem: The self-deceived schemes to misdirect, mislead, and fabricate the evidence on which he will believe. Try imagining Iago planting the handkerchief in an attempt to get himself to believe that Desdemona has committed adultery.

Table 2.1 illustrates how each of these problems emerges when we model self-deception on interpersonal deception.

As I will explain in detail shortly, it is *prima facie* implausible that a unified self would have the belief states of one who both maintains the truth, as real deception seems to require, and yet also succumbs to the falsehood (static problem). For related reasons, some have thought it is impossible to initiate the process of deceiving oneself in a way that could have any chance of succeeding (dynamic problem). Whether or not these elements stand in ineliminable tension, it is very common to characterize self-deception as an inherently unstable or tense state or process (Audi, 1982, 1985, 1988; Funkhouser, 2005, 2009; Lynch, 2012; Noordhof, 2009). (In §3.5.4 we will discuss this supposed tension in greater detail.) Many accounts of self-deception can be categorized by which of the three elements of the Basic Problem they end up mitigating: They divide the self, deflate the deception (e.g., to a motivated bias without intentional deception), or deny that successful self-deception results in belief.

Table 2.1 Interpersonal deception as the model for self-deception

Deceiver	Victim	Deceiver = Victim
• Believes that p	• Believes that not-p	• Believes that p and believes that not-p (Belief Problem)
• Motivated to mislead and intends to do so	• Unwilling and does not consent to be misled	• Motivated to mislead self and intends to do so, yet is unwilling and does not consent to be misled (Motivation/ Intention Problem)
• Takes deceptive measures	• Falls for deceptive measures	• Takes deceptive measures against self, yet falls for them (Deception Problem)

THE BASIC PROBLEM AND A CONCEPTUAL MAP   29

The overarching problem of self-deception – the Basic Problem – is to show how active measures to deceive can be taken against a single self with actual success in acquiring the deceptive belief. (The Belief, Motivation/ Intention, and Deception Problems are all more specific varieties of the Basic Problem.) One way to "solve" this problem is to dodge it – that is, deny one of the three elements. Possible solutions to the Basic Problem can be pursued under three broad headings, depending on which of the three elements it downplays or revises. Each option contributes to answering at least some of the more specific problems raised:

> *Sacrifice* **deception** *(intentional or purposive manipulation)*: It can be dif-
> ficult to see how an intentional project of self-deception could possibly
> get off the ground, let alone be sustained. Self-deception tests the limits
> of self-manipulation, and it often seems to demand a disturbing lack of
> self-knowledge. We could try to dodge the Basic Problem by denying that
> self-deception is robustly deceptive – it is neither intentional nor purpo-
> sive. This obviously eliminates the Motivation/Intention Problem straight-
> away, and by lowering the manipulation demands required for deception
> it avoids the Deception Problem as well. It is less clear that it addresses
> the Belief Problem, although it likely dodges this as well by eliminating the
> need for true belief possessed by a deceptive agent. In such a case, there
> would only need to be the one (false) belief.
>
> The immediate concern about such proposals is that they might not war-
> rant the label self-*deception*. It is not clear that such pheonomena would be
> any more deceptive than simple cognitive mistakes that arise due to cold
> biases. There is no duplicity (two minds, two beliefs) that is characteristic
> of deception.
>
> *Sacrifice* **the self**: Self-deception challenges the idea of a unified cognitive,
> conative, and emotional self. So why not just divide the self? This route
> can handle the Belief Problem by having different parts of the mind end
> up believing different things, much as the different people believe differ-
> ent things in cases of interpersonal deception. These proposed psycho-
> logical divisions can take various forms (the conscious and unconscious,
> the social self and the private self, the lustful self and the religious self,
> and so on), each with its own beliefs or data to draw from. Likewise, the
> Motivation/Intention Problem can be resolved by attributing different
> agendas to these different psychological divisions – one part intends to

mislead the other, which remains in the dark. Finally, the Deception Problem is resolved by segregating these beliefs and intentions throughout the deceptive process.

The immediate concerns about such proposals are that they might not be psychologically realistic, and they might not warrant the label *self*-deception.

*Sacrifice **belief***. Philosophers often take belief to be necessarily reasons responsive, but self-deceivers often distort or show a relatively high disregard for evidence and rational support. Such disconnect from rational norms strains the boundaries of belief. Maybe, then, the self-deceived do not end up genuinely believing that which they are motivated to believe. Instead, they bear some other attitude toward the object of their deception. Embracing this option obviously eliminates the Belief Problem. It also seems to mitigate the Motivation/Intention and Deception Problems by not requiring that self-deception aims at producing false belief. The substitute it offers instead might be much easier to achieve.

The immediate concern about such proposals is that if the self-deceived do not reach belief, then they might not warrant the label self-*deception*. These proposals might not do justice to the phenomenon, which many see as generating belief.

We will explore each of these strategies for dealing with the Basic Problem in Chapters 3–5.

Not everyone dodges the Basic Problem. Steffen Borge (2003) raises the Basic Problem and concludes that it rules out the very possibility of self-deception:[3]

> There is no such thing as self-deception ... The problem is that even though the notion of "self-deception" is part of our folk psychology, the folk-psychological notions of "belief," "deception," and "self" seem, on closer inspection, to rule out the very possibility of self-deception. How can you trick yourself to believe something you do not believe? Folk psychology seems to lack the resources for explaining what goes on in the cases that we call self-deception. (Borge, 2003: 1, 4)

This is a revisionary position, as it argues that ordinary folk are systematically mistaken in describing one another as self-deceived. Borge argues that the ordinary understanding of the component terms ("self," "deception,"

THE BASIC PROBLEM AND A CONCEPTUAL MAP   31

and "belief") lead to contradiction when we combine them into the concept of self-deception. For him, deception requires an actual intention or conscious effort to mislead, but he argues that it is impossible for a unified self to pull this off. Either there is no deception, or there is no self.

I think it would be better to preserve our ordinary classifications of people as self-deceived, if at all possible. Borge is correct that we ought to seek consistency in the totality of ordinary folk psychology. But we also should take into account the possibility of correction in light of systematic theorizing (e.g., by experimental psychology) and scientific data collection. It is conceivable that one could confront the Basic Problem squarely – like Borge, not mitigating any of the three elements – but, unlike Borge, argue that self-deception does, in fact, occur. On such views, the self-deceived are fully unified agents who possess contradictory beliefs, an intention to mislead themselves, and actual success. However, most theorists argue that the self-deceived are not fully unified, not fully deceptive (at least in the interpersonal sense), or not fully believers, but that the label "self-deception" is still justified. In the chapters to follow, we will discuss all three categories of proposed "sacrificial" solutions. These possibilities can also be combined with one another – e.g., one could sacrifice both the unity of self and the full-belief requirement. It is important to note that each sacrificial solution is at least psychologically possible, whether or not it is correctly labeled as "self-deception." So, we should not make the mistake of using armchair speculations to dismiss accounts out of hand, when, in fact, they could be empirically real.

Let's consider these various problems in further detail. Following Alfred Mele's framework, we will divide these problems into the *static* and the *dynamic*.

§2.1.1 *Static problems*

The static problems of self-deception are those that arise when our task is to describe the psychology of the self-deceived at a given time. The primary static problem is to describe the belief states of the self-deceived when they are successfully self-deceiving or self-deceived. (Belief Problem) If we take the interpersonal model seriously, then the self-deceived should have the beliefs of both the Deceiver and the Victim. This seems to imply that they both have the deceptive belief and lack it, an impossible state to be sure. Even if we do not take the interpersonal model seriously, the self-deceived at least have a complex relation to the truth that can be extremely difficult to characterize in ordinary psychological terminology.

Contradictions

It would be absolutely unacceptable if self-deception required a person to both believe some proposition and *not* believe that same proposition. We might find it appealing to say that the self-deceived bald man both believes that he is bald and does not believe that he is bald. But these cannot be literally, fully, univocally, and simultaneously true. By simple logic, for any proposition p, it can never be the case that p and not-p.[4] This is known as the *law of non-contradiction*. We are considering a particular value for p: "Telly believes that he is bald." It should be obvious that these two propositions cannot both be true:

(1) Telly believes that he is bald.
    Form: A believes that p.
(2) It is not the case that Telly believes that he is bald.
    Or: Telly does not believe that he is bald.
    Form: not-(A believes that p). Or: A does not believe that p.

The conjunction of (1) and (2) is a contradiction, and contradictions are never true. Significantly, the contradiction would be "in the world" and not merely "in thought." That is, we would not merely be attributing contradictory beliefs to Telly, but our description of him would itself be contradictory.

There is room to maneuver, however. Maybe our talk is non-literal, and we merely mean that it *seems* or is *as if* he both believes and does not believe that he is bald. Or we might want to say that he neither fully believes nor fully does not believe, placing him in some doxastic no man's land.[5] Or perhaps he believes it in some sense of belief, but he does not believe it in another sense of belief. Finally, he could believe it at one time and not believe it at another time. None of these possibilities would violate the law of non-contradiction, and each possibility is explained later in this book.

Contradictory beliefs

It is important to distinguish the contradiction just described from the logically possible – even if not psychologically possible – case in which the self-deceived believes contradictory things. In this case, the contradictories exist only in thought (that is, belief) rather than in the world. To describe this situation we take (1) and conjoin it with:

(3) Telly believes that he is not bald.
   Or: Telly believes that it is not the case that he is bald.
   Form: A believes that not-p.

The significant difference between (2) and (3) concerns where the "not" is placed. (1) and (2) combine to make for a contradiction because the former attributes a belief to Telly, whereas the latter denies (negates) that very attribution – Telly supposedly has and does not have the very same belief. In contrast, (1) and (3) do not contradict one another because they both positively attribute beliefs to him. This is a difference in *scope*, which, in this case, means the extent of the claim that is negated. What Telly *believes*, according to (1) and (3), is contradictory – the negation is *within* the belief (narrow scope). But *we* are not contradicting ourselves when we describe him as such.

Now, maybe it is impossible for a person to have those two beliefs, because believing that you are bald makes it impossible for you to believe that you are not bald. But if this *is* impossible, it is not because logic tells us so. Instead, it would have to be a *psychological* impossibility, something about the nature of belief specifically. Perhaps anything that counts toward attributing to someone the belief that they are bald equally counts against attributing to him the belief that he is not bald, and vice versa. But this demands further argument.

Believing contradictions

Finally, having contradictory beliefs does not necessarily mean that you believe a contradiction. As philosophers trying to capture subtle differences, we must make fine distinctions here. To believe a contradiction, you must put the contradictory beliefs together, so to speak:

(4) Telly believes that he is both bald and not bald.
   Form: A believes that (p and not-p).

From a logical point of view, at least, (1) and (3) could both be true consistent with (4) being false. With (4), the conjunction – "and" – is within the scope of the belief, yielding a belief that is not logically guaranteed by (1) and (3) alone. If Telly keeps his beliefs segregated in some sense, then he could both believe that he is bald and believe that he is not bald, but not believe that he is bald *and* not-bald. One could argue that the latter belief requires that he consider both propositions together in his consciousness or thought, but Telly might keep them segregated in his mind. He just does not put the pieces together to outright believe a contradiction, so he instead merely believes contradictory things.

The primary static puzzle for self-deception is determining which of the above belief attributions are typically true of self-deceivers. As we have seen, some combinations are either logically or psychologically suspect.[6]

Philosophers studying self-deception in recent years have tended to focus on the static puzzles for belief. But there are also be static problems when it comes to motivation, intention, emotion, or the other psychological states and processes at work in self-deception. For example, in interpersonal cases the Deceiver is motivated to mislead the Victim and does so intentionally. But, the Victim is not motivated to be misled and does not consent to it. Are the self-deceived motivated to mislead themselves, and do they do so intentionally (Motivation/Intention Problem)? As deceivers, they certainly seem to be so motivated. But the self-deceived are simultaneously victims of their own deception, and, in this capacity, it does not seem that they want to be misled. Otherwise, why would they have to be tricked at all? What do they *really* want?

Let's turn to the emotions to get one final example: A mother is self-deceived about her daughter's dancing ability, claiming that the daughter is much better than she is in fact. The mother proudly smiles when talking about the daughter's dancing, and she is eager to go to the recitals. Yet, she sullenly criticizes the daughter afterwards for her mistakes, and she abruptly avoids any conversations that could draw comparisons to the other girls or offer an objective assessment of her talent. It is unclear how happy the mother is as she sits in the theater.

§2.1.2 *Dynamic problems*

The dynamic problems are those that arise when we try to account for the psychological processes whereby the self-deception is achieved over time. The focus is primarily on belief once again, but this time we are attending to the dynamics of belief acquisition or retention via deception. As before, the interpersonal model leads us. In interpersonal cases, the deception succeeds only because the Victim does not know the Deceiver's intentions. Further, the Deceiver has information that he manipulates in order to mislead the Victim – e.g., the poor Victim does not know that I planted the fingerprints on the knife handle. But if the Deceiver and Victim are one and the same, then they should share the same knowledge regarding the

THE BASIC PROBLEM AND A CONCEPTUAL MAP   35

intention and the evidence. In that case, the deception would never succeed (Deception Problem). Surely, if you know that you intend to trick yourself and knowingly fabricate the evidence for yourself, then you would not be dumb enough to fall for it. It would be like a hustler fooling himself as he skillfully moves the cards in a game of three card monte.

Getting off the ground

As believers, we cannot be wholly indifferent to rationality and evidential considerations, and this at least puts serious limits on our ability to self deceive. In theory, the quickest way to get yourself to believe something is simply to decide to believe it. Just as I can decide to raise my arm and then immediately perform that action, why not just decide to believe what I want and immediately succeed at it? Well, things are not that easy. As Bernard Williams has argued, deciding to believe seems to be impossible, at least if it is supposed to be done immediately and in full consciousness:

> If I could acquire a belief at will, I could acquire it whether it was true or not; moreover I would know that I could acquire it whether it was true or not. If in full consciousness I could will to acquire a "belief" irrespective of its truth, it is unclear that before the event I could seriously think of it as a belief, i.e. as something purporting to represent reality. At the very least, there must be a restriction on what is the case after the event; since I could not then, in full consciousness, regard this as a belief of mine, i.e. something I take to be true, and also know that I acquired it at will. (Williams, 1973: 148)

I cannot simply decide to believe that I was born in California and immediately succeed at it. My knowledge of both my intention to so believe and the evidence in my possession dooms this to failure. I know that wanting something to be true is no reason to think that it actually is true. In general, belief becomes vulnerable when there is *recognition of its purely nonepistemic causal origins*. A further difficulty arises due to the *holistic nature of belief and evidence*. When I recall my childhood in Nebraska, the birth certificate in my file cabinet, and many other bits of evidence, it becomes virtually impossible to believe otherwise. Similar to how I cannot look at my hands and sincerely deny that they are there, I cannot "look" at the evidence and sincerely deny where it leads. At least, I cannot do these things without

THE BASIC PROBLEM AND A CONCEPTUAL MAP

telling a special story to explain away the perception and evidence. Notice that both of these difficulties are normative in nature (i.e., we *should* not believe for brutely causal reasons, and we *should* believe on the basis of the total evidence). While normative, these reasons also might limit what is even psychologically possible.

If we are to succeed at intentional self-deception, it seems like we will have to exploit some tricks. Forgetting our deceptive intention and our previous evidence is one tactic, yet deciding to forget is not any easier than deciding to believe. Instead, we could try exploiting brute psychological mechanisms. As mentioned earlier, Blaise Pascal famously argued that we have practical reasons to believe in God: It is the safe "wager," given the possibilities of eternal punishment or eternal reward. But what are we to do if we think there is no good evidence to support this belief? This is where brute psychological mechanisms come into play. We habituate ourselves to that belief by acting as if it is true. We repeat creeds. We associate with fellow believers. Through means like these, we can eventually acquire the belief even if it is not evidentially supported. But this is a process that takes time, and we are no longer simply deciding to believe in the same way that we can decide to raise our arm and have that action immediately follow.

Our prospects for getting self-deception off the ground critically depend on our ability to appropriately manage both the evidence before us and the chains of reasoning that it induces. Some philosophers (e.g., Bernard Williams) think that belief is *necessarily* sensitive to evidence and rationality. The idea is that what we believe to be true cannot – in the strongest sense of the term – be divorced from what the evidence and rationality support. Daniel Dennett (1978, 1987) and Donald Davidson (1984) reach this conclusion by endorsing an *interpretationist* account of belief. Their idea is that beliefs are psychological states that we attribute to others in order to make sense of their behavior. The fact that we are trying to make sense of their behavior brings rationality to the enterprise from the outset. We assume that people are rational and then assign beliefs on that basis. Indeed, Dennett and Davidson think that it is incoherent to assign beliefs to people in ways that violate the basic norms of meaning and rationality. Here is one of Dennett's examples:

> A biologist colleague of mine was once called on the telephone by a man in a bar who wanted him to settle a bet. The man asked: "Are rabbits birds?" "No," said the biologist. "Damn!" said the man as he hung up. Now could

THE BASIC PROBLEM AND A CONCEPTUAL MAP   37

> he *really* have believed that rabbits were birds? Could anyone really and
> truly be attributed that belief? Perhaps, but it would take a bit of a story to
> bring us to accept it. (Dennett, 1987: 14)

If someone were to assert such a thing, we would most likely insist that
they must mean something idiosyncratic by "rabbit" or "bird." Just by
understanding what those words mean, one has to recognize that they do
not overlap. So even if someone *says* that rabbits are birds, we should resist
interpreting their utterance as reflecting the belief that we characterize in
those terms. Similarly, if a traveler were to say that the destination is only
50 miles away, she could not simultaneously believe that it is more than
100 miles away. And this is because believing that something is 50 miles
away rationally entails that it is less than 100 miles away. We cannot make
sense of a point of view that sees rabbits as birds or 50 as being more than
100. And, in attributing beliefs to people, we are trying to make sense of
their point of view.

But one need not be an interpretationist to impose strong rationality
constraints on believers. David Velleman (2000), Asbjorn Steglich-Petersen
(2006), and Tamar Gendler (2007), in the spirit of Bernard Williams, have
argued that belief must have the aim or function of getting at the truth.
Further, they hold that respect for evidence and rationality offers the path
to truth. On their view, if you are not attempting to get at the truth, then
you are not in the game of believing – you are instead imagining, fantasizing, pretending, or the like. In these different ways, we see a tradition
that holds that judgments that conform to the demands of evidence and
rationality *constitute* belief or at least are *essential* to belief.[7]

Others, such as David Hume (1739/1978, 1777/1975), have argued that
our sensitivity to evidence and rationality, as believers, is simply a *contingent*
fact about human nature. Hume claimed that our acceptance of inductive
generalizations and the very fact that belief is not under voluntary control are psychological truths that could have been otherwise.[8] The contemporary Humean – represented, say, by the biological account of belief
favored by Ema Sullivan-Bissett (2017, 2018) – will hold that we are wired
to believe on the basis of evidence and rationality (for the most part, at
least) for Darwinian or otherwise strategic reasons. We are more likely to
thrive in our environments with such a psychology. But, on this Humean
view, disregard for evidence and rationality is always a possibility, and we
must turn to the empirical sciences to discover the degree to which our
psychology conforms to the dictates of rationality. (In contrast, for Dennett

and Davidson it is *a priori* that we believers strongly conform to the dictates of rationality. Of course, it is still an empirical matter whether the intentional or interpretative stance can be successfully applied to particular individuals.) The degree to which we are rational, on this view, is determined by the evolutionary constraints (e.g., time pressure, existent variations, etc.) and the extent to which true beliefs are valuable. Simon's emphasis on "bounded rationality" informed us that deviations from rationality are to be expected, and the subsequent "heuristics and biases" literature that started with Tversky and Kahneman has pointed us to their empirical reality. In light of these psychological realities, some have weakened the rationality requirements for belief to a minimal threshold, rather than having rationality strongly guide all belief attributions (Cherniak, 1986). And others have argued that deviations from the norms of formal reasoning are not always detrimental, as truth and formal rationality are not always desirable in real ecological settings (Gigerenzer et al, 1999; Stich, 1990).

Whether the respect we believers show for evidence and rationality is necessary or merely contingent, we are, by and large, creatures that must show some respect for reality. Few of us, if any, can self-deceive merely by choosing to believe whatever we prefer. Successful self-deception will then require using tactics to manipulate evidence or rationality. We will say much more about these means in the next chapter. But as you likely already anticipate, these will include evidence avoidance, evidence fabrication, selective memory and attention, and tricks of rationalization. And none of this will work, it seems, unless we remain unaware of the very process we are initiating.

Sustaining

The dynamics of self-deception are even more complicated than this. Once the self-deceived get off the ground, their self-deception will not sustain itself unless additional efforts are made to do so. Self-deception is not achieved once and for all, with an inertia that keeps it moving forever in the desired direction without additional assistance. No, it instead requires continual measures, as the kinds of obstacle that exist at its outset repeatedly will arise and threaten its stability. These obstacles include:

a   First, there is the threat of *becoming aware of the intention or efforts to self-deceive*. If at any time we become aware of the fact that we are making efforts to fool ourselves – either in the present moment or that we

THE BASIC PROBLEM AND A CONCEPTUAL MAP   39

did so in the past – the very success of these efforts is jeopardized. Self-deception seems to require a kind of mental opacity: One cannot continue to be self-deceived while becoming aware of how one got there.[9] So, this ignorance must be sustained.

b   There is also the risk that our *old evidence will return*, either before our senses or simply in our memory. Self-deceivers often resort to tactical avoidance of old facts and memories, or at least make efforts to downplay them.

c   The threat that the veil will be lifted is so real because we must repeatedly self-deceive in order to *accommodate new evidence*. Both old and new evidence must be avoided, ignored, downplayed, or rationalized away. As we will see later, this might demand that the self-deceived maintain a connection to reality and evidence, preventing them from becoming full believers in their deception.

d   Finally, *other people might challenge us* to defend our claims. As others very well might not share the motivation that drives our self-deception, they could have a more clear-headed assessment of the evidence and call us out for our biases. (Although, not always – there can be collective self-deception, or at least shared motives to believe.)

And when does this process end? Or is it never ending? We address these questions a bit later, in §2.5.

We have thus far focused on the dynamic problems for acquiring a self-deceptive belief. But there are also dynamic problems for motivation, intention, and emotion. For example, how can the motives and intentions persist as the deception unfolds? There is not just the worry of keeping up an elaborate charade. Additionally, if the deception is successful, then that very success could undercut the motive to continue deceiving. One needs to maintain access to the truth to better deceive. The worry is that successful self-deception could be self-undermining, as wholehearted false belief could lead one to no longer selectively avoid and attend to the evidence – call this the "letting one's guard down" phenomenon. And with respect to the emotions, they often need evidential or rational support – e.g., a reason to be happy or proud – just as do beliefs. So, we could have problems both getting deception off the ground and sustaining it for the sake of generating or regulating the emotions.

I have described these static and dynamic problems as they emerge on the assumption of the interpersonal model – that self-deception is like other-deception. This leads us into the immediate static problems with

40 THE BASIC PROBLEM AND A CONCEPTUAL MAP

contradictory beliefs and intentions (or motives, at least) to deceive, as well as the dynamic problems of achieving the deceptive outcome. While denying the interpersonal model can certainly mitigate these problems, it does not wholly eliminate them. It is still a muddle as to what the self-deceived believe, want, and intend; often there *is* the strong appearance of conflict and duplicity. The so-called sacrificial moves all have costs of their own. Finally, we know that there is *some* distinction between the cases that we would describe as self-deceptive and those that are merely cognitive mistakes.

§2.2 A classic picture: Freud and Davidson

One tactic that has recurred in the history of philosophical and psychological treatments of self-deception has been to fully embrace the interpersonal model: Self-deception is *even more like interpersonal deception* than we might have thought, in that the self is itself divided into distinct "persons," agents, or systems, each with its own agenda. If we thought that self-deception is like interpersonal deception, but for having one and the very same thing playing the roles of both Deceiver and Victim, then psychological and perhaps even logical impossibilities threaten. But by sacrificing the unity of self, self-deception becomes much more like unproblematic other-deception. The history of both philosophy and psychology has shown us that theorists often react to internal conflict by dividing the soul or mind into parts, with the result that the internal conflict more closely resembles interpersonal conflict. This can be done to handle phenomena like weakness of will, ambivalence, and temptation as well. These theorists hold that such commonplaces demand that we deny that even psychologically healthy people have truly unified selves. Let's begin our survey of views by considering some prominent philosophical and psychological treatments of self-deception in this tradition.

This self-splitting maneuver traces back at least to Plato's famous tripartite conception of the soul. Plato divided the self into three parts: the rational, the spirited, and the appetitive. The rational part is calculating; the spirited part contains emotions like disgust, pride, and anger; and the appetitive part lusts, hungers, thirsts, and seeks money. But why think these are distinct parts rather than different aspects of the same thing? One of Plato's main reasons for seeing conflict as reflecting a real psychic division was rooted in considerations of rationality or contradiction:[10]

> It is obvious that the same thing will not be willing to do or undergo opposites in the same part of itself, in relation to the same thing, at the same

time. So, if we ever find this happening in the soul, we'll know that we aren't dealing with one thing but many. (Plato, 1997, *Republic*: 436b)

The idea is that if we both want and do not want something, or both believe and do not believe something, then these contrary attitudes must reside in distinct parts of our mind. Logic alone, then, seems to dictate such a psychological separation.

Plato represented each of these three parts as a psychological agent in its own right. Metaphorically, they were represented as a little human being (rational), lion (spirited), and many-headed beast (appetitive). (*Republic*: 588c–590b) Each of these is the type of creature that can have its own desires, perceptions, and beliefs. Plato's overall approach offers what we would now call a *homuncular* theory – positing a little person (or in his case, sometimes a little beast) inside of you corresponding to different cognitive tasks or states. And for Plato there was a clear pecking order: Self-control demands that the little human being remains in charge and that the parts operate in harmony:

> [F]irst, that all our words and deeds should insure that the human being within this human being has the most control; second, that he should take care of the many-headed beast as a farmer does his animals, feeding and domesticating the gentle heads and preventing the savage ones from growing; and, third, that he should make the lion's nature his ally, care for the community of all his parts, and bring them up in such a way that they will be friends with each other and with himself. (Plato, 1997, *Republic*: 589a–589b)

To illustrate the tensions that can hold among these parts, Plato told an especially disturbing story. Leontius was a man full of unusually strong sexual desires for pale boys. One day he came upon a pile of corpses (pale, indeed!), and his appetite swelled with desire to stare upon them. But his sense of shame and disgust urged him to look away. He struggled, but eventually his lowly appetitive desires prevailed and his eyes gazed with lust (*Republic*: 439e–440a).

While the Leontius story is not a case of self-deception, it is not hard to see how the same general framework can be employed for that purpose. Among his examples of opposites, Plato includes these psychological states:

> Assent and dissent, wanting to have something and rejecting it, taking something and pushing it away. (Plato, 1997, *Republic*: 437b)

These are some of the very same opposing forces at work in self-deception. It is natural to say that part of the self-deceived assents to a proposition, while another part dissents to it. A part of the self-deceived wants to deceive, and another part rejects this project (which is the very reason why it has to be deceived or tricked). Finally, a part of the mind takes in the evidence, and another part pushes it away.

Over 2000 years later, Sigmund Freud hypothesized his own version of the tripartite soul: ego, id, and super-ego. Similar to Plato's model, each of these parts is said to possess its own versions of folk psychological states like beliefs and desires. The ego is the reality-centered, largely conscious self; the id unconsciously harbors our primitive desires – like the instinctual survival and sex drives (libido); and the super-ego serves as the conscience.

Plato's partitioned soul may have made self-deception *logically possible*, but more was needed in order to make self-deception *psychologically realistic*. Leontius's struggle is made sensible by positing different parts with different agendas. Still, Leontius was fully aware of his conflicting motives. Such awareness would undermine the very project of self-deception, so something more is needed. Freud's development of the unconscious, and the processes that make use of it (e.g., repression), provide us with some of these additional tools. The unconscious loomed larged in Freud's structural theory of mind – the id is wholly unconscious, and the ego and super-ego partially so. And his reason for positing the unconscious and a divided mind more generally was to explain psychological processes that otherwise seemed inexplicable:

> But we have arrived at the term or concept of the unconscious along another path, by considering certain experiences in which mental *dynamics* play a part. We have found – that is, we have been obliged to assume – that very powerful mental processes or ideas exist (and here a quantitative or *economic* factor comes into question for the first time) which can produce all the effects in mental life that ordinary ideas do (including effects that can in their turn become conscious as ideas), though they themselves do not become conscious ... Thus we obtain our concept of the unconscious from the theory of repression. The repressed is the prototype of the unconscious for us. (Freud, 1927/1960: 4–5)

Freud believed in *psychological determinism*, understood as the existence of psychological causes for every psychological event.[11] Indeed, he expanded the realm of the mental so as to causally explain phenomena that otherwise

THE BASIC PROBLEM AND A CONCEPTUAL MAP   43

would either only be random or due to physiological causes. While everything in the world may or may not have a cause, Freud was very bold in claiming that all psychological phenomena are determinatively explicable in terms of prior *psychological* states. Unconscious processes were posited to explain three kinds of phenomena in particular: parapraxes (e.g., slips of the tongue, overly convenient forgettings), dreams, and neuroses.[12]

Unconscious processes such as repression, if legitimate, could play a prominent role in self-deception by helping to hide motives and suspicions from the conscious self (ego). Freud saw evidence that the unconscious possessed both sophisticated reasoning ability and strategic powers:

> [W]e have evidence that even subtle and difficult intellectual operations which ordinarily require strenuous reflection can equally be carried out pre-consciously and without coming into consciousness. Instances of this are quite incontestable; they may occur, for example, during the state of sleep, as is shown when someone finds, immediately after waking, that he knows the solution to a difficult mathematical or other problem with which he had been wrestling in vain the day before. (Freud, 1927/1960: 20–21)

Freud then draws attention to unconscious processes that are even more germane to self-deception:

> In our analyses we discover that there are people in whom the faculties of self-criticism and conscience – mental activities, that is, that rank as extremely high ones – are unconscious and unconsciously produce effects of the greatest importance; the example of resistance remaining unconscious during analysis is therefore by no means unique ... If we come back once more to our scale of values, we shall have to say that not only what is lowest but also what is highest in the ego can be unconscious. (Freud, 1927/1960: 21)

Freud sees the ego as having to deal not only with an external world, but also with internal forces that are, in a sense, also external – the libido of the id and the moralizing of the super-ego. In managing these different forces, something that we might recognize as self-deception sometimes results:

> Whenever possible, it [the ego] tries to remain on good terms with the id; it clothes the id's *Ucs.* [unconscious] commands with its *Pcs.* [preconscious] rationalizations; it pretends that the id is showing obedience to the admonitions of reality, even when in fact it is remaining obstinate and

> unyielding; it disguises the id's conflicts with reality and, if possible, its
> conflicts with the super-ego too. In its position midway between the id and
> reality, it only too often yields to the temptation to become sycophantic,
> opportunist and lying, like a politician who sees the truth but wants to
> keep his place in popular favour. (Freud, 1927/1960: 58–59)

This ego is the source of censure and repression, keeping certain thoughts from consciousness. But this resistance – which resides with the ego – is itself unconscious.[13] The ego is not transparent to itself.

This is the Freudian picture of self-deception that so agitated the philosopher Jean-Paul Sartre, prompting his alternative theory of "bad faith" (*mauvaise foi*) and consciousness more generally. Sartre characterized bad faith as "a lie to oneself" (Sartre, 1943/1956: 87), and it can be seen as one variety of self-deception. It is an especially personal form of self-deception, however, as its subject matter is the person herself. Sartre gives especially vivid examples: As her date reaches for her hand, a woman attempts to avoid making a decision whether to willingly receive it. She remains passive, denying her radical freedom and pretending that she is not a bodily creature. In her passivity, she is in bad faith. In a second example, a waiter plays the part of being a waiter a bit too well. His movements are contrived, as if he is actively pretending to be a waiter – he is playing a game or becoming a robot. But he is not *merely* a waiter. In denying his freedom to choose how to act, he, too, is in bad faith.

Sartre denied that in these cases, or in similar ones that we might classify as self-deception, the phenomena are to be explained by making recourse to unconscious states. His target is the Freudian view, which sees these as acts of repression. Against the Freudian he argues, first, that lying to oneself requires that one and the same thing both possesses the truth and does not possess the truth at the same time, *and* knowledge of the truth must actively guide the deception. (Here recall the static and dynamic problems of self-deception.)

> It follows first that the one to whom the lie is told and the one who lies are
> one and the same person, which means that I must know in my capacity
> as deceiver the truth which is hidden from me in my capacity as the one
> deceived. Better yet I must know the truth very exactly *in order* to conceal
> it more carefully – and this not at two different moments, which at a pinch
> would allow us to re-establish a semblance of duality – but in the unitary
> structure of a single project. How then can the lie subsist if the duality
> which conditions it is suppressed? (Sartre, 1943/1956: 89)

THE BASIC PROBLEM AND A CONCEPTUAL MAP   45

This is a combination of both a conceptual point about lying and a psychological claim concerning the viability of a self-directed lie. The conceptual point about lying is that liars must both possess the truth and transmit a falsehood. Self-lying, then, requires that the self possesses the truth but simultaneously transmits a falsehood to itself.

Why is this psychologically impossible? First, for Sartre this is due to fundamental commitments about the nature of the mind that he inherited from René Descartes. Like Descartes, Sartre insisted that the mind is both unified and translucent to itself. For instance, Sartre writes that: "All knowing is consciousness of knowing" (Sartre, 1943/1956: 93). This seems to render the possession of contradictory beliefs, such as propositions (1) and (3) from our §2.1.1, psychologically impossible as they would remain unhidden within a single room of the mind, so to speak. The activity of self-lying also seems impossible to pull off, as the intention to lie would similarly remain before the same consciousness to which it lies.

In the end, the account of bad faith that Sartre offers is narrower and more idiosyncratic than how self-deception is normally understood. Bad faith is a very particular kind of lie to oneself – a denial of one's radical freedom. The woman on a date tries to escape making a choice, and the waiter passively accepts the waiter script. These are "lies," according to Sartre, because one cannot escape making a choice or escape responsibility – there are choices and there is activity even in these examples. But Sartre's ultimate characterization of bad faith makes it sound much less like a lie or intentional deception:

> In bad faith there is no cynical lie nor knowing preparation for deceitful concepts. But the very act of bad faith is to flee what it can not flee, to flee what it is. (Sartre, 1943/1956: 115)

It might be better to think of this activity as a pretense rather than as a lie. These people are pretending as if they are a thing-in-itself rather than a thing-for-itself, to use the Sartrean terminology. At best, this is just one kind of self-deception, albeit one intimately connected to the deep truths (supposedly) about the human condition.

Second, Sartre argued that even if there were robust unconscious mentality as on the Freudian picture, it would not solve the problem of self-lying. Sartre speaks of a "censor" within the mind that would have to mediate between the conscious ego and unconscious id in order to bring about self-deceptive (or self-lying) repression. The conscious ego is supposedly unaware of the hidden truth and is therefore incapable of executing any deception. And the id does not want to be repressed. For these reasons, Sartre insists that there must be a censor mediating the deception. But he argues that our original problem arises at the level of the censor, leaving us no better off for positing unconscious mentality:

> [T]he censor in order to apply its activity with discernment must know what it is repressing ... But it is not sufficient that it discern the condemned drives; it must also apprehend them *as to be repressed*, which implies in it at the very least an awareness of its activity. In a word, how could the censor discern the impulses needing to be repressed without being conscious of discerning them? How can we conceive of a knowledge which is ignorant of itself? (Sartre, 1943/1956: 93)

Sartre's reasoning here is flawed.[14] Sartre assumes – mistakenly – that the ego is fully conscious. In fact, the Freudian ego is partially conscious and partially unconscious. So, the censor, residing as a part within the ego, could very well be unconsciously aware of impulses or thoughts residing both within itself and elsewhere (e.g., in the id). Sartre also thinks that the censor must have second-order knowledge of its states and activities – i.e., it must know what it knows and what it is trying to do. But, in general, we do not think that knowledge demands higher order knowledge, or that the ability to perform a task (even a cognitive one) requires awarenesss that we are performing that very task.

But what if Sartre were correct and the censor must be consciously aware of its states and activity? On the Freudian picture, the ego and id are distinct entities – the id is like the Other, as Sartre himself recognizes. There is no incoherence or obvious psychological obstacle to the censor being consciously aware of a plan to repress the impulses or thoughts of a distinct entity like the id. Still, it does seem that a fully conscious or aware censor would have to be distinct from the conscious part of the ego that is deceived – the censor believes what the deceived denies. But we have already seen that there is no reason to insist that the censor has this consciousness and awareness. The Freudian will then likely want to separate the ego into conscious and unconscious aspects, as Freud himself did (see Figure 2.1).

This was the status of the debate over self-deception in the broader intellectual community by the middle of the 20th Century, and it can be couched in epic terms. On the one hand, we have Sartre representing the Cartesian view of the mind as unified, translucent, and radically free.

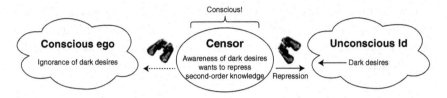

Figure 2.1 Sartre's critique of Freud

On the other hand, we have Freud representing the Platonic view, where the mind has distinct parts that can remain hidden from one another and manipulate us without our awareness. For Freud, unlike Descartes, the mind is governed by deterministic principles. While each side has its merits, neither side seemed to do full justice to the *irrationality* of self-deception. The Cartesian view – with its radical transparency – makes self-deceptive irrationality seem like a non-starter. The Freudian view, in contrast, turns apparent irrationality into rational thought and goal pursuit by mental faculties with their own information and agendas. This was the state of affairs that led Donald Davidson to focus on the irrationality of self-deception and highlight the problem for analytic philosophers.[15]

Davidson was probably the most accomplished 20th-Century analytic philosopher to venture into offering a philosophical treatment of self-deception. As a systematic philosopher, his approach was heavily influenced by his views on interpretation, belief, and rationality developed elsewhere.[16] To appreciate his account of self-deception, it is helpful to see how Davidson contrasts self-deception with wishful thinking. On his usage, wishful thinking is merely coming to believe something that you *want* to be true. Davidson thinks this is relatively commonplace, and not so difficult to explain. With wishful thinking we have a mental state (the desire or wish) that causes a cognitive state (belief) without rationalizing it. While self-deception often involves an element of wishful thinking, it involves much more – and this is where the theoretical difficulties emerge. Self-deception differs from mere wishful thinking in that the self-deceived must have had, at least originally, the non-deceptive belief. They then must have performed some *intentional* action in order to get themselves to believe otherwise. The self-deceived father originally believed that his son has a problem with alcohol, and, for *this very reason*, he intentionally set out to believe otherwise. Self-deception, for Davidson, must be intentional – steps must be taken by the self in order to produce the contrary belief. In this regard, self-deception becomes very much like interpersonal deception or outright lying.

THE BASIC PROBLEM AND A CONCEPTUAL MAP

It was important to Davidson that there be a strong connection between the true belief and the contrary, deceptive belief. In line with his intentional approach, he held that the true belief must somehow sustain the false belief:

> Self-deception is notoriously troublesome, since in some of its manifestations it seems to require us not only to say that someone believes both a certain proposition and its negation, but also to hold that the one belief sustains the other. (Davidson, 2004: 199)

Obviously, no belief will ever rationalize its negation, so this is a case of mental causation – one belief causing another belief – without rationalization. And note his choice of words: *sustains*. It is not just that the true belief prompts a transition to a false belief. Rather, the self-deceptive belief that not-p requires the simultaneous belief that p, as well as an ongoing causal connection between them. Davidson requires ongoing tension or opposition in the mind of the self-deceiver. If the self-deceived loses the truth, then she is no longer self-deceiving. The true belief is like a string that sustains a ball in midair.

This situation is irrational in a strong sense: It is irrational by the self-deceived subject's own standards. Indeed, this is the only kind of irrationality that Davidson recognizes. The irrationality at work in self-deception is similar to what Davidson previously diagnosed in cases of weakness of will (Davidson, 1980: Essay 2). With weakness of will, the subject acts contrary to her own best judgment. With self-deception, the subject believes contrary to her own best judgment. That said, however, she *also* believes in accord with her best judgment!

Davidson believed that this extreme degree of irrationality demanded mental partitioning. In the spirit of Plato, Davidson started by flatout refusing to ever attribute a contradiction – like proposition (4) from §2.1.1 – to any believer. Yet, he did allow that the self-deceived can have contradictory beliefs, such as propositions (1) and (3). In fact, he demanded it (Davidson, 2004: 200). And like Plato, Davidson thought that such opposing (contradictory) beliefs could be sustained only if they were segregated in different mental partitions. So we can see Davidson as operating in the tradition of both Plato and Freud, each of whom posited real divisions in order to account for inner conflict. The influence was explicit – indeed, one of Davidson's articles on irrationality appeared in a volume entitled *Philosophical Essays on Freud* and elsewhere he explicitly aligns himself with this tradition

THE BASIC PROBLEM AND A CONCEPTUAL MAP   49

(Davidson, 2004: 220). His partitioned yet highly rationalistic psychology is neither fully Platonic nor fully Freudian, but the influences are there.

Davidson pinpointed the irrationality of self-deception as residing in the very act that makes it possible: mental partitioning. The invocation of partitioning seems a bit contrived, as he takes it to be a necessary posit whenever confronted with blatant irrationality. In later writings, he even watered down this talk about partitioning:

> I spoke of the mind as being *partitioned*, meaning no more than that a metaphorical wall separated the beliefs which, allowed into consciousness together, would destroy at least one. (Davidson, 2004: 220)

So the psychological divisions are merely metaphorical, and elsewhere he says they are overlapping and fleeting (Davidson, 2004: 211) These are not the persisting and autonomous domains posited by Plato and Freud. And if the irrationality lies with partitioning the mind, what is the remedy? Logically, it seems that by unifying the mind the false belief will crumble under the weight of confronting the truth (although the converse could hold as well). But given the metaphorical nature of Davidson's account, unifying the mind might mean nothing more than being rational.

Putting this all together, we arrive at Davidson's official account of self-deception:

> An agent A is self-deceived with respect to a proposition p under the following conditions. A has evidence on the basis of which he believes that p is more apt to be true than its negation; the thought that p, or the thought that he ought rationally to believe p, motivates A to act in such a way as to cause himself to believe the negation of p. The action involved may be no more than an intentional directing of attention away from the evidence in favour of p; or it may involve the active search for evidence against p. All that self-deception demands of the action is that the motive originates in a belief that p is true (or recognition that the evidence makes it more likely to be true than not), and that the action be done with the intention of producing a belief in the negation of p. Finally, and it is especially this that makes self-deception a problem, the state that motivates self-deception and the state it produces coexist; in the strongest case, the belief that p not only causes a belief in the negation of p, but also sustains it. (Davidson, 2004: 208)

50   THE BASIC PROBLEM AND A CONCEPTUAL MAP

Notice the essential ingredients: there is the *evidentially supported belief* that p, this very thought *motivates* him to believe that not-p, *intentional* efforts are undertaken to achieve this end, he acquires the *unsupported belief* that not-p by *partitioning* his mind (among other things), and this psychological partitioning is *sustained* by the unwelcome, rationally supported belief. The mind is partitioned because of the egregious irrationality; but there still must be a causal connection between the beliefs residing in these different partitions.

This classic picture advanced by Freud and Davidson has what many will consider to be several virtues. Mostly, this is because it allows for the deceptive elements that we find in interpersonal cases. Both Freud and Davidson make self-deception out to be a strongly intentional and purposive act. The self-deceived are robustly deceptive in that there is deliberate scheming by one part against another. And the mental partitioning also allows for distinct beliefs corresponding to the mindsets of the Deceiver and the Victim. But all of this comes at some cost and risk. Foremost, the mind must actually be compartmentalized as they have argued. Internal conflict is very common, occuring even within the parts that Plato and Freud posit – e.g., there can be conflict within the spirited part of the soul or within the ego.[17] How many partitions will Davidson need to posit, and does this threaten to be merely an *ad hoc* "solution"? While their psychological posits were largely driven by speculative (Freud) or *a priori* (Davidson) considerations, one would think that empirical investigation should be able to either confirm or falsify the thesis of mental partitioning. And even if it is confirmed, one might object that this is no longer *self*-deception – i.e., in fragmenting the self, they have thrown out the baby with the bathwater. Finally, partitioning by itself is not enough to secure self-deception. It is also necessary that the distinct parts do not come into contact. Freud attempted to secure this by pushing the id into the unconscious. While Davidson is also happy to draw on the powers of the unconscious, he does not demand that any subset of the self-deceived's beliefs or motives remains unconscious. Rather, the opposing beliefs (and perhaps motives, too) must merely not be entertained *together* in consciousness.

§2.3 A minimal conception: motivated irrationality

Many eventually came to see the Freudian/Davidsonian picture as excessive. Chapter 3 is devoted to discussing the deflationary turn that followed – accounts that deflate the agency, practical rationality, and cognitive structure underlying self-deception. But before discussing those views we should mark a few other decision points along the way to constructing a theory of self-deception. In this section, I will explain what pretty much all theorists (should?) agree on as a starting point – the *Minimal Conception* of self-deception.

The first part of this conception concerns rationality. Deception must have something to do with truth and rationality, but there is no precise agreement as to whether the self-deceived must start with a true belief and end up with a false belief. It is arguable that this is not even required for interpersonal cases. In common parlance, *to be deceived* (state) is to have a false belief and *to deceive* (process) is to mislead. There is a sense, then, in which we could deceive someone (mislead them) without their acquiring a false belief. We might not be fully successful at inducing the false belief, but we could still take them away from the truth. Or, we could mislead them even if the belief we induce in them just so happens to be true.

Further, we could deceive someone in this process sense (mislead) without possessing the truth ourselves. This can happen in two ways. First, we could deceive someone when we ourselves are *simply ignorant* as to whether it is true or false. A salesperson might not have any idea whether the competitor's product – some other kind of smartphone, say – is any good, but she nevertheless might deceive a potential customer into thinking that this other option is of poor quality. The salesperson has an economic incentive, so she lies to the customer. Second, a deceiver could actually be *mistaken about what is true*, but deceive another nonetheless. An envious suitor might think that the princess's current lover has been faithful. But since this suitor wants to convince the princess to abandon her lover, the suitor deceives her into thinking that he has been unfaithful. The suitor might lie outright and manufacture evidence, but he could also draw her attention to misleading truths or simply raise suspicions to her without stating falsehoods outright. In these ways, the suitor deceives the princess even if, unbeknownst to him, the princess's lover really has been unfaithful.

We could use these same examples to argue that, not only is true belief not required of deceivers, the deceived need not actually believe what is false. Even if it happens to be true that the competitor's smartphone is inferior, there is a clear sense in which the customer has been deceived. And even though the princess has a true belief, there is also a clear sense in which she has been deceived by the suitor. Both of these lessons could be extended to self-deception as well: Self-deception might not require the original possession of true belief (qua Deceiver) or the acquisition of false belief (qua Victim).

52 THE BASIC PROBLEM AND A CONCEPTUAL MAP

Against these claims, some might insist that deception, simply in virtue of the meaning of the word, requires falsity – either false belief, or simply being pushed in the direction of falsity. But I recommend against this insistence. First, it is not too interesting to get into a verbal dispute over the meaning of the word "deception"; we should be much more interested in substantive debates over psychological possibilities and processes. And it would be better to be as inclusive as possible in characterizing self-deception. Second, this is especially so given that versions of both the static and dynamic problems can arise when we start with a false belief (based on misleading circumstanial evidence, say) and "deceive" ourselves into acquiring a true belief. Here is a fairly typical case of self-deception: Suppose that the bulk of the evidence available to Sam indicates that Sophie is not romantically interested in him. But he ignores that evidence, and he interprets other things she does in an overly optimistic manner. He indulges his fantasy that she would like to date him. Yet, contrary to what she has indicated, she really is quite interested in him – what he has "deceived" himself into believing is actually true. Would we really want to say that for that reason he is not self-deceived? I would discourage going down that path. The key ingredients of self-deception are still here: Sam has conflicting thoughts, a motive to believe, evidence contrary to that motive, and he has undergone a process of deception (i.e., evidence avoidance and distortion). If, contrary to fact, the evidence had instead been accurate – that is, she were not interested in him – that would clearly be a case of self-deception. But, in both cases, he would have been presented with the very same evidence and dealt with it in the very same way. It is better, then, to follow Davidson's characterization (given in the previous section) to the extent that it merely requires believing contrary to the evidence (but not necessarily coming to believe what is false).[18]

In formulating our Minimal Conception of self-deception, it is then better to focus on the irrationality rather than the falsity of the belief. Those who are deceived – in both interpersonal and intrapersonal cases – deviate from what it is rational (supported, justified, etc.) to believe, given the evidence available to them. The word "available" is important here. One can be self-deceived not only in irrationally responding to the evidence that they possess, but also by strategically avoiding unwanted evidence so that they do not have to deal with it in the first place. I will use "available" so as to include the evidence that people *could have had* as well as the evidence

THE BASIC PROBLEM AND A CONCEPTUAL MAP   53

that they in fact possess. As with any "could have" claim, it should come with qualifications. It is not that the person could have acquired the evidence only by taking extreme measures to do so. No, instead the evidence should be available by normal standards of accessibility – he easily could have acquired it, and likely would have done so had he not been motivated to avoid it.

Irrationality is part of our Minimal Conception of self-deception, but that is not enough. Self-deception must be distinguished from innocent cognitive mistakes that are not due to deception. There is a difference between merely being irrational and being self-deceptive, and one of the major problems of self-deception is to rigorously distinguish between the two. There is a strong consensus that the operation of cold biases alone does not count as self-deceptive. If I drastically overestimate the population of Israel or underestimate the population of Indonesia because of the ease or difficulty with which stories about the two countries come to my mind (availability heuristic), I am cognitively biased. But it would be very odd to say that I am self-deceived about their populations; I am merely wrong.

The most common way to distinguish self-deception from mere mistakes is to start by appealing to some incentive or motive that drives genuine self-deception. I have no incentive to underestimate the population of Indonesia, but I do have an incentive to be overly optimistic about my career prospects. Recall that hot biases are those biases that exist due to an incentive or motive.[19] We might then conclude that self-deception is irrationality that is produced by a hot bias. In interpersonal cases, people normally have an incentive or motive to mislead others, and this is a common way to distinguish deceiving someone from merely spreading misinformation to them. True, there are some people who lie to others compulsively, seemingly for no reason, and one might wonder if there also are compulsive self-deceivers. But if we press further, it is likely that we will find some incentive or motive – attention seeking? – driving the lies. If not, maybe we will want to say that these are more in the category of mere mistakes than that of deception.[20]

As with most things in life, matters are even more complicated. There is a range of cases within each of the two categories – mere mistakes and motivated misrepresentations – that we have distinguished. Mere mistakes can be due to the person being more or less epistemically negligent; motivated misrepresentations can be due to her being more or less deceptively

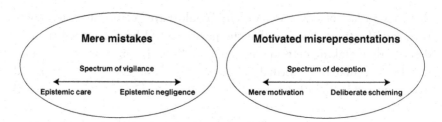

Figure 2.2 Some varieties of epistemic error and irrationality

scheming. (See Figure 2.2 for a depiction of these dimensions.) The distinction is evident in interpersonal cases as well: we can be more or less careful in the information that we spread to others, and we can be more or less misleading or deceitful toward others. These are different character flaws that we commonly distinguish in practical life. Sometimes we complain that someone is sloppy, lazy, or dim witted; other times we complain that someone is dishonest, manipulative, or deceitful. While these are different categories of criticism, they are not completely distinct. The sloppiness could be due to dishonesty, and extreme sloppiness might be indiscernible from outright deception. Extreme cases of epistemic negligence often call out for an explanation that points to a motive.

Combining the irrationality and motivation elements, we should all be able to agree on this Minimal Conception as a starting point:

> *Minimal Conception*: The self-deceived respond *irrationally* to the evidence available to them. This is not simply a cognitive mistake; it is a *motivated* misrepresentation.

While most accept that some kind of motivation is needed to make for self-deception, there is substantial debate over whether this formulation is *too* minimal. The next two subsections discuss the ongoing debate over whether something else is needed, such as an intention, to turn hot biases into full-throated self-deception.

§2.3.1 Intentionalism and motivationalism

We have already seen Donald Davidson clearly endorsing the intentionalist position: the self-deceived intentionally deceive themselves, and the deception itself is an intentional action.[21] Motivationalists, in contrast, think that

THE BASIC PROBLEM AND A CONCEPTUAL MAP   55

self-deception can be generated by motivation alone, and the self-deception need not be an intentional action:

> *Intentionalism*: Self-deception is an intentional action. The self-deceived have a specific intention to deceive themselves or to acquire the false or unsupported belief.

> *Motivationalism (anti-intentionalism)*: Self-deception is typically not an intentional action. Instead, self-deception typically is driven merely by a motivational state without an intention to deceive.

It may not be evident to you that there is a significant difference between being motivated to do something and having an intention to do so. But, the latter is supposed to involve greater *agency* on the part of the self-deceived. Davidson, who wrote highly influential articles on both agency and intention, builds his position on self-deception by contrasting it with mere wishful thinking. Wishful thinking is a kind of motivated irrationality, in which someone believes something merely because they want it to be the case. This is motivated, as the desire shapes the belief. And this is irrational, because wanting something to be the case is no reason to think that it actually is the case. Penelope believes that she will make the soccer team, say, simply because she wants to be on the soccer team. A motivationalist might count this as self-deception, but, at least as described so far, Davidson would demote it to the level of mere wishful thinking. This is because there is not yet any reason to think that the person has deliberately or intentionally done anything to acquire the unsupported belief.

As an example of self-deception that goes beyond wishful thinking, Davidson offers us a story about Carlos (Davidson, 2004: 209). Carlos has failed his driver's license test twice already, and he has received poor reports in the interim. The evidence does not support confidence that he will pass this next time. But it is discomforting to think that he will fail again, so Carlos positively *does* things to believe otherwise (e.g., redirects his attention and finds any bit of evidence he can that supports his preferred belief). Indeed, Davidson sees this as very rational behavior given Carlos's goals:

> His practical reasoning is straightforward. Other things being equal, it is better to avoid pain; believing he will fail the test is painful; therefore (other things being equal) it is better to avoid believing he will fail the test. (Davidson, 2004: 209)

So, this is all something Carlos *does* as a result of his *practical reasoning*. (Practical reasoning concerns reasoning about what to *do*, whereas theoretical reasoning concerns reasoning about what to *believe*.) While Davidson does not address the issue of responsibility, we very well might hold Carlos responsible for this erroneous belief, blaming him for it since he deliberately took steps to acquire that belief. (In Chapter 6, we will address the issue of responsibility in detail.) One complication, however, is that the practical reasoning and efforts seem below the level of his awareness. While they manifest purposefulness, they do not seem to be done with full awareness. And as we saw earlier, it might not even be possible to carry out a self-deceptive project in full awareness, given the connections between belief and rationality (see Figure 2.3).

There are various ways that the intentionalist could specify the content of the operative intention, as well as the role that it plays in the deception. Intentionalists could plausibly specify the intention driving the self-deception in at least these four ways:

a To acquire a *belief that not-p* (regardless of whether it is true of false). The self-deceived simply act so as to produce a belief that not-p, regardless of its truth or falsity (Bermudez, 1997, 2000). Using deceptive means is an incidental effect, not something that is specifically intended. Likewise, the falsity of the belief is incidental, as the self-deceived do not specifically intend to believe something false.

b To acquire a *false belief that not-p*. The self-deceived intend to acquire a false belief, in particular. That is, it is not just that the belief they intend to acquire happens to be false – they want and intend to believe something false.[22]

c To do *certain actions that lead to a belief that not-p*. The self-deceived might intend to avoid thinking about unwelcome evidence, intend to focus on happy thoughts, and so on. These behaviors can have the effect of being deceptive, even if the person does not intend to deceive herself (Mele, 2001, 18–19; Perring, 1997).

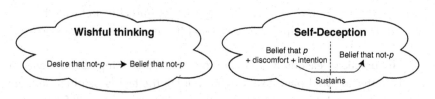

Figure 2.3 Davidson's contrast between wishful thinking and self-deception

THE BASIC PROBLEM AND A CONCEPTUAL MAP   57

d   To *deceive oneself into acquiring a (false) belief* that not-p. The self-deceived spe-
    cifically intend to acquire a belief (or false belief) through deceptive
    means. Here, the deception is not just incidental to the action. Davidson
    himself seems to endorse this option:

> Of course the relation is not accidental; it is not self-deception sim-
> ply to do something intentionally with the consequence that one is
> deceived, for then a person would be self-deceived if he read and
> believed a false report in a newspaper. The self-deceiver must intend
> the "deception". (Davidson, 2004: 207)

We can pair these candidate intentions according to whether they aim at
belief or deception: a) and b) are directed at belief; c) and d) are directed at
deception. And for each pair, the second member is more difficult to pull
off than the first. It is harder to intentionally acquire a false belief than it is
to intentionally aquire a belief that just so happens to be false (given that
we are sensitive to evidence and rationality). And it is harder to intentionally deceive yourself than it is to intentionally do things that just so happen
to be deceptive (because the trick of deception works better when the Victim is unaware of the plan). These are fine distinctions, to be sure, but if
a theorist demands that self-deception be intentional, it should not be too
much for us to ask what the intention is for.

There is a large philosophical literature on the nature of intentions and
intentional action, and we will touch on this later (§4.1). Intentions seem
necessary for action because one can have motives yet decide not to act
on them; and when one does act we can inquire as to what motive they
intended to act on. With self-deception, however, things become murkier
because these matters are not transparent to the self-deceived themselves.
Recourse is sometimes made to *unconscious intentions*, but others find this
notion psychologically problematic or unhelpful.[23]

Motivationalists deny that such intentions are necessary or even typical for self-deception. Instead, self-deception results merely from the right
kind of motive exerting its influence in the right kind of way. But what is
the motive for self-deception? Like the intentionalists, motivationalists can
offer different candidates for what drives self-deception. The usual candidates are some kind of desire or emotion:

a   *Desires.* As we saw with hot biases, desires can influence belief. In many
    cases of self-deception, it is fairly easy to identify the desire that skews

belief: he wants his kids to do well; she does not want to be played for a fool again. Or, we can appeal to a general desire to avoid discomfort. Freud and Davidson, for example, talk about the unpleasure or discomfort that always accompanies repression or self-deception. (It is irrelevant, to the point being made here, that they also posit intentions.) In §2.4, we will venture into the more fine-grained debate over the specific content of these desires.

b   *Emotions.* Emotions influence reasoning as well. One might think that there is a standard emotion associated with all kinds of self-deception. Annette Barnes (1997) and Mark Johnston (1988) claim that anxiety plays this role. Others are more liberal, allowing that various emotions can influence belief in ways that count as self-deceptive. Ariela Lazar (1999) discusses cases in which the emotions of anger, envy, grief, jealousy, rage, and cheerfulness serve as motives.

We should not think that the motives for self-deception must always be of the same limited kind. Hybrid and varied accounts are also possible, according to which desires and emotions of various kinds and in various combinations affect belief formation. Lazar (1999) presents such a heterogeneous view, appealing to the influences that desires, the emotions, and even the imagination have on belief.

Motivationalists can allow that self-deception is *sometimes* intentional. Alfred Mele, a prominent motivationalist, is open to this possibility, although he denies that intentions are typical of self-deception. He also claims that even when present, intentions are typically not directed at deception as such (Mele, 2001: 16–24). Motivationalists need only deny that such intention is necessary, although many do endorse the stronger claim that intentional self-deception is impossible to execute.

Motivationalists must also explain how these motives generate theoretical irrationality that rises to the level of deception. Desires are normally thought to generate action by presenting us with goals, and our beliefs then provide us with means to achieve those goals. For example, I desire to eat pretzels (goal), and I believe that there are pretzels in the pantry (means). So, I walk to the pantry – this is a rational action. Could desires play an analogous role in self-deception? Say, I desire to be successful. I believe that believing that I am successful is a means to being successful. (The embedded belief in the previous sentence is not an accident neither is it redundant.) So, I come to believe that I am successful. This is similar to the supposedly good practical reasoning that Davidson endorsed (Carlos

THE BASIC PROBLEM AND A CONCEPTUAL MAP 59

example), but here we have an obviously false premise – namely, believing that I am successful is not a particularly good means to making it happen.[24] There are such things as self-fulfilling prophecies, however, and maybe this is such a case. Still, there are many other self-deceptive cases – most cases, I would venture – for which believing that p is not a good means to bringing it about that p (e.g., believing that your spouse is faithful, in spite of the evidence, is not a good means to having her be faithful). So, the motivationalist might see desires as playing a different role in generating belief-like states. The means–end role for desires is more suitable for Freudian/Davidsonian intentionalist accounts. But these same problems arise – what rational purpose does self-deception serve, such that it would be practically rational to intend such a project?[25] We will return to this question in §2.4.

In addition to their goal-setting role in practical reasoning, desires and emotions can also act as mental causes that produce effects through associations or simple brute causal connections. This is the role to which many motivationalists appeal, and here they find extensive support in the empirical literature on motivated irrationality. Without question, such motives can skew belief. It is easier to find or recognize evidence supporting the hypotheses that we desire to be true (confirmation bias), we are more prone to optimism when experiencing the emotion of joy, and we are more likely to believe negative things about someone if we experience jealousy toward them. It is simply a fact about the human mind – perhaps covered by principles of association, or perhaps brute – that desires and emotions affect reasoning in such ways. The influence need not be a form of goal pursuit (e.g., there is no goal to confirm our hypotheses, be optimistic, or be pessimistic). The influence is not rational in either the theoretical or practical sense.

Mark Johnston (1988) argues against intentionalism in this spirit, objecting to the Davidsonian claim that self-deception is practically rational. In particular, he claims that coming to believe that not-p does not further the person's goals (except for cases of self-fulfilling prophecies or what he calls "positive thought"). Carlos is anxious about passing the test, and believing that he will do so does not make it any more likely that he will. The self-deception is not a rational, intentional action. Yet, it *does* alleviate anxiety:

> Our tentative conclusion is that wishful thought that is not positive thought is not rationalizable and so not intentional. But it does serve a purpose in that it reduces anxiety about the desired outcome. It is reasonable to be less anxious that not-p if one comes to believe that p. So although the

efficacy of the wishful thought or belief is intelligible only in terms of a rational connection between the attitudes involved, the generation of the wishful thought is not mediated by any rational connection. (Johnston, 1988: 74)

Self-deception is wishful thinking with some recognition of the truth (or evidentially supported belief), and therefore demands a divided or at least conflicted mind (recall Davidson). Johnston accepts this picture and speaks of the repression that is necessary to keep the truth out of consciousness. As Johnston describes it, these acts of repression are neither intentional nor simply causal. They are somewhere in between:

We should not treat repression, even in its complex manifestations, as an intentional act of some subagency guided by its awareness of its desire to forget. On the contrary, we should understand repression as subintentional, i.e., not guided by reasons but operating for the purpose of reducing anxiety. (Johnston, 1988: 76)

Johnston describes this subintentional mechanism as a *tropism*. This particular mechanism has a purpose, perhaps derived from evolution by natural selection, but its operation is merely mechanical rather than also being rational.

Motivationalists like Lazar and Mele hold that self-deception occurs whenever such motives influence our reasoning and cause us to believe contrary to the available evidence. But one could object that such influence alone is not truly self-deceptive. This is what Davidson thought, classifying such cases as mere wishful thinking.[26] Indeed, while hot biases are motivated and cold biases are not, why think that this difference makes the one category self-deceptive whereas the other is not? Further, others will argue that there simply *are* many other cases of self-deception that are not covered by the straightforward operation of such motives. Such cases involve greater agency, and they are described in our next subsection. This debate between intentionalists and motivationalists emerges again at various places in Chapters 3–5.

§2.3.2 *Degrees of deception*

The standard division between intentionalists and motivationalists might be a bit of an oversimplification. The deeper issue, I would suggest, is how much *agency* a person must exert in order for her motivated irrationality to count as self-deceptive. Intentions are supposed to get at agency, but agency also seems to admit of degree – one can be more or less involved in bringing about an action or outcome. So, we might want to look for ways to capture this sense of *degrees of agency* – and the correspondent notion of *degrees of deceptive activity* – that go beyond the customarily all-or-nothing depiction of intentional action. We can taxonomize self-deception based on the varying degrees of deceptive measures taken, and a more nuanced approach will be a slight improvement on the old intentionalist versus motivationalist debate.

To appreciate the possible degrees of deception invovlved in self-deception, let's turn back to the interpersonal model. There are various ways in which we can provide misinformation to others, and not all such ways count as lies. We could innocently spread a falsehood to others, where our mistake was unmotivated and this led to deception in the most innocuous sense. Say, I tell someone the incorrect start time for a ball game simply because I have a false belief and my spreading this misinformation is not to be explained by any prospect for gain or other incentive on my part. Next, someone could be under the influence of an emotion – joy, let's say – that causes her to be overly optimistic in reporting her academic expectations to others. The child does not necessarily paint this rosy picture in order to further some deceptive goal. It is simply that, as a matter of fact, her emotional state has this effect. But the interactions with others could be a bit more strategic, even if not intentionally coordinated. She could spread a falsehood – or simply a misleading picture of reality – to others because she wants them to share this belief, although she is not intentionally lying to them. Say, the child brags to her parents about her history quiz grade, although she did not think to tell them about the low test grade earlier in the week. The child may not be intending to deceive her parents, but she is nevertheless selectively providing them with biased information that generates a misleading picture of her academic performance to her own advantage. Finally, we could lie outright – knowingly and intentionally spreading a falsehood to others. The selective story told by the child was deceptive, but not as deceptive as an outright lie about her grades. As these examples progress from an innocent mistake to an outright lie, the person becomes more involved in a *deceptive project*. Similar to these degrees of interpersonal deceptiveness, motivationalists might be identifying a lower grade of self-deception, while intentionalists might be latching on to a more robust form (even if they misdescribe it as "intentional").

We can illustrate this by turning to examples of self-deceptive strategies. Self-deception can involve evidence avoidance or biased evidence search (among many other strategies). Evidence avoidance can be simply avoiding a likely source of disconfirming evidence, like not weighing yourself when you are on a diet. But it can also be very specific. A spouse, say, avoids driving past a particular woman's house because she suspects or even knows that her husband's car will be parked outside. The more specific the avoidance or the more that it demands deviations from her normal routine, the more likely it is that the self-deceiver has an inkling of what she would find there. Contrast this with a biased evidence search, in which a person seeks out favorable information by only watching news from a television station sharing his biases. Here the person need not possess the conflicting information; he never acquires it in the first place. And once he finds any bit of evidence supporting his favored view, he stops his search for evidence. Targeted evidence avoidance – e.g., not driving by a particular woman's house – is plausibly more deceptive than a merely biased search for evidence or a confirmation bias, because the former requires that conflicting information be repressed or withheld from the self (Funkhouser and Barrett, 2016). Regardless, it displays greater psychological complexity than does a biased evidence search. The biased news watcher might be single-minded in his delusions, but the self-deceiving wife is not so single-minded. It is not just that she might have general doubts or suspicions about her husband's fidelity; rather, she possesses specific bits of contrary evidence.

Some have argued for a *purposiveness* to self-deception that goes beyond its being a mere motivational bias, yet supposedly does not demand that it be an intentional action. At issue is the classic divide between merely causal processes and rational processes, and the possibility of murkiness in between. In action theory certain simple human and non-human behaviors (like a spider moving in on its prey) are described as purposive but not rational or intentional (Frankfurt, 1988). Such behaviors are purposive in that they involve the strategic pursuit of a goal in a way that is sensitive to environmental changes. But a spider does not reason, deliberate, or form intentions. Johnston's tropistic account might place self-deception in a similar category, although his description makes the process sound fairly dumb and mechanical. Dana Nelkin's view, discussed shortly, also takes self-deception to be purposive but not intentional.

Davidson, following Freud, thought of self-deception as involving an even greater level of deceptive activity or agential involvement, which goes beyond mere purposiveness. For starters, he thought that it required retention of the evidentially supported belief, an intention to form a contradictory belief, and actual success. Davidson is right that there are deceptions that go beyond mere wishful thinking, but we can certainly debate whether this demands that we admit something as robust as intentional self-deception, dual belief, and partitioned minds. We need not get into a verbal dispute over what counts as genuine deception, but we should at least recognize that deceptive activity comes in degrees. Figure 2.4 depicts these degrees of self-deceptive activity, understood in terms of the degree of agential involvement.

There is the *psychological* question whether all of these are even live possibilities, as some will deny that intentional self-deception is even possible (or at least typical). And there is also a *conceptual* question as to which categories deserve the label "deceptive." Each of these three – mere hot biases, purposive, and intentional – has been endorsed by some theorists as settting the threshold for genuine self-deception. But, again, the psychological issues about processes (possible, actual, and typical) should be of greater interest than the more conceptual issue of where to draw the line of deception.[27] We will return to this issue of genuine deception in §3.5.3.

Agential involvement is further complicated by the fact that distinct systems might be involved, and there might be significant differences between the *initiation* of self-deception and its *maintenance*. Self-deception could be intitiated or maintained by some combination of both System 1 and System 2 processes. Generally speaking, greater System 2 involvement will indicate greater agential involvement, as it is more associated with effort, control, consciousness, and the self. The relative contributions of these two systems can vary – some biases are automatic, some rationalization and evidence avoidance is effortful. Agential involvement can vary accordingly. It is also likely that the contributions of these systems change over time. Perhaps System 1 initiates the self-deceptive process, but System 2 steps up to maintain the bias over time. Matters could be reversed in

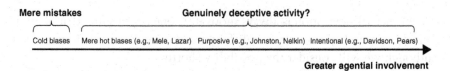

Figure 2.4 Degrees of self-deceptive activity

§2.4 What is the content of the motive? What is the proximate goal?

Both intentionalists and motivationalists take self-deception to be motivated. (Intentionalists just add something beyond the motive – intentions and intentional actions.) But what is the specific *content* of the motivation, and does it establish a *goal* for self-deceivers? It is common and perhaps intuitive to think that those who self-deceive toward believing that not-p do so because they desire that not-p. Donald self-deceives into thinking that he is not bald, because he desires that he not be bald. It is very natural to see that desire as both driving the self-deception and setting a goal for the self-deceiver. It is also natural to generalize the point to all cases of self-deception.

But the generalization is simply false. There are both *positive* (straight) and *negative* (twisted) varieties of self-deception.[28] As an example of the latter, a jealous husband might not have good evidence that his wife has been unfaithful, but he self-deceives into believing it anyway. He most definitely does not desire that she be unfaithful, though. Or a woman might have good evidence that she will get a job that she covets, but she self-deceives into thinking that she will not get that job because she does not want to raise her hopes and risk disappointment. The distinction between positive and negative concerns how the content of the deception aligns with the subject's motives and attitudes:

> *Positive self-deception*: Self-deception that not-p in which the person desires that not-p or has some other positive attitude (e.g., hope) toward not-p or negative attitude (e.g., anxiety) toward p.

> *Negative self-deception*: Self-deception that not-p in which the person desires that p or has some other positive attitude (e.g., hope) toward p or negative attitude (e.g., anxiety) toward not-p.

Given that self-deception is always motivated, one might think that neutral self-deception – where one is indifferent as to whether p – is impossible, although we will consider the possibility shortly.

We find negative self-deception not only in isolated cases, but also as a common symptom in various mental disorders: phobias, panic disorder, illness anxiety disorder, eating disorders (e.g., anorexia nervosa and

THE BASIC PROBLEM AND A CONCEPTUAL MAP   65

bulimia nervosa), paranoid personality disorder, and obsessive-compulsive personality disorder. Presumably, such people do not desire that they are in danger, trapped, sick, overweight, persecuted, or in a disordered environment. But they self-deceive in this direction anyway. Positive self-deception is less commonly found in mental disorders, but examples may include cases of narcissistic personality disorder. In these positive cases, the person likely wants to think that they have special significance or wants special attention, and they bias the facts accordingly. In Chapter 7, we will consider whether positive illusions – most of which do not rise to the level of a psychiatric disorder – are conducive to mental, social, or biological health. In addition to the mental disorder itself manifesting self-deception (e.g., someone is diagnosed with anoxeria nervosa, in part, because they have self-deceived beliefs about their body weight or shape), many others self-deceive so as to deny that they have any disorder at all (e.g., someone self-deceives that they do not have a substance/addiction disorder). See the American Psychiatric Association's DSM-5 for characterizations and diagnostic features for all these disorders; but the descriptions of these as involving self-deception are my own.

Let's return to the non-pathological cases. Our characterization of negative self-deception might be a bit confusing in that it might not be obvious how negative attitudes toward not-p or positive attitudes toward p could plausibly lead to self-deception that not-p. If you have anxiety about not-p, for example, why would you come to believe it? Or if you hope that p, why would you come to believe the opposite? Yet this commonly happens, either due to principles of association or as a defense mechanism. We can easily see how the woman who has great hopes for getting a certain job – and who also has evidence to justify these hopes – might self-deceive toward the negative (belief that she will not get the job) as a defensive or protective measure. This same case also illustrates how a desire that p (that she get the job) can motivate deception that not-p. This is similar to what psychologists call *self-handicapping*, except that rather than imposing obstacles to success the self-deceived impose obstacles to *believing* that they will be successful. In both cases, this could be for the sake of ego protection. In other cases, the effect is less strategic and could merely be due to psychological associations or contagion. If I have recurrent anxiety that not-p, that could contaminate my thoughts such that I overestimate the likelihood of not-p or outright believe it (Gendler, 2003). Here the belief does not further my goals, it is just a by-product of psychological principles (associations) at work. Lazar (1999: 281–282) offers examples of self-deception of this kind: A man who has recently lost his job is in a good mood when surrounded by friends, and his joy causes him to overestimate his prospects for finding a new job; a depressed woman feels inferior to her cousin, although the evidence does not support this.

The reality of negative self-deception might discourage us from seeking a unified account of self-deception, at least when it comes to motivation. Perhaps positive self-deception and negative self-deception are disparate phenonema in that they have quite different motives and goals. While positive and negative self-deception can be equally deceptive and exploit the same biases, one could easily come to think that they do so for different reasons. More generally, as we consider the variety of deceptive means, outcomes, and functions throughout this book, you should consider whether we are dealing with truly unified phenomena. When confronted with such diversity in the empirical world, some philosophers have a tendency to abstract away from differences and find unifying connections; others have a tendency to make fine distinctions and focus on the differences. Both approaches have their merits, but we should always ask what is the most fruitful way – in terms of theoretical and practical utility – to carve up this psychological space. And sometimes people find similarities or differences that simply are not there.

While there are superficial motivational differences between positive and negative self-deception, as we dig deeper perhaps there are motivational and teleological commonalities to discover after all. Mele – our exemplar motivationalist, whose position we discuss in detail in Chapter 3 – is completely open ended about the content of the motive driving deception, although the spirit of his view is that it is directed at the world being a certain way (e.g., not-p). But the primary motives driving self-deception could be either for the world be a certain way or to believe, think, or feel that the world is a certain way.

> *World-directed motives*: The self-deceived's motivation consists in a desire for the *world* to be a certain way (*p* or not-*p*) or in an emotional reaction to the *world* being a certain way.

> *Mind-directed motives*: The self-deceived's motivation consists in a desire or an emotional reaction to *believe, think, or feel* a certain way (that *p* or not-*p*).

We have already seen some views that offer mind-directed motives: Freud thought that repression, in general, served to mitigate psychic discomfort; Barnes and Johnston claim that self-deception aims at alleviating anxiety. These are motives that establish goals for the self-deceivers, and the goal is to change the mind rather than to change the world. In more recent years, Dana Nelkin (2002) offers the most perspicuous defense of a mind-directed theory that she calls the "desire to believe" account: The common motive driving all self-deception is a desire to so believe. One of the main advantages of this account is that it is supposed offer a unified motivational treatment of both positive and negative self-deception in that the motive is always for acquiring the belief that not-p, as opposed to world-directed motives that could be directed at either not-p or p. This desire to believe also establishes a common goal for all self-deception. The positively self-deceived father is motivated to *believe* that his son is an excellent student (psychologically comforting); the negatively self-deceived woman is motivated to *believe* that she will not get the job that she strongly desires (protection from disappointment).

The desire to believe is not necessarily or even typically conscious, but Nelkin (2002), Funkhouser (2005) and other belief-directed motivationalists think that these desires are real and efficacious states. These possibly unconscious, efficacious states are posited for the same general reason that other unconscious states are posited: to best explain behavior, especially behavior that is goal seeking. Indeed, the desire to believe establishes a goal for the self-deceived, allowing for self-deception to be purposive. This is analogous to interpersonal cases, in which the Deceiver, rather than being driven by a world-directed motive, is motivated to produce a belief in the mind of the Victim. Nelkin points out that this version of motivationalism also has strong affinities with intentionalism. Intentionalists (e.g., Pears, Davidson, Talbott, Bermudez) see self-deception as an intentional action aimed at producing a belief. Belief-focused motivationalists likewise see self-deception as purposive and aiming at belief, but somehow falling short of being intentional. Yet, one might think that such motivationalists are actually much closer to the intentionalists than they are to their supposed motivationalist kin (e.g., Mele, Lazar) who do not necessarily see self-deception as even being purposive. I suggest that we intepret Nelkin (2002) and Funkhouser (2005) as defending a middle ground position between world-directed motivationalists and intentionalists.

One might wonder: In what substantive sense do desire-to-believe motivationalists really differ from intentionalists? There are several points of agreement: Self-deception is driven by a motive to believe, the activity is purposive,[29] it manifests practical rationality, and (perhaps) subjects are responsible for it. Where are the differences? Most obviously, intentionalists posit an intention to deceive whereas motivationalists deny this. This means there must be some difference between purposive, practically rational behavior and that which is done with an intention. The desire-to-believe theorists can turn to the action theory literature on the distinction between merely purposive behavior and fully intentional behavior in order to defend their position. Nelkin (2002: 396) does not say much to distinguish the two, flatly claiming that there is an intention present in the one case but not the other. But what does this really amount to? More needs to be said about the roles of deliberation, cognitive effort, consciousness, and other aspects of agency in purposive and intentional behaviors. Nelkin thinks that the self-deceived can be responsible for their condition, because they can be aware of the influences that the desire to believe can have on their reasoning. Even if not an intentional action, Nelkin (2012) argues that self-deception can be due to negligence over which we have some control and can be responsible.

Desire-to-believe theorists like Nelkin and Funkhouser – as well as intentionalists like Pears, Davidson, Talbott, and Bermudez – all require that self-deceivers have preferences not only concerning the world, but also concerning their minds (beliefs). This is an example of what philosophers call *higher order thought* or what psychologists call *metacognition*: thought about thought. Metacognition requires a theory of mind – the capacity to attribute beliefs, desires, and other mental states to rational agents – in at least some sense. In the case of self-deceivers, the desire-to-believe view requires that the subjects: 1) possess the concept of belief, 2) are able to apply a theory of mind to themselves (e.g., attribute beliefs to themselves), and 3) have preferences concerning what they believe. Imposing these requirements fits with traditional views about self-deception as a failure of reflection and self-knowledge, which obviously demands the abilities to reflect and know one's mental states in the first place. These are fairly sophisticated cognitive capacities, capacities likely not found elsewhere in the animal world or in young human children. Nelkin (2002: 398) points out this consequence, seeing it as a virtue that her theory explains why only human beings of a certain age are capable of self-deception. While other animals might be capable of motivated irrationality, they are not capable of self-deception as these theorists understand it.

In summary, there are three main points in favor of the desire-to-believe account. First, it offers a more unified account of self-deception than do the world-directed alternatives in that it covers both positive and negative self-deception with the same kind of desire. Intentionalists, by citing an intention to bring about that belief, can better handle negative cases than can motivationalists, but desire-to-believe theorists can offer a very similar explanation. But for both intentionalists and mind-directed motivationalists, they need to explain why the self-deceived would intend or be motivated to produce a negative psychological state. Second, it makes the self-deception more deceptive to the extent that it posits a real motive to

THE BASIC PROBLEM AND A CONCEPTUAL MAP 69

bring about a change in mind. This also maintains a similarity to inter-personal deception, in which the motive is to produce a belief in the Victim. Motives to believe also distinguish self-deception from other forms of motivated irrationality in which a world-directed desire just so happens to distort belief but not for any strategic purpose of desiring a change in mind that would make this count as deceptive.[30] This higher threshold for deception also has the consequence that only reflective creatures with a theory of mind (in at least a minimal sense) are capable of self-deception. Third, it shows self-deception to be a purposive behavior for which the person can then be held accountable. On this view, the self-deceived are also practically rational, as producing a belief that not-p is a rational output of the desire to believe that not-p. In these regards, the desire-to-believe account is very similar to intentionalism.

Kent Bach (1981) advocates for a mind-directed motivationalist account that differs slightly from Nelkin's desire-to-believe formulation. Rather than being motivated by a desire to believe that not-p, he claims that the self-deceived are motivated to think that not-p. Bach's is *also* a world-directed account, as his analysis has it that the self-deceived also desire that not-p, which, in turn, motivates them to avoid the thought that p. In fact, it might be better to classify Bach as a world-directed motivationalist, as that is the more fundamental motive on his view. Having that as the fundamental motive also seems to take away the practical rationality of self-deception: the combination of desiring that not-p but believing that p does not make it rational to avoid the thought that p. This is a welcome result if one thinks that self-deception is practically irrational.

As he understands the term, belief is a dispositional state characterized by its functional relations to sensory input, behavior, and other psycho-logical states. This usage is certainly not idiosyncratic among philosophers of mind and action. Bach is not so concerned with the details of how this account is filled out, but behavioral dispositions are essential to belief. Thinking, in contrast, is an occurrent state – something that occurs at a time, an event. Thinking is close to being a purely phenomenological state for which the prospects of self-ignorance are low; you are more likely to be ignorant of your psychological dispositions than of your thoughts. How, then, is believing connected to thinking? When one believes that p, one is disposed to think that p. But this is not exceptionless. And one can certainly think that not-p without so believing.

Bach's claim is that self-deceivers merely want the psychological comfort of thought. Not only do they not want the behavioral dispositions that go with believing that not-p, they positively might want to preserve the behavioral dispositions of the evidentially supported belief that p. Funkhouser (2005) continued this theme, speculating that maybe the self-deceived merely desire the surface, phenomenological characteristics of belief (e.g., avowals and conscious thoughts) rather than the deeper behavioral dispositions. This is a qualified version of the desire-to-believe view. Funkhouser (2005) argues that the surface characteristics of belief (e.g., avowals and conscious thoughts) can often be indulged without jeopardizing the deceptive enterprise. But if the self-deceived came to acquire the full behavioral dispositions of a believer, they would have no reason to avoid fully confronting the evidence. This would likely end up undermining the deceptive project, as the person would have a difficult time overcoming the full weight of the evidence. This line of argument emphasizes strategic avoidance of the evidence, as such avoidance is supposed to demonstrate both a desire to maintain a certain state of mind (e.g., the thought that not-p) and the belief that p. Funkhouser (2005) draws on the interpersonal model to support this mind-directed form of motivationalism: Just as interpersonal deception aims at changing the mind of another, self-deception aims at changing one's own mind.

If the motivation for self-deception is mind directed, then there is at least the possibility of self-deception with respect to p when the person has no direct motive toward p/not-p. One could desire to believe that not-p without having any vested interest in whether p or not-p. Maybe it is socially desirable to have a certain religious or cultural belief, although you really do not care about the issue one way or another. You might then be motivated to deceive yourself toward that belief because of the advantages of social conformity while remaining indifferent about the matter itself. In this sense, *indifferent self-deception* is a possibility, consistent with self-deception always being a type of motivated irrationality. Typically, however, one will not have a motive to believe that not-p unless one also has desires or emotions directed at p/not-p itself. Similarly, for mind-directed theorists there could be cases of *ambivalent self-deception*, in which the person has a wholehearted desire to believe that not-p, but she is ambivalent at the world-directed level (i.e., desires that p and desires that not-p). Imagine a familiar case of world-directed conflict – a person desires to indulge the pleasures of the flesh while also desiring to remain pure (abstain). But their mind-directed thoughts are wholeheartedly behind the desire to think of themselves as pure. Ambivalent self-deception, unlike indifferent self-deception, is probably possible for world-directed motivationalists as well, although they will simply refrain from positing the mind-directed desire. They will have a harder time explaining, however, why the bias operates in one direction rather than another (see Table 2.2).

Table 2.2 Different accounts of the motives for self-deception

	Desire that not-p	Desire that p	Desire to believe that not-p	Desire to think that not-p
World-directed, positive motivationalism	X			
World-directed, negative motivationalism		X		
Mind-directed, positive motivationalism (standard)	X		X	
Mind-directed, negative motivationalism (standard)		X	X	
Mind-directed, ambivalent motivationalism (standard)	X	X	X	
Mind-directed, indifferent motivationalism (standard)			X	
Bach's world- and mind-directed motivationalism	X			X

In addition to desires for beliefs or thoughts, one could also hold that the motive for self-deception is directed at other states of mind. These could include desires for emotions, memories, pleasure, or other phenomenological states. But in practice, even theorists who posit motives like anxiety (e.g., Johnston and Barnes) still see self-deception as aiming at belief so as to alleviate anxiety. To my knowledge, philosophers have not developed theories that hold that the goal of self-deception is to directly achieve these other kinds of mental state rather than aiming to acquire belief-like states so as to satisfy such goals. But such theories would certainly be worth exploring.

§2.5 What is the end state?

As mentioned earlier, self-deception can be thought of as either a process (self-deceiving) or a state (self-deceived). It might be logical to think of the process of self-deception as ending once this state has been achieved.

THE BASIC PROBLEM AND A CONCEPTUAL MAP

But the relationship between process and state is not clear- cut. Is the state of being self-deceived the goal of self-deception, or is it simply the terminus? Does the state tend to persist once it has been reached, such that no further self-deceiving process is necessary? Or is self-deception an activity with no end? Or is self-deception simply a state of mind, with the path that led one there merely incidental?

As we saw in the previous section, some hold that the motives driving self-deception provide goals, such as to acquire the belief or thought that not-p. These are mind-directed motives. If self-deception is a practically rational activity, then achieving these goals would presumably end the self-deceptive process, much like eating a meal would satisfy one's hunger and end the search for food. But if the mind-directed motives that drive the self-deceptive process do not provide a goal, then the acquired beliefs (or whatever other mental states happen to constitute the self-deceptive state) are simply the terminus of a purposeless "deceptive" journey. Similarly, for world-directed motivationalists the acquisition of a belief that not-p might terminate the self-deceptive process, but it is hard to think of this as goal satisfaction if the motivation was a desire that the *world* be such that not-p. Believing does not make it so! Such views implicitly depict the self-deceptive process as practically irrational or, at best, arational: The terminal state that ends the self-deception does not actually satisfy the desire motivating the process.

As we will see later, whether the self-deceived ever acquire the deceptive belief that not-p is also in dispute. Here we are not talking about those who are merely attempting to self-deceive, but rather about those who are supposedly correctly described as self-deceived. According to some, self-deception necessarily requires a tension or conflict – in particular, a sustained connection to the truth throughout the deceptive process – such that the self-deceptive state is never a total victory. (This issue receives further discussion in §3.5.4 and §5.1.) Kent Bach insists on this point:

> In self-deception, unlike blindness or denial, the truth is dangerously close at hand. His would not be a case of self-deception if it hardly ever occurred to him that his wife might be playing around and if he did not appreciate the weight of the evidence, at least to some extent. If self-deception were just a matter of belief, then once the self-deceptive belief was formed, the issue would be settled for him; but in self-deception it is not. (Bach, 1997: 105)

Even if the self-deception results in a state of total self-deceit (i.e., belief that not-p), it is unlikely that the process can terminate and sustain itself without

THE BASIC PROBLEM AND A CONCEPTUAL MAP   73

the person making ongoing efforts. As we detailed in §2.1.2, sustaining the illusion will likely require the self-deceived to repeatedly distort or avoid new evidence and respond to new challenges from their peers. Intentionalists like Freud and Davidson saw repression or self-deception as an ongoing activity – e.g., the true belief must sustain the false belief, according to Davidson. But whether or not intentionalism is true, it is unlikely that the self-deceived state will persist without ongoing deceptive efforts. And, somewhat puzzling, some theorists think that if the self-deception were a total success – in the sense that the person comes to wholeheartedly believe that not-p – that would make her no longer self-deceived, but outright deluded instead.

We have started with the process of self-deception and asked when, if ever, it ends. But some think this entire approach is wrongheaded. Rather than being a process, these theorists hold that self-deception is just a state of mind. While there obviously is a process that leads people to being self-deceived, Robert Audi has argued that self-deception fundamentally is a state rather than a process. Audi (1997) is explicit about this, saying that whether someone is self-deceived is wholly determined by their current cognitive state rather than being even partially determined by the process that brought them there. He emphatically states that self-deception is not an historical concept: A cognitive duplicate of a self-deceived person must also be self-deceived, no matter how they came into that state. Audi's view has it that self-deception is achieved whenever the correct cognitive relations hold at a time. We might think this is insufficient because we think that a deceptive project – carried out in time – is also necessary for self-deception. Or we might think that Audi also needs to hold fixed the evidential factors that are extrinsic to the mind.

§2.6 Conceptual map

We can incorporate our discussion up to this point into a flowchart, mapping the conceptual space for possible views on self-deception or the multidimensional space of psychological possibilities for motivated irrationality (whether or not these possibilities are all best described as "self-deception"). As we delve further into these issues in subsequent chapters, we can add to this conceptual map. As we saw in the preceding section, self-deception either is a process or it is carried out through one. The process logically divides into three major stages: the initial conditions, the deceptive project, and outcomes. There are multiple decision points at each stage, and we

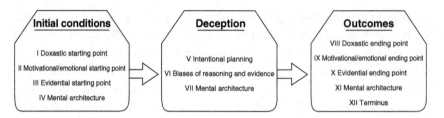

Figure 2.5 Conceptual map

can get a good sense of the space of possible positions on self-deception by considering the different ways in which these answers can be combined (adding to the options, if necessary). Not all combinations are viable, and these answers alone do not constitute a theory. But this logical approach serves to carve off terrain for further investigation and elaboration, and it might help us envision new possibilities (see Figure 2.5).

The concept of self-deception is fuzzy, as is almost every philosophically interesting concept (free will, morality, personhood, etc.). Multiple paths through this conceptual space might warrant the label "self-deception." But I urge that we try to keep our focus more on the philosophical problems and psychological possibilities rather than succumbing to terminological disputes.

Initial conditions

I   *Doxastic starting point*
    a S believes that p (where p is evidentially supported).
    b S believes that not-p (where not-p is evidentially unsupported).
    c S believes that p and believes that not-p.
    d S neither believes that p nor that not-p.
    e S's belief states with respect to p are indeterminate.
    f S suspects that p or doubts that not-p.

II *Motivational/emotional starting point*
    a S has a standing desire that not-p (or acquires such a desire in light of the unwelcome belief or available evidence pointing toward p).
    b S has a standing desire that p (or acquires such a desire in light of the unwelcome belief or available evidence pointing toward p).
    c S has a standing desire to believe that not-p (or acquires such a desire in light of the unwelcome belief or available evidence pointing toward p).

THE BASIC PROBLEM AND A CONCEPTUAL MAP   75

    d   S has a standing desire to think that not-p or have phenomenological experiences that not-p (or acquires such a desire in light of the unwelcome belief or available evidence pointing toward p).

    e   S has standing anxiety that p (or acquires such anxiety in light of the unwelcome belief or available evidence pointing toward p).

III   *Evidential starting point*

    a   S possesses or has available to her sufficient evidence that p.

    b   S is in an evidentially neutral position with respect to p.

    c   S possesses or has available to her sufficient evidence that not-p.

    d   S possesses deeply conflicting evidence as to whether p.

IV   *Mental architecture*

    a   S's mind is unified, at least in its beliefs and attitudes toward p/not-p.

    b   S's mind is partitioned regarding its beliefs or attitudes toward p/not-p.

    c   S's mind is transparent in its beliefs and attitudes toward p/not-p.

    d   S's mind is opaque in its beliefs or attitudes toward p/not-p.

Deception

V   *Intentional planning*

    a   S deliberates whether to acquire the belief that not-p.

    b   S deliberates whether to deceive herself into believing that not-p.

    c   S plans how to acquire the belief that not-p.

    d   S plans how to deceive herself into believing that not-p.

    e   S executes an intention to acquire the belief that not-p.

    f   S executes an intention to acquire the false belief that not-p.

    g   S executes an intention to engage in activities that are *de facto* deceptive with respect to believing that not-p.

    h   S executes an intention to deceive herself into believing that not-p.

VI   *Biases of reasoning and evidence*

    a   S is influenced by hot biases inclining her to believe that not-p.

    b   S is influenced by cold biases inclining her to believe that not-p.

    c   S takes steps to acquire or manufacture misleading evidence supporting not-p.

    d   S takes steps to avoid evidence supporting p.

THE BASIC PROBLEM AND A CONCEPTUAL MAP

e   S changes her epistemic or doxastic standards in regard to p/not-p.

f   S takes steps (e.g., rituals, social networks, etc.) to otherwise manipulate her thoughts regarding p/not-p.

VII *Mental architecture*

a   S's mind is restructured (e.g., partitioned) to allow for self-deception.

b   S draws on different functional parts of the mind so as to execute self-deception.

c   S represses certain thoughts or otherwise draws on the powers of the unconscious.

Outcomes

VIII *Doxastic ending point*

a   S ends up believing that p.

b   S ends up believing that not-p.

c   S ends up believing that p and that not-p.

d   S ends up partially believing that p and that not-p, or their belief states are indeterminate.

e   S ends up neither believing that p nor that not-p.

IX *Motivational/emotional ending point*

a   S continues to desire that not-p.

b   S continues to desire that p.

c   S continues to desire that she believe that not-p.

d   S's desire to believe that not-p is satisfied.

e   S continues to desire to think that not-p or have phenomenological experiences that not-p.

f   S continues to be anxious that p.

g   S's anxiety concerning p is alleviated.

X *Evidential ending point*

a   S possesses or has available to her sufficient evidence that p.

b   S is in an evidentially neutral position with respect to p.

c   S possesses or has available to her sufficient evidence that not-p.

d   S possesses deeply conflicting evidence as to whether p.

XI *Mental architecture*

a   S's mind ends up unified in its beliefs and attitudes toward p/not-p.

b   S's mind ends up partitioned in its beliefs or attitudes toward p/not-p.

THE BASIC PROBLEM AND A CONCEPTUAL MAP   77

    c   S's mind ends up transparent in its beliefs and attitudes toward p/not-p.

    d   S's mind ends up opaque in its beliefs or attitudes toward p/not-p.

XII *Terminus*

    a   S's self-deception terminates as a result of her ending doxastic state.

    b   S's self-deception terminates as a result of her ending motivational or emotional state.

    c   S's self-deception is ongoing, in spite of the doxastic and motivational/emotional outcomes.

The options under any given heading are not necessarily mutually exclusive (although in some cases they are), neither must a value be chosen under every heading (e.g., motivationalists need not endorse anything under the "intentional planning" heading). But we can track theories on this conceptual map, incomplete as it might be in its current form. Davidson's theory, for example, has the following values: Ia, IIc, IIIa, IVa, Vh, VI (any of a–f), VIIa, VIIIc, IXc/d, Xa, XIb/d, and XIIc.

§2.7 Nearby phenomena

While self-deception is a fuzzy concept, we can still distinguish it from proximate forms of irrationality, conflicted thinking, or fantasy. The following psychological and philosophical concepts are relatively near to self-deception, but they are also importantly different:

> *Cold biases*: Systematic deviations from the norms of reasoning that are not motivated, and therefore not deceptive. There is a difference between merely being wrong and being deceived.

> *Ambivalence*: This is to have mixed thoughts about something at a time. In the case of belief, this means that you neither fully believe nor fully disbelieve (at the same time). The self-deceived might be described as having mixed thoughts. But, ambivalence by itself need not be motivated neither need it be irrational. If the evidence is truly mixed, then ambivalence is the rational response.

> *Vacillation*: This is to go from believing that *p* to either disbelieving that *p* or outright believing that not-*p*. This process is carried out in time, and there need not be any time at which contradictory beliefs are simultaneously

held. Further, this vacillation need not be motivated. For that matter, it could also be rational, given subtle changes in the evidence or one's attention to it.

Hypocrisy: Hypocrisy can give rise to symptoms similar to self-deception. Notably, the hypocrite will say one thing and behave in a contrary manner. But the hypocrite is not lying to himself; he is lying to *you*. His words likely do not reflect his beliefs. And there need not be any irrationality in his beliefs. The hypocrite, unlike the akratic, need not think he should or needs to act as he claims to believe.

Weakness of will (akrasia): Weakness of will is intentionally acting contrary to your own best judgment. It is a form of practical irrationality – not acting on your best reasons. Self-deception is a form of theoretical irrationality – not believing on your best reasons. With weakness of will the mismatch is between thought and action. With self-deception, the mismatch is fully in thought. The weak willed have opposing desires. The self-deceived appear to have conflicting belief-like states.

Lying to yourself: Lying to yourself is an intentional act of deception. This is likely impossible to pull off, at least if performed consciously, as it would require that you knowingly tell yourself what you take to be a falsehood. If you know it is false or unsupported, it is hard to see how you could possibly believe it. Most theorists think that self-deception need not be this intentional, overt, or direct.

Bad faith: This is the Sartrean notion of denying your own radical freedom and mistakenly thinking that you have a pre-established essence – that you are a thing-in-itself rather than a thing-for-itself. At most, this is just one very particular form of self-deception.

Willful ignorance: This is when you take steps, such as avoiding evidence altogether, to preserve your own ignorance on some matter. This is often motivated by a fear of what you might discover. It is irrational to the extent that it discourages acquiring evidence to ground one's beliefs. This could be a type of self-deception. But as it stops the flow of information altogether, there need not be an evidentially supported belief to suppress or oppose. This situation is one in which the person has an absence of information altogether rather than the presence of unwanted information.

Willing belief: To will a belief is to acquire it directly simply by deciding to do so. Bernard Williams (1973) and others have argued that this is impossible. Fortunately, self-deception does not require such efficiency or such radical disregard for the facts. The self-deceived are normally depicted as being sensitive and responsive to evidential considerations, so they must deceive themselves by manipulating the evidence. Self-deception is a process that is drawn out in time, rather than following immediately from a decision.

Confabulation: To confabulate is to tell a story that may not be genuinely believed, but without any intention to deceive. The confabulator need not have any motives specific to the content of the confabulation (e.g., may not care whether it is true). They might confabulate merely to fill in gaps in memory or to cover other deficiencies, which could be thought of as a motive of its own.

Wishful thinking: This is thinking or believing that something is true merely because you want it to be true. Some will distinguish this from self-deception by requiring more robust efforts for the latter (Davidson). Others will deny that wishful thinking results in full belief, counting it more as a daydream or fantasy. Still others will classify some cases of wishful thinking as outright self-deception.

Imagination: To imagine is to represent something as true, but not to a belief-like level. Imaginings are normally known to be non-verdical. It may seem that the self-deceived only imagine or fantasize that what they want to believe is true – indeed, Lazar (1999) pursues this possibility. But, the self-deceived likely want something more robust than mere imagination. They seem to want something to really be true or at least to really believe it. Imagining is a harmless kind of insensitivity to the evidence, but self-deception seems more serious because it affects the person's behavior in more systematic ways.

Pretense: To pretend is to act as if something is true without actually believing it. Pretense behavior might resemble self-deception, since one might think that the self-deceived are acting insincerely and that they do not genuinely believe what they avow. Indeed, Gendler (2007) argues that self-deception is an act of pretense. But people are normally aware when they are merely pretending, and one might think that the self-deceptive condition is much more sincere than are acts of pretense.

Summary

- The Basic Problem of self-deception is how a single self can take deceptive measures against itself and actually succeed. We were introduced to specific versions of this problem: Belief, Motivation/Intention, and Deception. There are both static and dynamic problems of self-deception. What are the belief and motivational states of the self-deceived? How can a deceptive project directed against the self possibly succeed?
- Freud and Davidson represent one traditional and still common way of handling the Basic Problem: Divide the self.
- Minimally, self-deception is a form of motivated irrationality. Self-deception must be distinguished from mere mistakes. Theories can be divided into the intentional or merely motivational. Perhaps it is more accurate to say that self-deception can be more or less purposive.
- There is both positive and negative self-deception. This makes it harder to identify a common motive for self-deception. The motives could be world-directed or mind-directed. These motives might or might not set goals for self-deceivers. There is a lot of disagreement over the conditions under which self-deception terminates, or if self-deception must be an ongoing process.
- We can map positions on self-deception by identifying initial conditions, deceptive measures, and outcomes. Self-deception should be distinguished from other kinds of irrationality, conflicted thinking, and fantasy.

Recommended reading

For an authoritative discussion of the static and dynamic puzzles of self-deception, along with deflationary treatments of them, see Mele (1997, 2001). We will critically examine Mele's positive position in the next chapter.

As believers, we cannot totally disregard evidential and rational concerns. Williams (1973) makes the classic case against deciding to believe. Davidson (1984) and Dennett (1987) argue, in a series of essays, that rationality is the norm guiding belief attributions. These combine to support the view that self-deceivers, to the extent that they are concerned with belief, must manipulate evidence or reasons to achieve their objectives.

For an introduction to his theoretical reasons for positing robust unconscious processes, see Freud's *Introductory Lectures on Psycho-Analysis*. For a more informal and amusing series of examples with, at times, fanciful

THE BASIC PROBLEM AND A CONCEPTUAL MAP   81

explanations accompanying them, see his *The Psychopathology of Everyday Life*. Sartre's classic response to Freud and his positive theory of bad faith are presented in Chapter Two of *Being and Nothingness*. Davidson's intentionalist views on self-deception are presented in Essays 11–14 of his *Problems of Rationality* (2004).

Nelkin (2002) makes a very clear case for mind-directed motivationalism. There she makes her case that self-deception can be purposive (goal seeking) without being intentional. Lazar (1999) offers a good counter to the intentionalism of Davidson and the purposiveness in Nelkin's form of motivationalism.

Notes

1 Although some deny this, seeing "self-deception" as a fundamentally different word than "deception." Exploiting comparisons to words like "self-taught," Ruddick (1988) claims that self-deception is not a two place relation.

2 The distinction and the "static" and "dynamic" terminology originates with Mele (1987, 1997).

3 Kipp (1980) also argues that it is impossible to carry out a self-deceptive project, at least if we take "self-deception" *literally* (a word he repeatedly emphasizes). He recommends a metaphorical reading instead.

4 Although there are a few logicians who actually deny this! This view, dialetheism, is advocated by Graham Priest (1995). We will not explore this dark possibility.

5 "Doxastic" is a philosophical term for a belief-like attitude.

6 Davidson (2004, Essay 13) discusses (basically) these same four sentences and the logical or psychological problems they raise.

7 Velleman later backed off on this claim, in large part due to phenomena such as self-deception – he mentions wishful thinking in particular (Shah and Velleman, 2005). On his revised view, belief is more weakly regulated by the truth, and it is governed by the *norm* that truth is the standard of correctness for belief. Steglich-Petersen (2006) offers an excellent presentation of these issues.

8 Hume's view was a bit more complicated, given his formulation of the problem of induction, in that he thought that we are wired to ignore rational skepticism and believe on the basis of habit or custom instead. (1777/1975, Section V) His view seems to be that we are wired to believe according

to what most non-philosophical people would judge to be good evidence (e.g., regularities observed in the past), although his position is not always consistently stated.

9 But see Funkhouser (2003) for an empirically supported defense of the claim that believers might be even this extremely irrational.

10 Plato also claimed that the different parts of the soul can be distinguished by their distinctive pleasures and aims. (*Republic*: 580d–581c) It is this very feature – differing agendas – that explains the existence of conflict. Plato famously held that analogues to these psychological parts are also found, on a larger scale, with the three classes of a city.

11 See his *The Psychopathology of Everyday Life* (1960), Chapter XII for a bold statement.

12 These categories correspond to the three parts of his *Introductory Lectures on Psycho-Analysis* (1966).

13 See Freud (1927/1960: 8–9) for a particularly clear statement.

14 Both Neu (1988) and Wood (1988) elaborate on these objections.

15 He certainly was not the first analytic philosopher to investigate self-deception. Other prominent, systematic, early treatments include books by Herbert Fingarette (1969) and David Pears (1984), as well as Raphael Demos's (1960) article on lying to oneself.

16 Davidson's views on the kind of irrationality found in self-deception are ultimately presented in Essays 11–14 of his posthumously published *Problems of Rationality* (2004). His essay "Deception and Division" is most relevant to the problems of self-deception. To fully appreciate the Davidsonian position on irrationality and self-deception, one should understand the views of intention, weakness of will, mental causation, belief, and interpretation that he developed in his earlier work. These articles are collected in his (1980) and (1984) books.

17 This point is also made by Neu (1988: 88).

18 That being said, some do require that the self-deceived acquire a false belief. Mele (2001) includes it among his list of jointly sufficient conditions, as does Nelkin (2002). However, Nelkin (2012) rejects this requirement. There she agrees that if the psychological process is the same as a case that we agree is self-deceptive and leads to false belief (as most cases of self-deception do), it should not lose that label in those relatively rare cases in which the belief happens to be true by luck. Later, we will discuss various other philosophers and psychologists who require false belief for self-deception.

THE BASIC PROBLEM AND A CONCEPTUAL MAP   83

19 Things are a bit more complicated. While there is no incentive to be biased in estimating a country's population, there could be *general* incentives or benefits to some cold biases. For example, maybe we do have an incentive to have our beliefs confirmed and persevere in general (confirmation bias and belief perseverance bias).

20 In §2.4, we will more systematically address the question of motives for self-deception. In particular, we will distinguish between cases in which we self-deceive toward what we want to be true (positive cases) and those in which we self-deceive toward what we wish is *not* true (negative self-deception). A further important distinction is between self-deception that is driven by a desire for the world to be a certain way and that which is driven by a desire to acquire a belief. As we will see shortly, the motives can get quite complicated.

21 Other intentionalist accounts that we will consider later include Pears (1984), Talbott (1995), and Bermudez (1997, 2000).

22 Ariela Lazar – a motivationalist – denies that the intentionalist needs to go this far: "The intentionalist account requires that the subject have a desire such as 'that I believe that I will pass the test.' The subject's assessment that the belief in question is false need not be part of the content of the desire to believe. A similar point applies to the intention to form a belief. However, the intentionalist account views the self-deceived subject as being motivated by her conviction that the desired belief is either false or at least undermined by the weight of the evidence" (1999: 273, footnote 17).

23 This is the Freudian move embraced by the likes of Davidson and Pears. In §3.2, we will discuss Mele's arguments that such posits are unnecessary. Although, Mele (2001: 16–17) does grant that unconscious intentions are at least possible.

24 Of course, the belief that I am successful is not necessarily *theoretically* rational (e.g., supported by the evidence), and in cases of self-deception these beliefs will not be.

25 See Lazar (1999) for objections along these lines.

26 Although not all of these influences are in the positive direction. A jealous and insecure man is biased into thinking that his wife has been unfaithful when the evidence does not support this. This is something other than wishful thinking.

27 Krebs, Ward, and Racine (1997) also point out the spectrum of self-deceptive possibilities, warn against verbal disputes, and encourage giving greater weight to discussion of the psychological possibilities. Noordhof

(2009: 54–60) makes similar points while discussing the degreed or otherwise naunced nature of intention and agency.

28 Mele uses the vocabulary of "straight" and "twisted," but I think that "positive" and "negative" are better labels. (Sometimes "wishful" and "unwelcome" are used, as well.) The categories of positivity and negativity are a bit broader, more clearly covering the emotions. In this regard, they fit with the usage of Lazar (1999). And the deceptions or biases driven by the negative emotions are not always best described as "twisted" – e.g., there is nothing twisted about fear causing us to overexaggerate threats.

29 It is possible to be a desire-to-believe theorist and deny that the desire establishes a goal. But mind-directed theorists normally posit such motives to account for the apparent purposiveness of self-deceptive behavior and to fit with its ultimate product (e.g., a belief-like state).

30 Nelkin's (2002: 385) "Otis" and "Ben" cases are supposed to display this contrast.

3

DEFLATIONARY ACCOUNTS

3.1 **Motivated bias accounts: eliminating intention**
3.2 **Mele's account**
3.3 **Psychological details**
3.4 **Issues with psychological measures**
3.5 **Objections**
3.6 **Anxiety-based deflationary accounts**

This chapter presents and critically evaluates *deflationary accounts* of self-deception. At a minimum, deflationary accounts deny that self-deception is something that we intentionally do, so they are committed to motivationalism instead. Using our §2.1 distinctions, these accounts *sacrifice some of the deception (intentional or purposive manipulation)* that is sometimes thought to be essential to deception. Deflationary accounts not only abandon strong agential involvement, they also reject other claims associated with intentionalism. They often deny that the self-deceived have dual beliefs or that they ever believed the truth in the first place, that self-deception is goal seeking, that the mind is divided, and so on.

Alfred Mele (1987, 1997, 2001) has put forth the most well-developed deflationary account. I think it is fair to say that Mele has done more than any other philosopher to elevate philosophical discussion of self-deception these past few decades (i.e., post-Davidson and Pears). Accordingly, his views will be the primary focus of this chapter, and we will get into the nitty-gritty details of his proposal. His account draws on various psychological claims, so we will attend to those as well. While Mele's account is the primary focus, most of the objections that we raise against his view in §3.5 will generalize to other deflationary accounts. In §3.6, we will consider a couple other deflationary proposals before moving on to discuss more robust alternatives in the next two chapters.

§3.1 Motivated bias accounts: eliminating intention

The defining characteristic of deflationary views is that they are on the low end of the spectrum when it comes to agential involvement (see §2.3.2, Figure 2.4). This deflationary attitude toward agency will likely pervade many of the 12 categories from the conceptual map given in §2.6. The deflation often extends to cover:

a *Agency*: There is no intention to deceive, the deceptive activity does not manifest practical rationality, and perhaps the person is not responsible for it.
b *Belief complexity*: The self-deceived do not have dual beliefs, possess or retain the truth, or otherwise have robust doxastic conflict.
c *Motivational complexity*: The self-deceived do not have deception-specific or perhaps even mind-directed motives. They do not have motivational conflict between deceiving and unwilling parts of their minds.
d *Mental architecture*: The self-deceived do not have partitioned minds or robust unconscious processes playing essential parts in the deceptive project.

The deflationary approach is primarily defended on grounds of simplicity (Occam's Razor): Do not posit psychological complexity beyond what is necessary. Simplicity – in one's ontological posits and explanations – is a widely recognized explanatory virtue, so this approach is a reasonable one. The overall strategy is to argue that in order to account for the phenomena, it is not necessary to posit intentions, complex beliefs and goal-seeking motives, or psychological divisions. The deflationary option is supposed to be beneficial not only due to general considerations of simplicity, but also because the typical non-deflationary posits are especially problematic in their own right. It is hard to make sense of effective intentions to deceive

DEFLATIONARY ACCOUNTS   87

(dynamic problem), contradictory beliefs (static problem), or a self that is divided and opaque (yet nevertheless has interactive parts that are *somewhat* translucent).

Deflationists can turn to experimental cognitive and social psychology to show that intentionalism is unnecessary, mining their discoveries in an attempt to cobble together purely motivational, non-intentional explanations for various forms of self-deception. It should go without saying that our philosophical theories of psychological phenomena are better to the extent that they fit with and perhaps are even guided by well-established psychological results. And by the 1980s the central ideas behind the prominent intentionalist accounts were on shaky ground. Freudian psychoanalysis was a relic of a bygone era, at least in most academic circles. Freud's deep insights – of which there are many – were lost or diminished by his more extreme speculative proposals about drives, his total commitment to psychological determinism, and the often unfalsifiable "just so" stories of psychoanalysis that defied experimental testing. In the world of philosophy, Davidson's partitioning of the mind seemed a bit *ad hoc*, and he made no attempt to provide empirical confirmation for it. Instead, his psychological speculations were shamelessly *a priori* – coming from his theory of rationality – and he even conceded that his speculations about a partitioned mind were only "metaphorical." In contrast to such armchair theorizing, the "cognitive revolution" in psychology that replaced behaviorism and Freudianism offered, on solidly empirical grounds, new tools for thinking about the mind. The cognitivists posited inner mental states and processes (unlike behaviorists) that could actually be experimentally tested according to how they affected behavior (unlike Freudian psychoanalysis). It would be foolish for philosophers not to turn to the various new subfields that emerged – memory research, the heuristics and biases programme, social psychology, evolutionary psychology, and so on – in order to explain the mindsets, motives, and dynamics of self-deception.

Deflationists like Mele could piggyback on the successes of these psychological programmes, focusing on advances in motivated irrationality in particular (recall our Minimal Conception). Again, not just any kind of biased treatment of the evidence counts as self-deception. So, deflationists will have to make the case that the motives driving self-deception are sufficient to make it count as genuinely deceptive and that this deflationary approach can actually handle all, or at least the bulk, of the realistic cases that we would pre-theoretically classify as self-deception. Given that deflationists eliminate intentions and separate self-deception from mere mistakes by relying exclusively on motives (recall Figure 2.2), we should expect them to have a lot to say about *how* these motives function. It will be important that they defend answers to the diagnostic questions we have already raised: What is the content of the motives driving self-deception? Do these motives establish goals for the self-deceived, or do they instead influence cognition by manipulating pleasure, through principles of association, as a brute psychological fact, etc.? Their answers need not provide a fully unified account, as the world is often messy and self-deception could have many different causes and functions. Still, the deflationists have the burden of filling in these essential details.

§3.2 Mele's account

Mele frames the debate over self-deception around the static and dynamic problems. His approach is not so much to answer these problems as it is to avoid (deflate) them altogether. The static problem is primarily about how a person can simultaneously hold contradictory beliefs – the evidentially supported belief (*qua* Deceiver) and the evidentially unsupported belief (*qua* Victim). Mele's response is to deny this belief complexity, holding that only one belief attribution (the Victim's) is necessary. Not only does he deny dual belief, he also denies that the self-deceived must originally possess the truth. So, self-deception does not even require a change in belief over time. By denying belief complexity, he also undercuts one major motivation for dividing the mind and resorting to the unconscious. (Recall that Davidson held that the contradictory beliefs could not be entertained together, so the mind must be partitioned.) The dynamic problem is primarily about how one can intentionally and knowingly deceive themselves. Mele flatly denies this agential and motivational complexity as well, undercutting the need to posit strong unconscious processes and psychological partitions. In these regards, Mele emphasizes that self-deception is not like interpersonal deception: There are not two loci of beliefs, motives, and agency.

If he is against the assumptions that frequently lead to the static and dynamic problems, what is the positive picture the he offers in their place? Mele opens his (2001) book with this example:

> "A survey of university professors found that 94% thought they were better at their jobs than their average colleague" (Gilovich 1991, p. 77). Are university professors exceptionally adept at self-deception? (Mele, 2001: 3)

DEFLATIONARY ACCOUNTS 89

Mele assumes that this is a case of self-deception, perhaps even a paradigmatic example since he opens his book with it. Presumably, a hot bias is at work here. The vast majority of professors probably *want* to be better than average, but it is mathematically impossible for more than half to be so (let alone 94%!). But why think that this case fits the intentionalist pattern (e.g., Davidson's) for self-deception? There is no reason to think that these professors originally held the evidentially supported belief (to be precise, the belief that is evidentially supported for about 44% of them) that they are *not* better than average. There is no reason to think that they reacted negatively to that fact and thereby formed an intention to deceive themselves. And there is no reason to think that they (again, about 44% of them) retained the supported belief after deceiving themselves into believing that they are better than average. Or so Mele, quite reasonably, argues. These points against agency and dual belief generalize to a great variety of self-enhancing biases, attribution biases, optimism, and status quo biases. (These are the very psychological tendencies that we discussed in §1.2.)

As we see from this example, along with several others he provides, Mele's view is that self-deception can result merely through the operation of a hot bias without requiring elaborate motivation (e.g., to deceive or otherwise be mind directed) or agential involvement. Hot biases in general do not require deliberation, practical reasoning, the formulation and execution of an intention, or cognitive effort. Mele offers realistic vignettes of self-deception that fit and apparently support this deflationary approach:

- Don's article has been rejected by an editor. Of course, he *wanted* it published. Don's desire causes him to read the reasons for rejection in an uncharitable light. He believes that the rejection was unwarranted.
- Betty works for a political campaign and has heard rumors that her candidate is sexist. She selectively seeks evidence (e.g., his voting record) that indicates he is not sexist. This selectivity is supposed to occur naturally, without Betty *attempting* to deceive herself. Due to this confirmation bias, she retains her belief that he is not sexist. (Mele, 2001: 26–27)

Mele argues that self-deception is typically just the result of such motivated irrationality, so the intentionalists introduce unnecessary psychological posits and complexity. It is not just the intentions that should go, but all the other psychological claims that accompany them: dual belief or (in many cases) even changes in belief, motivational complexity, and psychological

DEFLATIONARY ACCOUNTS

partitioning. His deflationary account does not go much beyond the Minimal Conception, holding that self-deception is merely a special class of hot biases (i.e., those that lead to evidentially unsupported, false belief).

Mele (2001) does not offer a set of necessary and sufficient conditions to cover all cases of self-deception, which is what philosophers traditionally require for an "analysis." But he does offer jointly sufficient conditions for the self-deceptive acquisition of a belief.[1]

1 The belief that not-*p* which S acquires is false.
2 S treats data relevant, or at least seemingly relevant, to the truth value of not-*p* in a motivationally biased way.
3 This biased treatment is a nondeviant cause of S's acquiring the belief that not-*p*.
4 The body of data possessed by S at the time provides greater warrant for *p* than for not-*p*. (Mele, 2001: 50–51)

Some of these conditions are not required (necessary) for all cases of self-deception. Mele allows for the self-deceptive *retention* of belief, and he is open to the possibility that one can be self-deceived although the *evidence actually possessed supports* the deceptive belief (say, due to a biased evidence search). Still, he clearly takes these conditions to cover most "garden variety" cases of self-deception, even if they are not absolutely required.

Notice how Mele diverges from Davidson, Bach, and Audi right at the outset by not requiring that the self-deceived possess the true belief or in any way have the truth "dangerously close at hand." Whereas Bach and Audi think that the self-deceived never come to believe the content of their self-deception (instead, they only avow or think it), Mele has the acquisition of a false belief built into Condition 1. While not all these conditions are supposed to be necessary for self-deception, given his semantic understanding of "deception," Mele is committed to the self-deceived acquiring or retaining a false belief – to be deceived just is to be mistaken. Condition 4 then gets at the lack of rational or evidential support, which he holds is not strictly necessary due to the possibility of biased evidence search (Mele, 1997: 102, footnote 18; 2001: 51–52). We might recommend rewording Condition 4 so that it is a claim about the *available* evidence, as we characterized that concept earlier, rather than having it be a claim about the evidence that is actually possessed. In this way, it too could become a necessary condition for self-deception. (Of course, there may be difficulties in specifying what it means for evidence to be available or to what extent it must be accessible.) Together, Conditions 1 and 4 commit the self-deceived to believing a *falsehood* that is *not supported by the available evidence,* where these are semantic constraints on the state of being self-deceived.

Conditions 2 and 3 get at the *motivated irrationality* of the self-deceptive process. First, notice that the content of the motive introduced in Condition 2 is not specified neither are any restrictions placed on it. Any kind of motivationally biased treatment of the evidence, when combined with the other three conditions, is sufficient for self-deception. The motive could be a desire that the world be such that not-p, or it could be a desire to believe that not-p. But somewhat shockingly, as Condition 2 is written the motive could also have nothing whatsoever to do with p/not-p, so long as the motive still affects how evidence relevant to p is processed. Of course, desires that explicitly are about p/not-p are much more likely to result in a biased treatment of the relevant evidence than are desires without such content. One might find it hard to imagine why a father would treat evidence concerning his son's drug use in a biased manner unless he desired that his son not be on drugs (or desired to at least believe this). Still, it is very possible to be biased in that way without having desires so specific or on target. Desires for the son's *general* well-being or the father's concern about *someone else's* possible drug use could also bias his thoughts about his son. Here we still see a connection between the motive and the bias. It is hard to imagine a motive influencing reasoning with respect to p unless there were *some* such logical, similarity, causal, or other associationistic connection tying them. Mele does not go into these details, however. In formulating these conditions, he does not specify candidate motives or the relations they must bear to the content of the deception.

Condition 3 is supposed to rule out weird causal connections between the motive and the resultant false belief that are not deceptive. This is similar to complications that arise for causal theories of pretty much anything. For example, a causal theory of perception might hold that you see a coffee cup only if there is the right causal connection between that coffee cup and the visual imagery you experience – that constitutes perceiving the coffee cup. But it is very important that the causal connection be of the right kind. If a coffee cup on the other side of world causes some virtual reality technician to feed input into a computer and transmit that information to the virtual reality headset that you are wearing, causing you to have imagery as if perceiving the coffee cup, you are not *seeing the cup.* Even though the coffee cup (indirectly!) caused visual experiences just as if you were looking at it, this causal influence did not play out in the right way to count as perception of the cup. (Compare: My daughter is not seeing Paul McCartney while she watches a recorded performance by The Beatles on television.) Philosophers or psychologists of perception need to explain how in cases of genuine perception the light reflects off the cup that I hold in my hand, comes into contact with the eye, is encoded in the brain, and gives rise to the phenomenological experience of the cup. The same issues arise for deception. A motivationalist theory of self-deception should explain how it is that the motive causally interacts with the reasoning process so as to give rise to a false belief in a way that properly counts as a deceptive process. The content of the motive should be relevant to this. Mele does address this challenge, and, in the next section, we will discuss the ways in which he thinks motives influence reasoning so as to constitute self-deception.

Conditions 2 and 3 do not require that the motive establishes a goal for the self-deceived to pursue. This contrasts with the role that motives like desires play in intentional action. When we act intentionally our desires commonly provide us with goals that are achieved through our actions (desire for coffee: goal to drink coffee: intentional action to seek coffee: goal satisfaction). But Mele does not think that the self-deceived must have a desire *to believe* that not-p, for example. Such a desire could provide a goal that is then achieved when the self-deceived come to believe that not-p (Condition 1). Mele's approach is quite contrary to this intentionalist picture; the motives driving self-deception do not, or at least need not, make the process goal seeking or purposive. He instead focuses on other ways in which motives influence thought and action. The motives he has in mind are more means – simple tools – to deception than reason-providing incentives for deception. These motives can even have a "twisted" effect in that they lead people to self-deceive about things that are definitely not their goals, such as getting them to underestimate their chances for success or the likelihood that others truly love them. These are the cases we have termed *negative self-deception*.

Fundamental to Mele's account is the claim that self-deception is not deceptive in the same way that interpersonal deception is deceptive. Interpersonal deception is goal seeking or purposive (intentional, even). Interpersonal deception *does* require that there be a doxastic and evidential disparity between Deceiver and Victim. We deceive others by pursuing these goals (e.g., instilling false beliefs in their minds) and hiding our beliefs and the evidence from them. Mele thinks that self-deception is radically different:

> Stock examples of self-deception, both in popular thought and in the literature, feature people who falsely believe – in the face of strong evidence to

the contrary – that their spouses are not having affairs, or that their children are not using illicit drugs, or that they themselves are not seriously ill. Is it a plausible diagnosis of what transpires in such cases that these people start by knowing or believing the truth, *p*, and intentionally cause themselves to believe that ~*p*? (Mele, 1997: 92)

Mele thinks not. His conditions 2 and 3 do not require that the motive provides the self-deceiving with a goal, let alone an intention to achieve it. And Conditions 1 and 4 do not require doxastic or evidential disparity. The account is unapologetically deflationary. As these conditions are supposed to be sufficient *and* cover many cases of self-deception, the dynamic and static problems are avoided.

In §3.5, we will raise objections against the supposed *sufficiency* of these four conditions. But we will also consider challenges that deny that Mele's theory has appropriate *scope*. That is, while his conditions might be sufficient for self-deception, some argue that the account is deficient in that they do not cover many very common cases of self-deception. A set of sufficient conditions need not also be necessary in order to be of interest. Still, they should cover a large swath of the common cases that raised the theoretical problems driving the investigation in the first place.

§3.3 Psychological details

Mele's work on self-deception was quite a bit different than many of the philosophical efforts preceding it. Prominent treatments of self-deception by Sartre, Davidson, and others were psychological only in a speculative or *a priori* sense. More than any other philosopher, Mele is responsible for bringing experimental psychology to the philosophical debates over self-deception. And this, I submit, is how it should be. If our minds are divided, if robust unconscious processes are at work, if we hold contradictory belief-like states – in all such cases, there should be some empirical evidence to be found supporting these speculations. If, instead, other well-confirmed psychological processes can explain the phenomena (positive case) *and* there is no such evidence for the non-deflationary alternatives to be found (negative case), then we should embrace deflationism. This is exactly how Mele argues. In this section and the next, we will examine Mele's positive and negative psychological case for deflationism.

94 DEFLATIONARY ACCOUNTS

§3.3.1 *Biases, hot and cold*

The self-deceived have motives that give rise to hot biases – that is the core of Mele's account. But he also points out that these motives can trigger the activation of cold biases. Mele (2001: 28–29) singles out three cold biases in particular:

- *Vividness*: Striking or vivid data carry greater weight in our reasoning and judgments.
- *Availability heuristic*: Judgments of frequency or likelihood are influenced by the availability of positive instances (i.e., how readily they come to mind).
- *Confirmation bias*: People search for and give undue weight to evidence that confirms rather than disconfirms the hypothesis they are testing.

These biases can be individually triggered by the motives driving self-deception, but it is not uncommon for them to work together. An athlete vividly remembers the one time she won a pole vaulting competition. It is thereby more available to her mind, and she overestimates the frequency with which she wins. This tidbit is given too much weight, resulting in biased confirmation of the hypothesis that she will win her next competition. As Mele would interpret her, she self-deceives. In these ways, cold biases can become lukewarm, or perhaps it is even better to say that what are typically cold biases are hot on these occasions.

More obvious are the ways in which these motives stimulate biases that would not exist but for such a motive – true hot biases. Mele (2001: 26–27) flags four such biases:

- *Negative misinterpretation*: When we desire that not-p, we tend to misinterpret or dismiss evidence that we would otherwise recognize as counting against not-p. Don does not recognize the accuracy of the editor's decision, although he would acknowledge the validity of the reasons were it not his article that was rejected. He confronts the evidence, but he does not see it as disconfirming.
- *Positive misinterpretation*: Worse yet, when we desire that not-p, we might interpret evidence that we would otherwise recognize as counting against not-p as positvely supporting it. Rather than seeing her rejection as good evidence that she is not interested in him, he misinterprets it as her "playing hard to get." The misinterpretation is motivated, and the misjudgment would not occur in a motivationally neutral frame of mind (let us suppose).

- Selective focusing/attending: Because we desire that not-p, we will selectively focus on the evidence that supports that belief and selectively ignore the contrary evidence. An insecure professor rereads the most favorable student evaluations while ignoring the more critical ones.
- Selective evidence gathering: The desire could also cause us to avoid disfavorable evidence in the first place, while actively seeking out confirmatory evidence. A spendthrift makes sure not to check her bank balance due to her desire for extra funds. A gun advocate searches for the cases in which the "good guy" stopped the "bad guy" with a gun.

Significantly, in characterizing each of these biases, Mele describes the motive as a desire that not-p. While his four sufficient conditions are neutral on this point, it is here revealed that he tends to think of the motive as being world directed (i.e., that the world is such that not-p).

These biases can operate without the person knowing the truth "deep down." And Mele claims that all of these biases can be activated and unfold without any intentional planning or effort. He appeals to hedonic considerations to explain at least some of their dynamic effects. Given the desire that not-p, attending to certain bits of evidence is simply pleasurable while attending to other bits of evidence is unpleasant. No intention, planning, or special effort is needed to garner these pleasures. We can compare and contrast his positive view here with that of both Freud and Davidson. Freud thought that repression was driven by pleasure seeking or pain avoidance, and Davidson thought that the self-deceived find the evidentially supported belief unpleasant. But they nevertheless thought that much more robust agency is necessary to gain this pleasure. Mele seems to be emphasizing that the *means* to self-deception (e.g., the selective attention) is pleasurable in itself, not just that the ultimate end – repression, wishful belief – is pleasurable. Freud and Davidson could accept this as well, but for them this is an intentional effort aimed at a greater pleasure. Mele denies that this is typically, if ever, the case.

§3.3.2 Hypothesis framing and confirmation biases

Hedonic considerations can also influence the hypotheses we test. "Hypothesis" is a scientific and formal sounding word, but here it is used modestly for *any* speculation about how the world is. You might have a hypothesis about where you left your cell phone, for example. When you investigate some topic, it often is not the case that you are testing *whether p or not-p*

96   DEFLATIONARY ACCOUNTS

(e.g., whether you left your phone on your nightstand or not). Instead, you often pick a particular option and test it – e.g., you test whether you left your phone on your nightstand (or you test whether you did not leave your phone on your nightstand, where this is a distinct hypothesis). This is no mere logical trick, as it makes a real difference to what you come to believe. And if one hypothesis is more pleasant to consider, it can thereby become a more likely hypothesis to test.

There are really two stages of bias to this story. First, a desire that not-p can bias one to preferentially *hypothesize* that not-p – this is a hot bias. Second, the confirmation bias – which could be cold or could become lukewarm (i.e., heightened) due to the presence of the desire that not-p – can then lead one to unduly *believe* that not-p:

> Given the tendency that this bias constitutes, a desire that not-*p* – for example, that one's child is not experimenting with drugs – may, depending on one's other desires at the time and the quality of one's evidence, promote the acquisition or retention of a biased belief that not-*p* by leading one to test the hypothesis that not-*p*, as opposed to the hypothesis that *p*, and sustaining such a test. The desire's role in the production of the biased belief is its prompting and sustaining a test of a specific hypothesis. With the hypothesis in place that one's child is not experimenting with drugs, one will be more likely to search for, recognize, and attend to evidence for this hypothesis than evidence against it, and more likely, as well, to interpret relatively neutral data as supporting the hypothesis than as challenging it. This obviously will increase the probability that one will come (or continue) to believe that one's child is innocent of drug use. (Mele, 2001: 32)

And this entire process can unfold without any intention to deceive or other forms of robust agential involvement.

§3.3.3 *Belief thresholds and errors*

The biases due to hypothesis framing and confirmation search are pretty tame "deceptive" processes. At least in part, they can arise even when no motive is present. Fortunately, Mele (2001) invokes a final category of psychological mechanisms that could influence belief formation, and they would do so in ways that I think show the motive playing a much more strategic role than what we found even with the hot biases.

He draws on work by psychologists James Friedrich, Yaacov Trope, and Akiva Liberman, which argues that ordinary folk often strategically regulate their thresholds for belief according to the costs of getting things wrong. If the costs of getting a particular belief wrong are especially great, then we will tend to have higher evidential standards for accepting or believing in that way. For example, airport security officers are trained to have high standards for accepting or believing that a passenger is not a terror threat, simply because the stakes are so high. If they erroneously believe that someone is not a terror threat, then lives could be lost. Similar logic justifies the skepticism of those in quality control positions, be they examining the quality of a drug, vetting a potential job applicant, or safety testing an automobile. Conversely, if the stakes are rather low, our evidential standards for acceptance or belief are correspondingly much lower. I will readily accept someone's testimony concerning when the basketball game starts, in large part because there is not much to lose in being wrong.[2]

Friedrich (1993) argues that we are fundamentally pragmatic thinkers rather than being fundamentally truth-directed reasoners. The explanation for this is Darwinian – we were designed to be survival mechanisms first and foremost, not truthtrackers. Friedrich's proposal, then, is a bit of *evolutionary psychology*.[3] As believers, he expects that we will have "inference strategies" (roughly, belief-forming tendencies) that seek to gain rewards and avoid costly errors in real world ecological environments. This can lead to deviations from the standards of ideal reasoning that a logician or experimental scientist would recommend in the idealized or controlled environments in which they find themselves pursuing the truth. Friedrich names his theory PEDMIN – primary error detection and minimization. Evolution wants what is merely "good enough," and, as believers, we require evidence sufficient to allow us to hold onto our preferred hypotheses while avoiding costly errors. Costs to consider include not only the costs of acquiring a false belief, but also the costs involved in information search itself. Some inference strategies simply take more time and resources to execute, but since both are limited trade-offs are necessary:

> If normative accuracy is difficult to achieve given the real world's constraints on the quality and availability of data, a reasonable alternative goal would be one that places attainment of desired outcomes and avoidance of harmful consequences ahead of truth detection. (Friedrich, 1993: 301)

Besides information search costs, Friedrich gives special attention to costs that impact self-esteem or self-image. We should be especially resistant to falsely believing negative things about ourselves – such mistakes often (although not always) are costlier than falsely believing something positive about ourselves. This observation can partially explain self-enhancing biases, and it has obvious application to self-deception in that we often self-deceive concerning our self-image. However, in environments in which it is costly to miss a fault in oneself – and this costliness is made salient to the person (e.g., the person is about to give a public performance or interview for a job) – we should not expect such biases.

Significantly, as these costs change or become more focal, our thresholds for belief also vary. These variations in costs and their salience could explain why some people are biased or perhaps even self-deceived on a certain topic and others are not (varying importance). Mele (2001: 36–37) applies this point to a young man accused of treason. For his parents, the costly error is to believe that their son is guilty when he is innocent. So, they are biased toward believing in his innocence. But for an FBI agent, the much more costly error is to believe that the young man is innocent of treason when he is, in fact, guilty. So, the agent is biased toward believing that he is guilty. The effect is much more sophisticated than what we find with simple confirmation biases, and it can be manipulated by changing the relevant costs:

> [S]tudents led to believe that a certain trait (extraversion or introversion) promoted higher academic performance subsequently perceived themselves as having the trait to a greater degree. There are clear emotional costs to mistakenly believing that one lacks this desirable trait, but what cost is incurred in the experimental task if people mistakenly believe that they possess the trait to a greater degree than is in fact true? Thus, self-deception might not occur out of a need to construct justifications for a preferred self-image (Kunda, 1990) so much as out of a method of testing that reflects a reasonable lack of concern for errors associated with giving oneself the benefit of the doubt. (Friedrich, 1993: 314)

But we should not assume that PEDMIN is *always* the operative strategy or that, more generally, people always employ the same belief-forming strategies. It could be that strong desires or emotional reactions trigger more pragmatic approaches, such as PEDMIN-like strategies, that lead to heightened concern for costly errors.

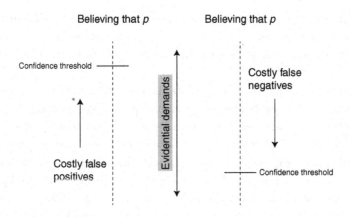

Figure 3.1 Confidence thresholds and errors

The Trope-Liberman (1996) theory is very similar to PEDMIN. Trope and Liberman posit *confidence thresholds* – the point at which no further evidence or testing is necessary – for accepting and rejecting a hypothesis, and these two thresholds will often vary in their demands (see Figure 3.1). As with Friedrich's theory, confidence threshold values depend on the costs of false acceptance (e.g., missed opportunities or negative affect) and the costs of information search. Trope and Liberman note that hypothesis testing is also influenced by our prior confidences. Even if the costs or thesholds change, we will not hypothesis test if our prior confidence is already above that level (1996: 253). But their main difference with Friedrich (1993) is that they do not see one type of error as dominating decision making. Rather, Trope and Liberman (1996: 264) argue that hypothesis testers are motivated to avoid both kinds of error (false positives and false negatives), although there very well might be different confidence thresholds at work.

The Friedrich and Trope-Liberman theories deal with costs that are specific to individuals, costs that vary according to their life histories and interests. But others have discovered more universal belief-forming tendencies relating to thresholds and error tolerance. This is the project of *error management theory* (Haselton, 2007). The belief-forming tendencies at work here are more a part of human nature, and as such they concern recurring matters important to survival and reproduction – e.g., mate selection and risk avoidance:

> [D]ecision-making adaptations have evolved through natural or sexual selection to commit predictable errors. Whenever there exists a recurrent

> cost asymmetry between two types of errors over the period of time in which selection fashions adaptations, they should be biased toward committing errors that are less costly. (Haselton and Buss, 2000: 81)

Recurring situations, from an evolutionary perspective, include decisions such as whether to eat berries of a certain type, engage with aggressors of a certain size who bare their teeth, or mate with a male displaying signals of fitness. Asymmetrical costs between false positive and false negative errors can lead to the natural selection of strategies that play it safe. If food is relatively abundant, it might be better to err on the side of caution and pass up questionable berries – there is little to gain, but much to lose.

Haselton and Buss (2000) focus on cross-sex assessments of sexual interest by humans. This might not come as a shock to you, but heterosexual men have a tendency to overestimate female sexual interest. This is a bias that is, in some sense, motivated: Mother Nature has learned that it was better for males to err on the side of a false positive (with little to lose by briefly pursuing a female who does not reciprocate interest) than to err on the side of a false negative (and miss a quality opportunity for sexual reproduction). There is a contrary bias in the case of women: to underestimate the level of a suitor's intended commitment. The costly error for women was the false positive: to think that a man is committed when he is not. These asymmetries exist because females (more specifically, eggs) were in greater demand in our ancestral environment than were males (sperm). In further support of the strategic occurrence and value of the bias, Haselton and Buss found that men did not overestimate the sexual intentions of their sisters with respect to other males.

These cases of biologically grounded biases are not so different from the PEDMIN-based biases that Mele classifies as self-deceptive. Human males and females have strategic incentives for these biases because such biases further their reproductive success. The costs mirror those in Mele's treason case. Just as the parents are motivated to avoid false positives (treason), females are motivated to avoid false positives (commitment). And just as the FBI is motivated to avoid false negatives (not treason), males are motivated to avoid false negatives (not interested). Granted, in the sexual interest case the incentives lie more in the domain of biology than psychology. As such, it is more likely that PEDMIN is driven by desires that are identifiable within the person's psychology, whereas error management could be due to more primitive motives or behavioral dispositions. Still, given that an incentive is in place – grounded either in psychology or biology – the very same deceptive manipulation of the evidence can occur. A man can negatively misinterpret a woman's discouraging remarks and selectively remember and focus on the times she simply smiled at him, all so as to further his biologically motivated belief that she has a sexual interest in him. In §5.2, we will discuss biological motives for self-deception in greater detail.

PEDMIN, confidence thresholds, and error management theory can all be employed to help explain negative self-deception as well. Negative self-deception has generally been viewed as problematic for motivationalists, since the person believes against what that they want to be the case, and, in many cases, one could be skeptical that the person is really motivated to so believe. The jealous husband does not want his wife to be unfaithful, and it is not always clear that he even wants to believe this. Costs and confidence thresholds can offer strategic explanations of the negative bias. If the costs of being a cuckold are so high, then the costly mistake for the husband would be to falsely believe that his wife is not having an affair. This is psychologically realistic, as such self-deception seems to be a defense mechanism grounded in insecurity. The error management theory example of women underestimating the intended commitment of male suitors also fits this category. They might want the males to be committed, but the costly mistake is to falsely believe that a male is committed. This psychological mechanism can explain many biases that we would describe as showing defensiveness, caution, or insecurity. For a person who does not take failure well, the costly mistake is to falsely believe that she will succeed. So, she underestimates her chances for success.

This ends our discussion of Mele's positive case for a deflationary psychology underlying self-deception. Note that he does not make an empirical case for self-deceivers possessing or acquiring the false belief. As we discussed earlier, he assumes Condition 1 as a semantic requirement of deception. However, this point is actually in great dispute. It would be better, then, to make an empirical case that Condition 1 is met in the bulk of the examples classified as self-deception. If it is not met, then we would be better served with a new definition of "self-deception" rather than saying that we were mistaken in classifying them as such.

For those interested in charting theories in conceptual space, we can plot Mele's theory according to our §2.6 diagnostic questions. It is striking how open ended or tolerant he is in answering these questions. For most, Mele would accept multiple possible answers: I (any of a–f, although probably not c), II (any of a–e), III (any of a–d), IV (any of a–d, although inclining

102   DEFLATIONARY ACCOUNTS

toward a/c), V (typically, none of these but g), VI (any of a–f), VII (typically, only b), VIIIb, IX (any of a–g, although typically a/b), Xa, XI (any of a–d, although inclining toward a/c), and XIIa/c. Notice that the only decisive answers are for VIII and X, which concern the resultant belief state and evidential position of the self-deceived. This decisiveness is only due to semantic considerations; on the theoretical or empirical questions, he is much more non-committal.

§3.4 Issues with psychological measures

Mele's negative case against robustness is rather limited in scope: He argues against alleged empirical demonstrations of dual belief. Remember, Mele denies that the self-deceived must believe the truth at the outset of self-deception or retain some connection to the truth in the end. But what about the other respects in which one could be non-deflationary? Mele does not make a direct negative case against the existence of (unconscious) intentions, efforts to deceive, or partitioned minds. His attitude on all these issues is one of tolerance, but held in check by Occam's Razor: Such psychological complexity might be possible, but it is (at least typically) unnecessary to posit such things to explain self-deception.

Mele singles out for special criticism two sets of psychological studies that purport to demonstrate motivated dual belief: Ruben Gur and Harold Sackeim (1979) and George Quattrone and Amos Tversky (1984). These experimental studies have received quite a bit of attention within the literature on self-deception. Although they are somewhat dated now, they still deserve our attention as well. For one, we should see how those in other fields view the phenomenon – maybe philosophers have a peculiar understanding that should be tempered or augmented with interdisciplinary input. Additionally, we should consider ways in which self-deception can be empirically tested. This includes tests for: dual belief, an intention to deceive, unconscious processing, motivation, and irrationality. The studies discussed here are ingenious in these regards, even if some unwarranted conclusions are drawn in the end.

Gur and Sackeim (1979) set themselves the task of demonstrating the empirical reality of self-deception. Their first step was conceptual: they had to provide a rigorous characterization of the phenomenon. Much like an analytic philosopher would, they provided four conditions that they took to be necessary and jointly sufficient for self-deception:

1 The individual holds two contradictory beliefs (that *p* and not that *p*).
2 These two contradictory beliefs are held simultaneously.
3 The individual is not aware of holding one of the beliefs.
4 The act that determines which belief is and which belief is not subject to awareness is a motivated act. (Gur and Sackeim, 1979: 149)

Notice that while they require contradictory beliefs, their conditions do not demand an intention to self-deceive. And while Condition 4 clearly shows them to be in the motivationalist camp, their version is different from the motivationalism of Mele and other philosophers. They do not demand that the motive influence the acquisition of one of the beliefs. Instead, the motive simply explains why the subject *lacks awareness* of one of their beliefs. (Gur and Sackeim seem to go out of their way to speak of a lack of awareness rather than speaking of one of the beliefs being unconscious.) Not only do they not demand that the irrationality be motivated, they do not even require that either belief be formed irrationally – there is no irrationality requirement at all. While one might think that some irrationality must be involved whenever a subject simultaneously holds contradictory beliefs, this is not so clear when we examine their watered down grounds for belief attributions.

Whatever the merits of this analysis of self-deception, Gur and Sackeim came up with an ingenious way to test whether these conditions can actually be met. Previous work had shown that attitudes about the self affect one's willingness to self-confront. For example, those who have just received negative feedback will turn away from a mirror sooner than do those who have received positive feedback – they do not want to face themselves. But visual confrontation is just one form of self-confrontation, and Gur and Sackeim decided to test self-confrontation in another form: identifying one's recorded voice. Participants were recorded reading an assigned passage, and edited versions of the recordings containing snippets from multiple participants were constructed. Participants were then tested, tasked with identifying recorded snippets as either their own voice or that of another. They were also wired to measure their galvanic skin responses (GSRs), as arousal levels had previously been identified for self-confrontation (e.g., hearing one's own voice) as opposed to other-confrontation (e.g., hearing the voice of another).

The participants were not perfectly accurate at identifying their own voices, and the pattern of mistakes was revealing. Some participants made false positives (mistook the voice of another for their own); others made false negatives (mistook their own voice for that of another); some made both kinds of mistake; and others pretty much got it right. But, in the mistake cases, the skin still got it right. That is, if it *was* their voice, they had the GSR appropriate for recognition, even if they reported that it was not their voice. If it was the voice of another, they lacked the GSR of self-confrontation, even if they reported that it was their voice. And, very significantly, the pattern of errors corresponded to attitudes toward the self. Those who were narcissistic or who had been experimentally manipulated so as to have higher self-esteem (by receiving positive feedback) tended to make the false positive mistakes. Those who had received negative feedback tended to make false negative mistakes. This is where we find the relevant motivation: willingness to self-confront.

> In short, when people are made to feel good about themselves, they tend to "project" and see themselves in places where they are not. When people are made to feel bad about themselves they tend to "deny" seeing themselves in places where they are. (Gur and Sackeim, 1979: 165)

Putting this all together, Gur and Sackeim think that most of the cases in which participants made mistakes fit their four conditions and, hence, count as self-deception. They attributed beliefs to participants on the basis of self-reports that a voice either was their own or another's, and contradictory beliefs were attributed on the basis of the simultaneous GSR levels that did not match their self-reports. Further, participants were not aware of the belief attributed on the basis of the GSR. Finally, they were aware of the reported belief either because they were motivated to self-confront or, conversely, motivated to self-avoid. Gur and Sackeim contended that these participants were self-deceived.

But this interpretation has some serious flaws when it comes to the belief ascriptions. The authors take both the verbal reports and the physiological responses to be sufficient for belief. Philosophers have long doubted, however, whether sincere assertions are infallible guides to belief, especially when they conflict with behavior (as is common in cases of self-deception). In an era in which we no longer think that the mind is wholly transparent to itself, we no longer have philosophical reasons for thinking that people have infallible self-knowledge about their beliefs. While psychologists understandably want a way to measure beliefs and attitudes, they too have recognized the limitations of self-reports. It is not just that people lie outright, they are also influenced to respond in socially desirable ways or otherwise self-deceive without consciously intending to mislead (Paulhus, 2002). So, self-reports should be taken with a grain of salt.

Matters are even worse when we turn to the GSR evidence. Many philosophers will object that the inference from simple physiological responses to outright belief is much too quick. Gur and Sackeim seem to recognize this worry, at times making the weaker claim that there is merely some kind of self-recognition:

> This would indicate that when subjects committed such errors, at some level of processing correct identifications had also been made. (Gur and Sackeim, 1979: 150)

This must be correct *at some level of processing*. But, Mele (1997: 96) objected, why think that this processing rises to the level of belief? We often have physiological reactions that are typically indicative of a certain belief, but that do not reflect our beliefs on a particular occasion. Goosebumps, hair standing on end, a pounding heart, perspiration – these are physiological symptoms of fear. When people experience them, it typically means that they *believe* that a threat is present. Yet, when someone presents these symptoms while watching a horror movie, the person does *not* believe that a threat is present.[4] It is simply too crude to take basic physiological responses as sufficient for belief.[5] Such responses are not necessarily reasons responsive, neither do they drive our behavior in the way that belief-like states do. They are more in the category of brutely caused responses (like a leaf turning toward the sun) than being a cognitive state to be evaluated by the standards of rationality. We can criticize a belief for being irrational and applaud it for being rational, but many are reluctant to call a simple physiological response either irrational or rational.

It is also a bit odd to claim that there is a motivational explanation for why these participants are aware of the one belief (corresponding to their report) and not aware of the other belief (corresponding to their GSR levels). These GSR levels are simply not the kind of things that people could be aware of, at least without significant training. No motive explains this lack of awareness. Instead, we are unaware that we are processing this information because it occurs at such a low level – it is not properly cognitive. It is similar to why we are not aware of subliminal recognition and processing: Our lack of awareness is due to simple biological constraints that have nothing to do with motivation.

Quattrone and Tversky (1984) offered further studies that were supposed to demonstrate dual belief and self-deception more generally, working

106   DEFLATIONARY ACCOUNTS

with the Gur-Sackeim conditions for self-deception. Quattrone and Tversky were particularly interested in cases in which people are motivated to achieve a certain diagnosis even though manipulating the diagnostic test does not make it any more likely that the desired outcome actually obtains. For example, people might be motivated to manipulate their answers on a health quiz so that they receive a more favorable diagnosis, even though this manipulation obviously does not make it any more likely that they actually are healthy. This defeats the purpose of the test, and if the matter in question is high stakes (e.g., a heart test), then such manipulation is manifestly irrational. One would benefit most from accurate information.

In their study, Quattrone and Tversky initially tested participants' tolerance to cold water by measuring how long they were willing to keep their forearm immersed in a cooler of circulating ice water. Participants then performed a short exercise task on a stationary bicycle. Next, they were fed (among other things) misinformation about heart types and tolerance to cold water. Depending on the group to which they were randomly assigned, they were told either that increased or decreased tolerance to cold water following exercise was associated with a type of heart that is prone to disease and results in a shorter life expectancy. They immersed their forearms in ice water for a second time, again to test their tolerance. As you might expect, those who were told that increased tolerance to cold water following exerecise was diagnostic of poor health outcomes had significantly less tolerance (measured in time duration) as compared to their earlier test. For those who were told that decreased tolerance was indicative of poor health, the opposite effect (i.e., greater tolerance) was observed. This seems to be a motivated bias, if not of belief, then in action.

But Quattrone and Tversky thought that biased beliefs were also at play, and they went so far as to argue that these participants met Gur and Sackeim's dual-belief condition. Participants were queried as to whether they had purposefully tried to alter their cold tolerance on the test after exercise. Only about a quarter of the participants claimed this; most people who did alter their performance did not admit to it. Quattrone and Tversky claim that such people hold contradictory beliefs: They believe that they purposefully altered the diagnosis, and they believe that they did not purposefully alter it. Quattrone and Tversky assume something close to intentionalism here: that the change in behavior was purposive. Accompanying this claim about agency, they add that the participants believed or were aware of their own purposes.

But is this truly a case of dual belief and purposive manipulation? Mele (2001: 85–91) denies both of these claims. He first claims that even if the participants were aware of the motives that led to the change in their tolerance for cold water, it does not follow that they believed that they were purposefully altering the test results. The motive could just operate on its own, perhaps unconsciously – belief is not necessary for this effect, neither is it inevitable. Mele offers this apparently analogous case:

> Ann, who consciously desires her parents' love, believes they would love her if she were a successful lawyer. Consequently, she enrolls in law school; in enrolling she is trying, unconsciously, to please her parents. But Ann does not believe, at any level, that in enrolling in law school she is trying to please her parents. (Mele, 2001: 86)

Mele also denies that participants should be interpreted as *purposefully* manipulating the test results in the first place. For example, he thinks that motives could affect the confidence thresholds for belief by establishing what counts as costly errors, producing the alteration without any robust agential involvement.

While Mele is likely correct in arguing against the dual-belief claim, the Quattrone and Tversky experiments can teach us something else very significant about the motives for self-deception. The studies seem to show that people are highly motivated to maintain a state of mind, in the form of receiving favorable diagnostic results. I would argue that in the cold tolerance study the participants have a mind-directed motive – they want to think that they are healthy. Of course, they also want to actually *be* healthy – this is what we have called a world-directed motive. But this study seems to show that people will alter results so as to preserve or achieve a certain state of mind, even if such actions jeopardize their important world-directed health motives. This preference is not rational, at least if treatments are available or other preparations should be made. I would think that for most people falsely believing that they have a healthy heart, rather than falsely believing that they have an unhealthy heart, is the truly costly error. In this regard, we could challenge Mele's (2001: 90) application of PEDMIN-like mechanisms to explain the deception.

Mele is correct to point out the inadequacies of these psychological investigations of belief, with the general worry being that they posit belief on much too flimsy grounds. Self-deception, along with many of the related phenomena defined in §2.7, stretch the boundaries of belief and our rationality. One lesson is that we – philosophers and psychologists, perhaps working together – need to develop a more sophisticated account of belief. We will return to these concerns about belief in §5.1. While Mele's points against dual belief are well taken, he could have made a stronger negative case for his overall deflationism by turning to the empirical evidence on matters besides belief. He denies that strong agential involvement is necessary or typical for self-deception, but is there any empirical evidence that supports their absence? Mele (2001) often simply states that it is unnecessary to assume that the self-deceived are making an effort to deceive themselves, but more recent empirical work since then directly bears on the issue.

There has been an explosion of work on automatic and controlled processes (dual process) since the bulk of Mele's work on self-deception was published. (Recall our Chapter 1 discussion of System 1 and System 2 processes – this is basically the same distinction.) The automatic processes are supposed to be fast, effortless, and largely unconscious (System 1); the controlled processes are supposed to be deliberate, slow, effortful, and often conscious (System 2) (Kahneman, 2011: 20–21). We should apply this to self-deception, for it might offer a way to empirically test the deflationary thesis about agency. The suggestion is that if self-deception is largely driven by automatic processes, then there is relatively little agential involvement. However, if self-deception significantly involves controlled processes, this would indicate effort and, hence, greater agential involvement. This would bolster the idea that the activity is robustly deceptive. But how can we test the issue?

Experimental psychologists frequently test to see if a process is effortful by imposing *cognitive load* on participants. Cognitive load is extra mental work – like a problem to solve or a temptation to resist – that takes mental effort to perform. If imposing cognitive load leads to impaired performance on the main task, then this suggests that the main task takes effort as well. Performance is impaired because the cognitive load draws on the limited resources that the self has to execute effortful tasks. However, if peformance on the main task is not impaired even when participants are under cognitive load, this suggests that performance of the main task is automatic and does not require special effort.

Piercarlo Valdesolo and David DeSteno (2008) tested whether a common self-serving attribution bias – moral hypocrisy – operates automatically or under effortful control. "Moral hypocrisy" here refers to a person's tendency to downplay a moral transgression performed by the self as compared to those performed by others. Participants were divided into two main groups: one distributed tasks between themselves and others, and the other observed such distributions. Afterwards, both groups were asked about the fairness of these actions (their own or the observed actions of others). Moral hypocrisy was operationalized as a discrepancy in evaluating the fairness of the actions performed by the self as compared to those same actions as performed by others.

It is widely accepted that moral evaluations are influenced by two systems: an intuitive, reactive system and a controlled, reflective system (dual process). Valdesolo and DeSteno tested whether moral hypocrisy is due more to the intuitive and automatic system or the controlled system. Specifically, they wanted to test whether moral hypocrites have a biased intuitive reaction when the moral behavior is their own, or if their bias instead emerges at the level of controlled processing (e.g., effortful rationalization). If spontaneous moral emotions evolved in humans and our nearby kin in order to manage social relations, then it would be expected that moral hypocrisy is more of a controlled and deliberate process. The idea is that they would have an intuitive response that their own behavior was unfair, and they would need to make a controlled effort overcome that reaction and manifest moral hypocrisy.

Some participants (self-group) had to perform either a ten-minute photo search (easy task) or a 45-minute logical-mathematical task (hard task). These participants were given the opportunity to assign the more arduous task to themselves, the next participant (whom they did not know or would they interact with), or to have the assignment determined randomly. But either they or the next participant would do each of the two tasks. Participants made their decisions about how to assign these tasks privately. Afterwards, they were asked a series of questions, including judging (on a Likert-type scale) how fairly they thought they had acted. Other participants (other-group) were tasked with observing such choices being made by others. Later, these participants assessed the observed actions for fairness. Each of these two groups was subdivided such that half performed a memory task that imposed cognitive load on them (after the choice that they would judge had already been made, but before making their judgment). The striking results were that those under cognitive load did not manifest the moral hypocrisy bias when evaluating their unfair behavior, although those not under cognitive load did manifest hypocrisy. (Valdesolo and DeSteno, 2008: 1337) The suggests that the bias is effortful, at least in the sense of drawing on resources that can be depleted. The moral hyopcrisy is not an automatic reaction.

110   DEFLATIONARY ACCOUNTS

I do not want to suggest that a single experiment is in any way deci-sive. Rather, the point is that there are empirical means to test the degree of agential involvement in biases and, potentially, self-deception itself. Discerning the contributions made by automatic and effortful processes has significant practical consequences for treating (as either a therapist or epistemologist) bias and self-deception. That is the good news. But, on a negative note, such knowledge can be exploited so as to more easily spread bias and deception. Advertisers and propagandists – perhaps even one's own children! – can be especially skilled at exploiting vulnerabilities in either our automatic responses or our tendency to deliberately rationalize.

§3.5 Objections

Now that we fully understand Mele's deflationary theory, it is time to turn to objections. Since his account is deflationary, most of these objections will be against the sufficiency of his conditions for self-deception. That is, theorists have objected that Mele does not include enough to adequately capture self-deception – he has deflated the phenomenon too much. Some have also objected that he does not offer a unified account of self-deception, and on at least one point there has been resistance to his proposed nec-essary condition (i.e., his claim that the self-deceived acquire or retain a false belief). In this section, we will consider a variety of such objections: Mele does not adequately explain how/why *negative self-deception* occurs; or the account does not explain why the self-deceived are so *selective* in their deception; or his conditions do not rise to the level of being genuinely *decep-tive*; or his conditions do not capture the necessary or characteristic *tension* of the self-deceived. We will consider all these as objections to Mele's theory in particular, but many of them also generalize to other motivationalist accounts.

§3.5.1 Negative self-deception

The first objection to consider is that the motivationalist treatment does not seem to readily extend to cases of negative self-deception, like the jealous husband or the self-deprecating woman who do not seem to have a desire that matches their deception. While Mele tends to downplay negative self-deception, saying that it is "much less common" (2001: 94) than posi-tive self-deception, it is common enough to likely arise in several recognized psychiatric disorders (as we discussed in §2.4). Insecurity, defensiveness, jealousy, hate, anxiety, fear, and sadness give rise to many non-pathological cases as well. So, negative self-deception is likely more common than Mele acknowledges. The objection is either that Mele's account cannot handle these cases at all or, if it can, that the account is problematically disjoint.

While Mele's stated sufficient conditions for self-deception do not demand that the motive be a desire that not-p (instead, the content of the motive is left completely open), in practice, this is the motive he frequently provides. By definition, the negatively self-deceived lack this kind of motive. Mind-directed motivationalist accounts, such as Nelkin's desire-to-believe version, seem to fare better in this regard. She offers a unified account of the motives driving self-deception: Both the positively and negatively self-deceived are driven by a desire to believe as such. Mele does not embrace this option, however, and he claims (2001: Chapter 5) that the motives for self-deception are not so unified – self-deception is messier than that.

Mele recognizes that, from his treatment of positive cases, he might already have the tools to handle negative cases as well. Negative self-deception can be explained in the very same way as positive self-deception, by psychological mechanisms that establish confidence thresholds in anticipation of costly errors. As he argues (2001: 101), it may be that a jealous husband's negative self-deception (i.e., belief that his wife is unfaithful, where this is false and not evidentially supported) makes it more likely that the relationship will be saved. Losing the relationship is a costly error to guard against, so perhaps jealous vigilance that results in biased belief is incentivized (Pears, 1984: 42–44). In effect, the claim here is that the motive to have a biased belief is itself motivated by its relationship-guarding consequences. If we think about this a bit, we should see that this point could easily be denied – jealousy obviously undermines many relationships. We might want to consider the alternative possibility that the man simply does not want to be played for a fool (cuckold), so the costly error is to believe that she is faithful when she is not. This belief-focused motive could set low thresholds for believing that she is unfaithful, leading to the negative self-deception. There is a sense in which this latter approach is similar to mind-directed motivationalist accounts like Nelkin's desire-to-believe, because the costly errors it considers are false beliefs. So, the motive supposedly has the effect of biasing toward a certain belief. This is not so different from desiring to so believe.

But negative motives and emotions could also straightforwardly trigger the cold and hot biases that Mele drew on in his account of positive self-deception. A fear that not-p can make evidence for not-p salient and command our attention. The fear can dominate our thoughts, leading us to worry that not-p, hypothesis test that not-p (rather than p), and trigger confirmation biases. What goes for fear also holds for jealousy, anxiety, and strong desires to avoid a certain outcome. Mele is well aware (2001: 98–99) that this offers yet another path to explaining biases that skew toward believing what is unwelcome.

It is interesting that Mele does not invoke the emotions as serious causes of biased reasoning until he discusses negative self-deception. For his earlier discussion of positive self-deception, he was content to speak of desires alone as creating the cognitive distortion, and it was relatively easy for him to always find a relevant desire for each of his examples. But is there any reason to think it more likely that emotions are critically involved in negative self-deception as opposed to the positive cases? When we start considering the positive emotions – pride, joy, hope, love, and the like – it should be relatively easy to think of cases in which they distort reasoning so as to generate positive self-deception. Hope gives rise to irrational optimism about one's chances for succeeding as an artist; joy gives rise to irrational confidence that the world is fundamentally just. Lazar (1999) did a good job of emphasizing this very role for emotions. Perhaps Mele, among many others of us, has underestimated the role the emotions play in positive cases because it often is so easy to posit a sensible desire that aligns with the deception. Mele (2001: 113, 118) does acknowledge that emotions can play a similar role in positive self-deception, still he mostly invokes the emotions to account for the negative cases. Indeed, they were not a part of his multipronged account of "garden variety" self-deception.

§3.5.2 *The selectivity problem*

Jose Bermudez (1997: 2000) raises an objection against Mele's account, but one that he thinks also generalizes to other motivationalist accounts. The worry is that some essential ingredient is missing from Mele's brand of motivationalism, since the motives could be in place although no deception occurs. One could desire that not-p, although not in any way mistreat the evidence relevant to p/not-p. Bermudez points out that one could even desire to *believe* that not-p, again without necessarily manifesting any bias. Remember that Mele's four conditions were supposed to be *sufficient* for self-deception, but the selectivity of self-deception suggests that they are not.

Examples should be easy to generate. I want to be in excellent shape – heck, I even want to believe that I am in excellent shape. But I am not at all biased or self-deceived toward actually believing that I am. (If you think I am unknowingly biased, it is nevertheless commonplace that many others with these desires are not biased.) Maybe you think that the reason I am not biased or self-deceived in this example is simply because the evidence is too obvious. I clearly am not in excellent shape, so the bias or deception can never really even get off the ground. Yet even when the desire concerns something that could reasonably be true from the person's evidential perspective, it is still far from guaranteed that the desire produces a bias. You want to believe that today is the day that you finally start your exercise program. And it easily could be the day. But as the day unfolds you see that it is not going to happen, and you harbor no illusions. Others in your same motivational (i.e., they share your relevant motive *and* neither of you has relevant countervailing motives) and evidential situation sometimes *are* biased or self-deceived, of course. That is the point of the selectivity objection.

Recall the specific ways in which Mele thinks that motives distort reasoning: They trigger cold or hot biases, skew hypothesis framing and testing, and they alter confidence thresholds. Bermudez (2000: 317–318) acknowledges that all these things happen, but he makes two points in response. First, it is not *guaranteed* that the motives will produce such *biases* at all. This is what the fitness and exercise examples just given were supposed to show. Second, even if the motives do produce biases – such as lower thresholds for acceptance – it does not follow that they will actually produce a self-deceptive *belief*. In some cases (e.g., self-deception), the motives lead to both effects, but, in others, they have neither effect or only the former.

Bermudez raises the selectivity problem not only as an objection to Mele's theory, but as a major premise in a positive argument for intentionalism. The form of argument is an inference to the best explanation: Intentions best explain the selectivity of self-deception. Bermudez (2000: 318) recognizes that this posit is "speculative," and he admits that future anti-motivationalists might find a way to account for selectivity. The posited intentions also should be truly explanatory. It is not enough simply to say that there must be an intention that explains why self-deception occurs whenever it does. There should be some further evidence that such intentions exist, or further work for the intentions to perform, otherwise it risks becoming a vacuous explanation.

114   DEFLATIONARY ACCOUNTS

The motivationalist does have some options at hand besides accounting for selectivity exclusively in motivational terms. It could simply be a fact without further *psychological* explanation that sometimes motives influence reasoning in these ways and sometimes they do not. True, those *types* of motive would no longer be causally sufficient for self-deception. But Mele and other motivationalists could argue that these motivational explanations nevertheless provide the strongest psychological conditions available, and they sometimes are enough to induce self-deception (Mele, 1997: 130). This response holds that no further psychological states are necessary, and it is simply a fact – determined by lower level conditions, say – that these motives sometimes bias reasoning and sometimes they do not. This kind of situation is actually fairly common in the sciences, especially the human sciences, where generalizations are qualified by *ceteris paribus* clauses. Strictly sufficient conditions for any general or higher level phenomenon are rare.

§3.5.3 Is this even deception?

There are extreme forms of intentionalism or eliminativism that will deny that any motivationalist account could possibly be correct, simply for semantic reasons. Haight (1980) and Borge (2003) argue that, by semantic or conceptual necessity, deception requires an intention to mislead or at least an effort to do so. On this view, non-intentional deception is no more possible than a square circle – it is a contradiction in terms. If they were correct, then all motivationalist theories of self-deception would be nipped in the bud. (Although there would still remain the phenomena so-classified, simply under a new name.) Theorists often counter by presenting cases of apparent interpersonal deception without intentions to deceive, hoping that we share their intuitions that these are cases of genuine deception rather than cases in which someone is merely misled. In §2.3.2, we were presented with some examples of these kinds of interpersonal cases that varied in their degree of agential involvement – e.g., innocently spreading a falsehood, being influenced by emotion when talking to others (leading to overoptimism, say), selectively sharing information with others due to a desire to please rather than deceive, or finally outright lying. Are these all cases of genuine deception?

We need not enter that foray here. Instead, it might be better to point out that "deception" is widely used outside of psychology to cover cases in which psychological intentions are clearly absent. For example, a Batesian mimic (e.g., a butterfly that mimics the coloration signaling toxicity, but which is not itself toxic) is commonly described as deceptive. Other examples of deception in nature are easy to come by: camouflage, anglerfish, playing possum, broken-wing displays, and so on. Maybe some teleology or simple advantage is necessary for these to count as genuine deception, but they can all arise without the presence of psychological intentions to mislead.[6] Common usage rightly classifies these as deceptive, as specific measures are taken *because* they mislead others to the animal's benefit. The "because" here is ultimately understood in terms of natural selection. Still, we can imagine some denying that the *individual animals* are engaged in *deceptive acts* (while granting that deception is occurring), so long as they are not actively involved in purposefully generating misleading appearances. The idea is that the camouflage, say, is deceptive, but the camouflaged *moth* is not engaged in any act of deception. This subtle line is a tough sell. But it is true that individual animals can be involved in the deceptive ruse to varying degrees: from merely growing a colored pattern, a lure, etc.; to responding to a threatening stimulus by fainting or going into a broken-wing pretense; to actively deliberating a novel plan to mislead.

Let us grant for the time being that deception does not require a psychological intention to deceive. Still, does Mele's motivational account do enough to establish deception? Motives can influence reasoning in various ways, with some of these causal pathways being more deceptive than others. Mele's sufficient conditions for self-deception are highly deflationary, requiring only that a motive cause, as a matter of fact, a biased treatment of the evidence. He does add that to count as self-deception the motive must be a "non-deviant" cause of this bias, but the distinction between genuinely deceptive and non-deceptive causal pathways is not spelled out. Mele allows for many direct causal connections between motives and rationality that require very little, if any, agential involvement – e.g., motives that bias reasoning by enhancing the vividness of evidence or by causing us to test a favored hypothesis over its disfavored alternatives. Lazar (1999: 280–284) argues that emotions function in a similar way in the cases that she takes to be paradigms of self-deception. As she describes it, the influence the emotions have on reasoning is neither practically rational (e.g., purposive) nor effortful:

> Appeal to practical reasoning in order to explain these effects is hopeless in light of their prevalence and variety. In contrast to the predictions of the intentionalist approach, the formation of emotion-induced (or desire-induced) beliefs is highly uniform, quick and effortless. (Lazar, 1999: 283)

When motives or emotions operate in this manner, there is little agential involvement in a deceptive ruse.

Other motivationalists are more restrictive when it comes to specifying the motive, and some of these restrictions seem to make the process more deceptive. These motivationalists might insist that self-deceptive activity aims at the manipulation of the subject's own mental states, often in ways that heighten the agential involvement of the self-deceived. Nelkin's desire-to-believe account fits this description, and it seems to better capture the deceptive element of self-deception. Indeed, Nelkin touts her view over Mele's by pointing out how motives sometimes cause biases, but not in a way that is genuinely deceptive. If deception requires the pursuit of a deceptive goal (e.g., acquiring a belief irrespective of its truth), then Mele's conditions are too weak. A view like Nelkin's, with its mind-directed motives, can more plausibly refute the objection that this is not even deception by pointing out that the motives she insists on produce purposive or goal-seeking behavior. The activity more plausibly counts as deceptive if the person is making an *effort to produce a change in* mind. As noted earlier, this form of motivationalism is not so far from intentionalism. It seems to make self-deception something that we *do* as a *rational* means to achieving some *goal* or *purpose*. This matches what we find in interpersonal cases, where Deceivers pursue the goal of producing a false or irrational change of mind (or preserving a false or irrational mindset) in their Victims.

There are many ways to distort belief, and some of these ways are more aptly described as "deceptive" than are others. These distorting effects can be brutely causal – meaning that they influence belief through non-rational and non-evidential means – or they can arise within rational inquiry itself:

> *Brutely causal belief distortion*: acting as-if; repetition; peer association; mood-inducers (e.g., anti-depressants); hypnosis

> *Belief distortion within rational inquiry*: hypothesis formation biases; belief threshold manipulation; evidence search, avoidance, and attention biases; evidence fabrication; memory search and recall biases; interpretation biases and rationalization

The brutely causal belief distorters need not be part of any deception. Your social, cultural, and religious beliefs might be distorted by the environment into which you were born, but these brutely causal influences on your beliefs – which are highly significant, but not necessarily rational

DEFLATIONARY ACCOUNTS   117

or evidence based – need not be deceptive. At least not *all* enculturation is deceptive. (Although lots of history-denying, culture-enhancing, folk cosmology, and the like might be calculated for deceptive effect.) Whether a brutely causal belief distorter is deceptive depends on the reasons, or lack thereof, for why it occurs. Pascal's wagerer selects her associates so that they have the belief that she currently thinks is unjustified but yet she wants to acquire. Her peer association is deceptive as it aims at producing a belief irrespective of its truth (she even thinks it is unjustified and false). But when a child simply associates with the other kids in the neighborhood and has her beliefs influenced by that association, the association distorts her belief without being part of any deception.

Belief distorters in the second category directly bear on rational inquiry, as they concern hypotheses, evidential standards, evidence handling, and reasoning. At least some of these can occur without deception. Cold biases can skew evidence attention, distorting belief but without deception. So too for certain memory biases and confirmation biases. But these can also occur in the service of deception, such as purposive attention to favorable evidence or memories. For some of these belief distorters, it is unlikely that they would emerge were they not in the service of deception – e.g., evidence fabrication and evidence avoidance. Yes, these might occur because they "feel good" (or confronting the evidence would "feel bad"), but this is in league with employing such tactics toward the end of preserving a certain state of mind. If you avoid evidence that your boyfriend is lazy, this might be because it is depressing to dwell on that evidence. But it is depressing because that evidence leads you to thinking or believing that he is lazy.

Funkhouser and Barrett (2016) introduce the concept of what they call *robust deception*. This concept has three essential ingredients: the *strategic* pursuit of a deceptive goal in a way that is *flexible* to situational changes and shows some *retention of the truth*. Robust self-deception would then preserve many of the features of typical interpersonal deception, in which the Deceiver rationally pursues the deception of the Victim (strategic) by selectively manipulating evidence so as to create an illusory presentation for the Victim's particular perspective (flexibility). The Deceiver is successful because he has access to the truth or at least a broader or more accurate evidential perspective. Some means of belief distortion are intrinsically more likely to be in the service of robust self-deception than are others. Outright evidence fabrication is highly strategic, and it is unlikely to occur unless the person were aware that the real evidence does not support the motivated belief. By the same token, self-deception by means of evidence fabrication is much harder to pull off. This is the dynamic problem in full force, which comes with seeing self-deception as analogous to interpersonal deception. It is difficult to see how a mind can grasp the strategic value in manufacturing evidence so as to mislead, but yet still believe on the basis of that very evidence.

Self-deception by evidence fabrication is perhaps an extreme, and many critics of Mele have focused on deceptive evidence avoidance instead (Bach, 1997; Funkhouser, 2005; Funkhouser and Barrett, 2016; Gendler, 2007). Evidence avoidance is often fairly robust in that the person knows or strongly suspects that undermining evidence is to be found somewhere and takes measures to avoid it. But whether it is truly robust depends on the specificity of the avoidance – sometimes people avoid a whole class of evidence (e.g., they will not look at the science) and other times they will avoid very specific pieces of evidence (e.g., the mother will not look in the closet where her son stores his marijuana). Greater specificity in the avoidance indicates more robust deception in virtue of being more strategic, flexible, and informed. Contrast the robustness of evidence fabrication and avoidance with the more modest evidence interpretation and confirmation biases, which need not be so tactical or demand as much evidential awareness. Mele's cases tend to fall in this territory. The self-enhancing university professors need not be pursuing a goal of deception, need not take special measures in different contexts so as to maintain their mindset, and can be single-mindedly biased without in any way possessing the truth.

Mele offers several ways in which motives can bias reasoning so as to produce self-deception. Among these, I would argue that his use of confidence thresholds and costly errors gives him the best opportunity to meet the present objection. There are two reasons for this. First, changing confidence thresholds is immediately aimed at manipulating belief. The manipulation is fully mind directed, in accord with the nature of deception (i.e., producing or maintaining a state of mind). Second, this manipulation is strategic in that it is responsive to costly errors. The individual's motives determine what counts as a costly error for her. As these costs are highly individual and even context dependent, the resultant manipulation of confidence thresholds is intelligently calculated. Such intelligent scheming is another hallmark of robust deception.

But several of Mele's examples do not seem so strategic. In his diagnosis of "garden variety" self-deception, Mele often reduces the deception to no more than the operation of a hot bias – indeed, he opens his treatment of garden variety self-deception (2001: Chapter 2) by appealing to simple hot and cold biases. Or a certain hypothesis is pleasant to consider, so it is framed for testing and confirmation biases ensue. Don wants his paper to be published, and this motive biases him so that he does not recognize the force of opposing evidence. Granting that motives distort reasoning in these ways, why think that this is deceptive? If it were only a cold bias in play, Mele would not classify it as a case of self-deception. Those who drastically underestimate the population of Indonesia due to the availability heuristic are not self deceiving – they are merely biased. Hot biases might similarly be *merely caused* rather than purposive in their operation. It feels good to entertain one hypothesis as opposed to another or to interpret evidence in a self-serving way rather than on its face. Are these biases significantly different than giving an erroneous estimate due to the ease with which positive instances are available to mind? It is not clear that the mere fact that a motivational state is triggering the bias – but not in a goal-seeking or otherwise strategic manner – is enough to make a process that would otherwise be non-deceptive count as genuinely, or at least robustly, deceptive.

§3.5.4 *Tension is necessary*

Mele's sufficient conditions for self-deception depict it as a single-minded and non-complicated state: the self-deceived simply possess the false belief that not-p due to a motive that typically aligns with it (e.g., a desire that not-p). Several have objected that this single-minded depiction does not account for the tension that, on their view, is characteristic or even necessary for self-deception.

Doxastic conflict, shallow and deep

One of the most unsettling facts about philosophical debate over self-deception is the radical disagreement over what the self-deceived end up believing. Recall diagnostic question VIII (doxastic ending point) from our §2.6 conceptual map. Every possibility in logical space is in play:

a   The self-deceived believe that p. (Audi, Bach, Gendler)
b   The self-deceived believe that not-p, though they might *suspect* that p. (Mele, Van Leeuwen)
c   The self-deceived believe that p and believe that not-p. (Davidson)

d   The self-deceived partially believe that p and that not-p, or it might be indeterminate what they believe. (Schwitzgebel, Funkhouser, Lynch)
e   The self-deceived neither believe that p nor believe that not-p. (Archer)

It is fair to say, then, that at least sometimes there is doxastic conflict in the self-deceived, and it is not exactly clear what they believe. Given this wide disparity in answers, it is also very questionable that all these theorists are even investigating the same phenomenon! A recurring objection against Mele is that he does not do justice to this doxastic conflict or tension. This objection takes a stronger and weaker form. On the stronger version, the claim is that tension is *necessary* for self-deception. The weaker version claims that tension is merely *typical* or at least *common* of self-deception.

We need a bit more clarification as to what we mean by "tension" here. Our primary focus will be on doxastic tension, but there are other forms of tension to consider. Our beliefs manifest themselves in many ways, including within at least these categories: the cognitive, behavioral, emotional, and physiological. Often our belief manifestations and underlying dispositions across these categories will cohere with one another. I believe that I have a dentist appointment at 8:00 a.m., so I plan accordingly (cognitive), leave the house early (behavioral), feel some anxiety (emotional), and sweat a bit (physiological). All these reactions align with what we would expect of a believer who shares my motives and emotions. But other times our bodies and minds are more fragmented. Doxastic tension arises when there is inconsistency or conflict among these belief-relevant manifestations and the dispositions underlying them.

This is exactly what a few critics of Mele's theory have argued is typical of self-deception:

> Bach (1981, 1997): The self-deceived have the true belief that *p*, where this is understood as a disposition to think, reason, and act as if *p* is true. But the self-deceived overcome the first disposition and do not have the thought that *p*. In fact, they may actually think that not-*p*. Self-deceptive avoidance of the thought that *p* requires repeated efforts given that the true belief persists.
>
> Audi (1982, 1997): Ann is dying of cancer. But she does not want to face this truth, so she avoids receiving a precise diagnosis from her doctor. She speaks of recovery and living a long life, but she also experiences anxiety that tells against these avowals. The self-deceived unconsciously believe the truth, but they are disposed to avow what is false (and all of this has a

DEFLATIONARY ACCOUNTS 121

> motivational explanation). Like Ann, they manifest tension in their behavior, avowals, and emotional experiences.
> Funkhouser (2005, 2009): Nicole claims that her husband is not having an affair with Rachel, yet she avoids driving by Rachel's house to confirm this. The self-deceived have certain behavioral dispositions that indicate they believe the truth, but they avow otherwise.
> Gendler (2007): A person who is self-deceived in denying that they are suffering from a dreaded illness is careful to avoid illness-relevant evidence. If he were a genuine believer, he would be willing to confront the evidence. Instead, he is merely pretending that what he wants to believe is true. This pretense plays a belief-like role in his thoughts and at least some of his behavior.

Each of these theorists denies that the self-deceived have the false belief, in direct opposition to what Mele simply assumes in his sufficient conditions for garden variety self-deception.[7] Each of them also thinks that the doxastic picture is not only different than Mele envisions it, but also more complicated. While they see tension or conflict, they tend to think that an all-things-considered psychological analysis favors attributing only the true belief to the self-deceived. This is the position of Bach, Audi, and Gendler. Funkhouser (2009), following in the spirit of Schwitzgebel (2001), concludes that it is often indeterminate what the self-deceived believe.

Paul Noordhof (2009) argues for something close to doxastic tension, what he calls *instability*. He claims that the self-deceived necessarily fail to consciously attend to evidence that would cause them to lose their biased "cognitive endorsement" (his more general term, intended to cover both belief and sincere avowal). But this instability need not produce actual tension – it just shows the state to be vulnerable. Also, his view differs from the others grouped here in not requiring a stronger connection to reality (e.g., true belief).

It would be helpful to distinguish between different degrees of doxastic conflict. With what we can call *shallow conflict*, the manifestations or dispositions of belief conflict to some degree, yet it is clear that the person believes one way or the other. For example, a person boarding an airplane sweats more than we would expect of one who does not believe that they are in danger. Yet, they clearly believe that they are not in danger – they know the statistics about commercial flight safety, and they are willing to act accordingly. Their rational assessment, avowals, and behavior, all of which align with the belief that they are not in danger, trump their conflicting physiological reaction (sweating). With *deep conflict*, the situation is murkier. In these cases, there is substantial and perhaps even widespread inconsistency in the manifestations or dispositions typical of belief. This makes it unclear or indeterminate what the person really believes. The distinction between shallow and deep admits of degree, with variance along multiple dimensions – e.g., the several types of manifestation or disposition and their relative weight. While there are clear cases of shallow conflict and clear cases of deep conflict, I would suggest that it is hopeless to search for any natural fissure that cleanly divides the two categories.

Deep conflict cases, by their very nature, make belief ascriptions more difficult. There are a few ways to respond to deep conflict. One way is to divide the mind and see different subagents within it as possessing their own beliefs, beliefs that conflict and exert themselves in divergent ways. This is the Freud/Davidson picture. A different response to deep conflict is to argue that something besides belief is playing at least some of the roles typical of belief (e.g., avowal, thought, behavior). This move will be further discussed in §5.1. Deep conflict can also be accepted as irresolvable, in which case, it reveals the vagaries or indeterminacies of belief.

Another way to attempt to deal with these matters is through a combination of degrees of conviction and more rigorous weightings of the dispositions of belief. This is the proposal of Kevin Lynch (2012), who argues that often there is shallow conflict among the self-deceived that can be captured by appealing to the fact that belief admits of degree. Motivated biases often do not result in full-fledged belief, but will nevertheless alter the degree of confidence with which someone believes a proposition. Lynch claims, quite plausibly, that these changes are often appropriately described as self-deceptive. In fact, he claims that a change in degrees of confidence, rather than a total change from belief to disbelief, is the norm in psychological studies like those cited by Mele. This is because self-deception is a non-pathological condition, and as such the self-deceived are not radically disconnected from evidential considerations. Belief is often measured by self-reports on Likert-type scales, and self-deception is found when there are statistically significant differences in degrees of conviction that seem to be due to motivation. These middling self-reports are relatively fine grained and empirically legitimate ways to get at the nagging doubts or tension hypothesized by Bach et al. Inconsistent cognitive and behavioral tendencies will likely result in lower degrees of confidence.

Lynch recognizes that there are cases of deeper conflict in which, say, verbal behavior radically departs from non-verbal behavior. Following

Audi (1982), Funkhouser (2005), and Gendler (2007), he argues that in these cases the non-verbal behavior should be privileged as indicating what the person genuinely believes. In particular, the person's behavior in high stakes situations – how much risk they are willing to tolerate when they have something significant at stake – indicates their beliefs. There often is not much to lose by just saying or thinking something, which is why we can have those typical belief manifestations without genuinely having the belief that typically underlies them. A person who denies an illness does not genuinely believe this if they would seek the necessary medical care when it really matters. Unlike in the degrees of conviction cases, these people genuinely have the true belief (i.e., as opposed to merely having an unwarranted degree of confidence in the false belief that they are not sick or an unwarranted skepticism about the true belief). But Lynch says this is not self-deception at all. Instead, this is the avoidance of something that one knows to be true – what he calls *escapism*.[8] So, the deep conflict cases pushed by Bach, Audi, Funkhouser, and Gendler as being paradigmatically self-deceptive are not examples of self-deception at all!

What does Mele himself have to say in response to these kinds of objection? His response to such apparent counter-examples is twofold. First, he denies that such tension indicates contradictory beliefs or undermines the attribution of the false belief. That is, he downplays the significance of the tension. We saw this in his discussion of Gur and Sackeim's (1979) voice recognition study. There is tension in that subjects avow one thing but give an inconsistent physiological (GSR) response. Still, he holds that the voice deniers likely fully believe that it is not their voice and do not have the contradictory true belief. But in that example, the conflicting response is merely physiological, detached from the person's rationality and motor behavior. The doxastic conflict is shallow. What about deeper conflict, such as behavioral avoidance or emotional anxiety? Mele says that such conflict can be accounted for by mere suspicions or doubts that do not necessarily undercut the false belief (Mele, 2001: 71–72, 79–80). The terminally ill man's avoidance of accurate diagnostic information shows that he only *suspects* the worst, not that he knows his true condition. In these ways, Mele thinks the conflict is resolvable in favor of attributing the false belief. Second, he seems to think that in many cases of self-deception, there really is very little tension at all. This appears to be the case in many of his examples of hot biases – the university professors who think that they are better than average are single-minded in their biased (and often false) beliefs. But, Mele has not made a positive case for the rarity of deep conflict cases.

Deception and delusion

Those who emphasize deep conflict cases recognize that there are also Mele-type cases in which the person, due to a motive, single-mindedly acquires a false belief. But they either deny that these are cases of self-deception at all, or they argue that they are only a subset of self-deception. The most common word that deep conflict theorists use to describe Mele-type cases is *self-delusion*. The transition from self-deception to self-delusion is supposed to be the move from doxastic conflict to full false belief, although this can be understood in slightly different ways. Audi (1982: 140) states that the transition occurs when conscious false belief is achieved, where this is understood as an evidential judgment combined with the absence of conflicting talk and behavior. It is a single-minded state. Funkhouser (2005) and Gendler (2007) also use this vocabulary, adding that self-delusion occurs when the person is willing to act on the avowed (false) belief even in high stakes situations. It is in this context that Gendler (2007: 244–245) considers the illness denier. If there is no cure for their disease and they maintain the pretense that they are illness free, then Gendler will describe them as self-deceived. But if a medicinal cure for their disease is suddenly developed and they see no reason to take the pill, then they show themselves to be self-deluded. Those who stand behind their words when the stakes are high are genuine believers.

"Delusion" is a strong word, and it is also a clinical term. The DSM-5 (2013: 87) defines delusions as "fixed beliefs that are not amenable to change in light of conflicting evidence." Noordhof (2009) makes a good case for distinguishing self-deception from self-delusion on the basis that with the former, but not the latter, the person still accepts and properly applies the norms of good evidential reasoning. His account fits well with the DSM-5 usage. Appropriate as it may be, this use of "delusion" is stronger than what the philosophers who push the tension issue against Mele have in mind. Gendler's illness denial case is serious, and in one version the belief persists even when the stakes are especially high. The condition might even be pathological. But, it is unlikely that the illness denier is completely immune to evidential changes. Just because the denier follows through with belief-concordant behavior in high stakes situations, and thus might be said to genuinely have the false belief, it does not follow that he could maintain that denial when the test results are before him, his symptoms deteriorate, etc. Most of the subjects in the Mele-type cases that do not involve any doxastic tension are pretty clearly still amenable to changes in the evidence. For example, most of the biased professors would probably abandon their inflated self-enhancements if the right evidence were put before them. So, the philosopher's "self-delusion" should not be read as indicating a highly irrational, pathological condition. The cases the objectors would classify as self-delusional range from: biased belief but with sensitivity to the evidence (e.g., professors who self-enhance); biased belief that is insensitive to the evidence, but yet is benign (e.g., a culturally sanctioned religious belief that runs counter to the evidence); biased belief that is insensitive to the evidence and moderately harmful, but is not pathological (e.g., a mother who is delusional in denying her daughter's drug use); and biased belief that is insensitive to the evidence, harmful, and pathological (e.g., a man who believes that government agents are manipulating his family via radio waves).

Some philosophers and psychologists deny that the more extreme forms of clinical delusions – say, Capgras delusion (e.g., the apparent belief that one's spouse has been replaced by an imposter) or the Cotard delusion (the apparent belief that one is dead) – are even beliefs. The main reasons for these denials are that clinical delusions seem to be strongly insensitive to counter-evidence that would lead most rational people to abandon them, and the clinically deluded often fail to act as we would expect them to if their delusions were genuine beliefs. In these regards, delusions fail to *integrate* with the rest of the person's theoretical and practical life. (Currie and Jureidini, 2001; Dub, 2017) Nevertheless, the view that delusions are irrational *beliefs* remains the dominant position. (See Bayne and Pacherie 2005 as well as Bortolotti 2010 for a defense; DSM-5 for an authoritative statement from outside of philosophy.) Regardless, self-deception is normally not this extreme. It is normally a non-clinical condition arising within largely rational, relatively well-integrated, properly functioning individuals. For these reasons, self-deceptive activity itself often is largely rational, with belief distortion arising *within* the realm of rational inquiry. So, it seems to concern belief. (Although, see §5.1 for dissenting views.) Bortolotti (2010: 37–41) makes the case that certain motivated, clinical delusions (e.g., persecutory delusions) might overlap with self-deception, at least to the extent that each can generate belief by means of motivation and biases that arise within the normal range of inquiry.

Let's return to our main discussion concerning doxastic tension. All parties to these disputes will likely agree that there are cases in which motivated biases result in: i) outright false belief, ii) false belief with shallow conflict, iii) as well as deep conflict. (Mele is skeptical, or at least non-commital, regarding robust unconscious processing. But he can still recognize that there are cases involving deep conflict between thoughts, avowals, emotions, etc. and dispositional belief, regardless of the underlying cognitive architecture generating this conflict.) There is disagreement, however, concerning the relative frequency of each. Also, there is disagreement as to where to place these categories with respect to self-deception. Mele and Lynch emphasize that self-deception requires full deception – outright false belief, with at most shallow conflict. Oddly, this is a place at which Mele – a great denier of comparisons to interpersonal deception – insists that self-deception must be like interpersonal deception. Gendler's (2007) theory and vocabulary demands conflict, and she explicitly labels the cases of outright false belief as self-delusional in contrast to being self-deceptive. Funkhouser (2005) recommended this usage as well, but his (2009) switched to including deep conflict cases as merely a subset of self-deception. Likewise, Jordi Fernandez (2013: 399) accepts a liberal understanding of self-deception that includes self-delusion, though he has greater interest in the conflict cases. In contrast, Lynch (2012) denies that Funkhouser-Gendler cases are examples of self-deception for the very reason that such people have the justified, (typically) true belief. This is in direct opposition to the Bach-Audi theories, which insist on conflict between thought or avowal and dispositional belief, so like Gendler they do not count cases of outright false belief (perhaps with only shallow conflict) as self-deceptive.

Clearly, there is a real problem with the same terminology being used in different ways. These different uses of "self-deception" and "self-delusion" are depicted in Figure 3.2. One might very well wonder what is at stake in this dispute, which might have the appearance of being only semantic. In some senses, these are different phenomena, but, in other senses, they are also the same. Are there good methodological, explanatory, or theoretical grounds for favoring one way of carving the space of motivated biases over the others?

Even if Mele's sufficiency conditions capture some cases of what we would call self-deception, many others that we could describe as self-deceptive seem to resist assimilation to the deflationary model. We sometimes do have psychological evidence of division, fragmentation, and scheming well beyond the deflationary characterization. And some – such as Davidson, Bach, Audi, Funkhouser, and Gendler – have argued that these have presented the most interesting and challenging cases all along. Both parties to this debate make claims about what they think are the *interesting*

DEFLATIONARY ACCOUNTS   127

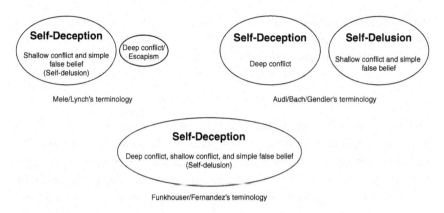

Figure 3.2 Self-deception and self-delusion

and *typical* cases of self-deception. Mele sometimes suggests that those who challenge him on grounds of tension and robustness are dealing in "mental exotica" and are preoccupied with "the outer limits of logical or conceptual possibility." It is much more interesting, he claims, "to understand and explain the behavior of real human beings" (Mele, 2001: 4). His account is aimed at what he thinks are the typical or "garden variety" forms of self-deception. Of course, the objectors *do* think that they are accounting for the behavior of real human beings, and their examples are often derived from supposedly everyday experiences. Gendler (2007: 233–234) thinks that conflict between pretense (which can mimic the cognitive and behavioral role of belief – see the discussion in §5.1.3) and belief "often" occurs in "the cleanest and most interesting cases of self-deception."

In some sense, the two parties are talking past one another. Bach, Audi, Davidson, and Gendler do not think that Mele's deflationary cases are typical cases of self-deception because they do not think they are self-deception at all! They are not thereby saying that their cases of tension and conflict are more common than Mele's cases of single-minded hot bias. They simply think that they are distinct phenomena. Conversely, Lynch denies that Funkhouser-Gendler deep conflict cases are self-deception, instead classifying them as escapism. There is the simple quantitative issue of which variety is more commonplace, and it would be good to have some way of quantifying just how common their deep conflict cases truly are. But there is also the question of which variety is more theoretically interesting, because more problematic. Mele seems to hold that his cases are more interesting because he thinks they are more common. The objectors, by

DEFLATIONARY ACCOUNTS

way of contrast, might think that their cases are more interesting because they raise greater theoretical problems. In sharp contrast, Mele's theory was largely motivated by its ability to evade the static and dynamic problems.

Other forms of tension

There is a tendency for philosophical accounts of self-deception to privilege one particular kind of tension as essential and symptomatic. The self-deceived say one thing but do another; they entertain one thought, but dispositionally believe otherwise; they attribute one belief to themselves, but actually have another; they avoid one kind of evidence and seek out another; they consciously believe one thing and unconsciously believe another. Even limiting ourselves only to doxastic tension, it can take many possible forms:

> *Evidential tension*: The total available evidence points one way, but the person believes otherwise. This is due to acquisition, avoidance, attention, and interpretation biases. There can be some recognition of this evidential tension in the form of nagging doubts and suspicions.
>
> *Conscious/unconscious tension*: The conscious mind contains one belief-like representation of reality, and the unconscious mind contains its contrary.
>
> *Higher order (self-knowledge) tension*: The person does not know what they believe. They have a false second-order belief (i.e., belief about what they believe).
>
> *Tension among the various other components of belief*: Belief has systematic connections to (non-linguistic) behavior, avowal, emotions, and physiological responses. There are many ways in which there can be tension among the various possible manifestations within each category.

Besides such doxastic tension, other forms of tension have been offered as symptomatic of self-deception as well. Sometimes a particular emotion – anxiety and fear are often offered as examples – is said to exist in tension with a related belief. A person is anxious that she will fail, so she is biased to believe that she will succeed. Other times the emotion aligns with the belief – she is anxious that she will fail, and she is thereby biased to believe that very thing! Motivational conflict often occurs in self-deception as well – the person may be conflicted about what they *want* to believe or be true. Their conflict could also be more abstract or theoretical: there could be deep conflict between motives to be rational in the first place and other motives to be led, as believers, by non-rational considerations – e.g., whether to follow scientific evidence or personal faith. And there might simply be motivational conflict built into the very idea of deception: a part of them is a willing participant in a deceptive ruse that the other part resists (and, hence, *needs* to be deceived).

Beliefs, motives, and emotions are the main psychological sources of tension. It is always possible for them to be in conflict among one another, and with our behavior and physiology as well. On further consideration, we should recognize that the self-deceived can have various kinds of tension; none of these forms is absolutely essential. Every one of the self-deceptive scenarios presented by Bach, Audi, Funkhouser, and Gendler might seem to exhibit a familiar kind of tension that we can associate with self-deception. Yet, there is no reason to think that any one of these stories captures a specific form of tension that is absolutely essential to self-deception. And a deflationist like Mele will argue that no such tension of any stripe is necessary.

§3.6 Anxiety-based deflationary accounts

Mele's deflationary account posits a generic motive driving the irrationality, but we have considered objections arguing that this motive does not necessarily capture the purposefulness of genuine self-deception. The desire could be for almost anything, and it could influence cognition in almost any causal – and not necessarily purposive – manner, as many examples of both hot and cold biases show. Nelkin's desire-to-believe theory better captures the deceptive nature of the process by requiring that there be a motive specifically aimed at producing a belief regardless of its truth. This motive fares better at putting the *deception* back in self-deception, as deception is about aiming to change minds (beliefs) in ways that are not rationally supported.

There are other deflationary theories that aim to capture the purposefulness of self-deception as well as its distinctive phenomenology. In his influential article "Self-Deception and the Nature of Mind," Mark Johnston (1988) claimed, as if it were a necessary condition, that self-deceptive belief that not-p is driven by an anxiety concerning p. He did not so much argue for this, instead assuming it as a starting point on the way to developing his tropistic account of self-deception. Annette Barnes (1997) greatly elaborated on his suggestion that self-deception is prompted by anxiety, arguing that an *anxious desire* is necessary for any kind of self-deception. Barnes slightly modified Johnston's motivational account, carefully articulating that the anxiety concerns some issue, q, which may be the content of the self-deceived belief but may instead be something closely related to it. She also went beyond Johnston in giving several examples that are supposed to illustrate the different forms this anxiety can take. As she understands the concept, anxiety requires *uncertainty* as to whether q or not-q, combined with a *desire* that q (Barnes, 1997: 39). For example, a student might desire that she be very intelligent, yet be uncertain whether it is true. Consequently, she is motivated by this anxiety to treat the evidence in a biased manner and come to believe that she did particularly well on a standardized test. Note how this example shows that the anxious desire need not have the exact same content as the self-deceptive belief. In this regard, she departs from Johnston (1988), who held that the anxious desire and self-deceptive belief have the same content. But otherwise, his view largely aligns with hers and even provided some inspiration.

Barnes claims that self-deceptive biasing and the resultant self-deceived belief have the *function* of alleviating the associated anxiety. This means that the self-deception must be purposive (unlike on Mele's view), even though not performed intentionally. This feature was also empahsized by Johnston. His tropistic (subintentional) account of self-deception (briefly discussed in §2.3.1) was supposed to show that self-deception has the purpose of alleviating this anxiety:

> In short, how could the desire that *p* lead the main or primary system to be favorably disposed toward believing *p*? And there seems no other answer but the anti-intentionalist and tropistic one: this is the way our minds work; anxious desire that *p* simply leads one to be disposed to believe that *p*. (Johnston, 1988: 85)

The challenges of the dynamic problem loom for this account, however, and Johnston and Barnes both grapple with it directly. For Johnston this requires repression on the part of the self-deceived that utilizes some combination of rationalization, evasion of disconfirming evidence, and overcompensation (bias toward producing confirmatory evidence or otherwise defending the favored proposition) (Johnston, 1988: 75). Barnes talks of a "false consciousness" – the self-deceived's lack of self-knowledge concerning the role that anxious desire plays in his belief formation

(Barnes, 1997: 99). The spirit of their views certainly allows Johnston and Barnes to draw heavily on the psychological biases discussed by Mele. They just add a bit more to the story.

Anxiety gets at many paradigmatic features of self-deception that are not necessarily explained by Mele's brand of deflationism. First, it does justice to the phenomenology of self-deception. Self-deception is often driven by an uncomfortable feeling. Although Barnes (1997) does not develop this obvious component, Lazar (1999) can be seen as a step in that direction. The role of the emotions in motivating self-deception still calls out for further development. Second, anxiety can deliver on the tension in self-deception. Barnes claims that anxiety necessarily involves uncertainty as to whether what one wants to be true actually is true. In this sense, at least, the self-deceived experience some tension. Whereas, Mele's self-deceivers typically experience little uncertainty (say, the university professors who self-enhance) and are sometimes described as self-deluded instead. Third, her account explains that self-deception is a purposive act that serves a function: It aims at alleviating anxiety.

Although she does not go into details concerning the phenomenology or etiology of anxiety, it is unlikely that Barnes has articulated everything that is required for anxious desire. That is, it is often the case that we want something to be true and are uncertain whether it is or will be true, yet we experience no anxiety. Mele observes that Barnes's characterization of anxiety is oddly devoid of any phenomenological specification. With this in mind, Mele (2001: 54–56) argues that his own motivational account can meet her stripped down version of anxiety as mere uncertainty plus desire. He too requires a motivating desire, and he holds that the self-deceived, prior to successfully deceiving themselves, are uncertain about the object of their deception (and, presumably, any relevantly related q). If anxiety is understood in a richer sense, such as requiring a feeling of anxiety, Mele simply denies that this is a necessary condition and that the self-deception occurs to alleviate it even when present. He sees no empirical grounds for thinking anxiety always prompts self-deception, and he claims that Barnes offers no conceptual justification. On the latter point, he may be a bit unfair. Barnes (1997: 64) does appeal to anxious desires so as to distinguish genuine self-deception from cases that are mere mistakes. Although someone sympathetic to Barnes's position should make a stronger conceptual case that Mele's examples of motivated irrationality, even if not mere mistakes, do not have the purposiveness required of real deception.

132 DEFLATIONARY ACCOUNTS

While Barnes gives several examples that are supposed to show how her theory can cover negative cases of self-deception (e.g., a husband's belief that his wife has been unfaithful) as well as positive cases, it is unlikely that many cases of negative self-deception function so as to alleviate anxiety. Scott-Kakures (2001) presents plausible examples – such as a man who self-deceives into thinking that he is having a stroke or a woman who comes to believe that she left the stove on – in which the negative self-deception seems to only increase anxiety. It is not just that they have missed the mark of alleviating anxiety concerning some q, it seems rather clear that the self-deception does not have the function of alleviating anxiety for any such q. Indeed, some of Barnes's purported candidates for q are rather strained and implausible. Regarding a man who self-deceives into believing his wife has been unfaithful, she writes:

> By believing that *p*, Mary is unfaithful, John [the husband] can believe that *q*, George [the other man] does not have a higher regard for Mary than for him ... The self-deceptive belief that *p*, that Mary is unfaithful, enables John to believe that it is more likely that his anxious desire that *q*, that George does not have a higher regard for Mary than for him, is satisfied. (Barnes, 1997: 42)

The idea is supposed to be that the husband is anxious that the other man might have higher regard for his wife than he does for him. This story, to my ear, strains credibility – I cannot easily imagine such an anxiety driving his self-deception. It is at least much more common that such a negative self-deceiver is furthering, if not indulging, his own anxiety or jealousy. Scott-Kakures argues that this can also be very strategic – say, motivating vigilance so as to be cautious about high stakes risks (infidelity, leaving the stove on, health threats). This alternative explanation sees much negative self-deception as having a non-hedonic basis, instead arising as a defense mechanism.

Summary

- Mele and others have argued that intentions are not necessary to explain self-deception. Hot and cold biases, framing effects, pragmatic approaches to belief, and other advances in cognitive and social psychology might point to cognitive and motivational explanations without robust agential involvement.

- Some psychological studies claim to establish dual belief, yet philosophers have challenged these belief attributions. Tests for purposefulness and effort have proved promising.
- One worry about deflationary accounts is that they might not do justice to the conflict or tension in self-deception. Some philosophers distinguish self-deception from self-delusion in this regard. Another recurring worry is that these deflationary accounts do not rise to the level of real deception.
- Some deflationary accounts see self-deception as purposive – alleviating anxiety or reducing costly errors, say – whereas others do not. We should further explore the extent to which regulation of the emotions and self-esteem can factor into deflationary accounts.

Recommended reading

Alfred Mele's book *Self-Deception Unmasked* (2001) is an accessible yet authoritative presentation of his deflationary account of self-deception. That book connects with much of the philosophical and psychological literature, up to that time, in a short space. Mark Johnston's "Self-Deception and the Nature of Mind" (1988) is a fine article, especially as it argues for a deflationary account of agential involvement in contrast to Davidson's intentionalism.

Audi (1997) and Bach (1997) present short critiques of Mele with respect to the supposed conflict or tension found in self-deception. Lynch (2012) is a more recent assessment well worth reading.

Gur and Sackeim (1979), Quattrone and Tversky (1984), and Valdesolo and DeSteno (2008) are all well worth reading for their psychological tests of self-deception. Parts of the DSM-5 (2013) could also be mined for insights on negative self-deception and delusions, in particular.

Notes

1 I have changed his notation here and in other quotations so as to conform with my usage throughout, having "not-*p*" stand for the deceptive or evidentially unsupported belief. He switches our use of "*p*" and "not-*p*."
2 In this paragraph, I have spoken about both belief and *acceptance*, a distinction recognized by some philosophers. The low evidential standards of the self-deceived might be better described as thresholds for acceptance

rather than for belief. The idea is that we sometimes accept things that we do not really believe, sometimes even to the point of acting on them. You might accept a premise for argument's sake, for example, without really believing it. Or you might accept that the enemy is positioned to your left, so as to plan a defense, but without really believing it. This notion of acceptance is further explained and applied to self-deception in §5.1.3.

3 Evolutionary psychology is psychology that is informed by the logic of evolution, in particular, natural selection. As such, evolutionary psychologists might investigate whether a particular psychological trait is an adaptation. The logic of natural selection is most associated with biology, although it can be applied to cultural evolution and even individual learning as well. Psychological adaptations are traits that helped us survive in our ancestral past, especially the Pleistocene, when psychological variations were competing against one another.

4 This point is especially emphasized by rationalistic philosophers of belief, such as Williams, Velleman, and Gendler as discussed earlier. These points also re-emerge in §5.1.

5 Sackeim (1988: 161–162) eventually granted this, as Mele (2001: 132) points out.

6 See Artiga and Paternotte (2018) for an account of deception that aims to cover human and non-human, as well as intentional and non-intentional, varieties under a single functional account.

7 Van Leeuwen (2007a) provides positive argument for attributing the false belief to self-deceivers, arguing specifically against Audi's avowal view. In large part, his argument is driven by the apparent fact that self-deceivers act as if they are genuine believers even in high stakes situations (e.g., investing in a business or flying an airplane).

8 His usage is inspired by Longeway (1990).

4

INTENTIONALISM AND DIVIDED MIND ACCOUNTS

4.1 Intentionalism: the general case
4.2 Divided mind accounts
4.3 Temporally divided selves
4.4 Other intentionalist and dual belief views

In the next two chapters, we will consider robust alternatives to deflationary accounts. Non-deflationists might embrace intentionalism, often because they take the interpersonal analogy seriously or want to keep a stronger form of deception in self-*deception*. They also might feel the pull of the claim that the self-deceived experience deep doxastic conflict, which can approximate if not entail dual belief. Indeed, like Davidson they might hold that the self-deceived intend the false belief *because* they have the true belief.

Theorists often think it is necessary to divide the mind in order to accommodate these tensions – this is the *sacrifice the self* move to the Basic Problem described back in §2.1. It might be a bit of an exaggeration to say that they *sacrifice* the self, as they can supplement or revise it instead. But they do deny that there is one thing that plays both the Deceiver and Victim roles, or which believes both p and not-p. Intentionalist accounts do not perfectly coincide with divided mind accounts, but there is substantial overlap. While divisions in the mind are often posited or appealed to so as to explain how intentional self-deception or deep doxastic conflict is even possible, one can also accept divided minds for independent reasons.

In this chapter, we will consider both intentionalist approaches and divided mind accounts. The next chapter considers robust accounts that are more revisionary (especially with respect to belief and purpose), albeit not demanding psychological intentions to deceive. Many of these different non-deflationary accounts can be combined with one another.

Non-deflationary accounts hold that self-deception is, at least not infrequently, *robust* in its psychological complexity. Specifically, it is robust with respect to those psychological elements that contribute toward the activity counting as deceptive. Recalling the categories from §3.1, this robustness can take the form of: agential involvement (e.g., intentional or purposive), belief complexity (e.g., deep doxastic conflict), motivational complexity (e.g., mind-directed motives or emotional nuance), and mental architecture (e.g., the unconscious; opacity). These certainly are not mutually exclusive options, and many non-deflationists embrace robustness along multiple dimensions. Their motives for so doing could be either largely *semantic* (coupled with common sense theorizing) or *empirical*.

As we saw with one of our objections to Mele (§3.5.3), some have argued that semantic considerations lead us to robustness. The idea is that one might appeal to what "deception" means, insisting that on semantic grounds alone it requires an intention to mislead, a division between Deceiver and Victim, or contradictory beliefs or motives. This understanding could be supplemented with appeals to paradigm examples of interpersonal deception that appear to have these very attributes. But semantic considerations alone cannot get us to robustness, as we also must be convinced that self-deception so understood actually occurs. This is basically how Davidson and Pears (to be discussed shortly) argue: Deception requires an intention to deceive and contradictory beliefs, and everyday life shows us that such self-deception really does occur. So they divide the mind, but not (especially for Davidson) based on any *empirical* psychological theorizing. Rather, they do so on a combination of semantic considerations and armchair speculation. Significantly, *eliminativists* about self-deception (e.g., Borge, 2003) sometimes argue against the very possibility of self-deception on purely semantic grounds as well. They might understand deception in robust terms but hold that such conditions, requiring a division between Deceiver and Victim, would no longer warrant the label *self*-deception. Alternatively, they could argue that

INTENTIONALISM AND DIVIDED MIND ACCOUNTS   137

it is psychologically impossible for a single mind to meet the conditions for literal deception.

Semantic considerations alone do not give us good enough reasons to accept psychological posits. But they can give us decent reasons, especially when coupled with folk psychological truisms, to look for such complexity. They can also put us on alert to make distinctions that deflationists might gloss over by reducing self-deception to hot biases. If there is a robust form of self-deception that genuinely requires doxastic and motivational conflict (static or dynamic), then we should see if it occurs within a single self and, if so, distinguish it from its less robust kin. One could make the case by directly appealing to findings in empirical psychology. Suppose that empirical psychology has demonstrated the reality of unconscious intentions, the unconscious execution of plans, segregated beliefs, and the like. If we have independent reason to think that these robust phenomena exist outside of self-deception, then we might think it likely that these tools are used in at least some cases of self-deception as well.

Philosophers have a tendency to go to extremes, sometimes misled by the methodology of analysis to look for all-or-nothing or exceptionless conditions. It would behoove both parties to at least consider a hybrid approach: Some self-deception is deflationary, some is robust. People often think that what they find to be of theoretical interest is the "real" phenomenon, rejecting or overlooking the rest. That being said, there is a real division between those who think that *all* self-deception can be accounted for with a deflationary approach and those who deny this.

§4.1 Intentionalism: the general case

Let's start our investigation of robust accounts by considering what intentionalism demands, some reasons for thinking it is true of self-deceivers, and what this would tell us about the structure of the mind.

§4.1.1 *What are intentions?*

To determine whether self-deception is always, typically, or even ever performed intentionally, we need to understand what is required for intentional action in general. This is incredibly nuanced terrain, as philosophers make very subtle distinctions between different varieties and degrees of agency. They also have substantial disagreement over the nature of intentions and the roles they play in generating action.[1] Recall

138   INTENTIONALISM AND DIVIDED MIND ACCOUNTS

that Nelkin, for example, required that self-deception be purposive – seeking belief – but yet she denied that it was intentional. If this is a real possibility, it means that something besides a merely causal and rational connection between a belief-desire pair and subsequent purposive action is needed for it to count as intentional. What more, then, do action theorists require of an agent to transform purposive (goal-seeking) behavior into intentional action?

Many different attributes have been taken to be distinctive, if not essential, to intentional action. (We broached this topic back in §2.3.1, when we were introduced to the debate between intentionalism and motivationalism.) The following attributes have all been offered as candidates:

1   *Effort.* Intentional actions are things people *do* in a fairly robust sense of that term. Other things merely *happen* to a person, like being shoved. Perhaps some mental events – say, the influence of a cold bias or even that of a hot bias – are like a shoving that merely happens to one. Not only are intentional actions things that we do, they are things that we *attempt, try* or *make an effort* to do. We can intend to do things that we do not actually succeed at doing. There are *foreseeable outcomes* of these attempts, and we intend at least some of what we anticipate to be a consequence of our actions. Putting this all together, intentional actions are things that we make an effort to do for some foreseeable outcome.

2   *Deliberation, decision, and planning.* Intentional actions display *practical rationality.* With intentional action there is some goal, normally provided by a desire or other "pro-attitude," and a means-end belief about how to achieve that goal. There may be *deliberation* about means, and perhaps even about goals. The reasoning might not be explicit or conscious, but whenever there is intentional action it is at least implicitly present or retroactively constructible. The reasoning at play is practical rather than theoretical. To be clear, the self-deceptive belief that not-p is *not* theoretically rational – the available evidence does not justify that belief. But someone could have good practical reasons to believe what is not theoretically rational, as so-believing could further the person's goals. Recall Davidson's Carlos example and Pascal's wager for such cases.

    When we do something intentionally, we have a *commitment* to that action. This is why we can intend to do something in the future. When we intend to do something we might *will, decide,* or perform some similar volitional act that establishes our intention. We frequently form a

INTENTIONALISM AND DIVIDED MIND ACCOUNTS 139

plan for how to achieve this end, as it might take a while to achieve this end and there might be several steps along the way.

3 *Control and responsibility:* As we act, we *control* or *guide* our activity. We may (consciously) *know what we are doing* while we are doing it. Accordingly, we are typically held *responsible* – morally and legally – for our intentional actions. This is because they are things that the agent did "on purpose." (But one could also do something on purpose without doing it intentionally – recall Nelkin's view.) Claims of responsibility are defeasible, however, as they might depend on further facts about the person's knowledge (e.g., maybe the action was intentional, but he was not fully aware of its consequences) or situational factors that may be beyond the agent's control (e.g., he had extremely limited options).

Obviously, these attributes do not always go together – e.g., someone might be responsible for something they did not plan on doing, or one might make an effort to do something without any deliberation or foresight. This is just a sketch of intentional action, and we need not fix on definite answers or draw sharp boundaries of agency. The idea is that some weighted clutster of these attributes mark off intentional action, and, roughly speaking, the more of them that are present the greater the agency. Again, I recommend thinking of a spectrum of agential involvement. The above three categories contain attributes that can be added to mere goal pursuit – of the kind performed by many other animals – to turn mere purposiveness into more robust action.[2]

Rather than immersing ourselves in these deep waters, it might be best to turn to how intentions and intentional action are understood by the participants in the self-deception debate. What are *they* affirming or denying when they embrace intentionalism or motivationalism? Among intentionalists, there is variation in how they understand intentional activity and what they take to be the specific intentions for self-deception We have already seen (§2.3.1) that there is disagreement over the latter: Are they trying to deceive themselves? Are they trying to acquire a belief (regardless of its truth)? Are they merely trying to do things that are *de facto* epistemically misleading?

Mele's understanding of intentional action focuses on the concept of *trying* or *attempting* to do something, holding that if people try to do something and they succeed, then they did that action intentionally. Conversely, if someone does not try to do something but they do it anyway, then they did not perform that action intentionally (Mele, 2001: 15). This is to take *effort*, in at least some sense of that term, as a mark of intentional action. This should be a welcome insight, as it allows for a psychological test for intentional action – experimental psychologists have methods that they believe test for cognitive effort (among other forms of effort). Although Mele does not pursue this possibility, we should then be able to resolve the question of intentionalism through empirical testing rather than philosophical debate (at least if we assume that intentional action requires an effortful attempt).

The two most prominent intentionalist theories have been those of Donald Davidson and David Pears. We should turn to Davidson, in particular, as he also wrote a hugely influential series of papers on action, intention, agency, and related issues. (These are collected in Davidson, 1980.) Davidson's account of intentional action makes rather thin demands. For him, to act intentionally is simply to act on a belief-desire pair (primary reason) that rationalizes the action. It is not further required that the person is aware of this primary reason or that any distinct mental act has been performed that counts as the intending. (Davidson, 1980: Essays 1 and 5.) He also speaks of intentions to perform future actions, where these are *caused* by belief-desire pairs, although are not reducible to them. But we need only concern ourselves with his account of intentional action, not intending to act in the future. For Davidson, intentional actions are those behaviors that are explicable, both causally and logically, by reasons-giving explanations that cite a goal (Davidson, 2004: 185). In effect, then, Davidson's thin notion of intentional action may not be so very different from what we find with Nelkin's purposive (but supposedly not intentional) self-deception.

Davidson repeatedly describes self-deception as an intentional activity, but what is the real force of this claim? We get a sense of the level of agential involvement that he has in mind when he says things like: self-deception requires "intervention by the agent;" "self-deception requires the agent to *do* something with the aim of changing his own views;" "The self-deceiver must intend the 'deception'"; and the self-deceived must take measures like intentionally directing their attention or searching for evidence with the goal of producing false belief (Davidson, 2004: 206–208). But it is not so helpful to merely assert that the deceptive activity is an *intentional* directing of one's attention. For, what does this amount to? What Davidson describes as an intentional activity, another might describe as merely goal seeking.

§4.1.2 *The case for intentions*

Stepping back from these particular theories for a moment, we can discern at least five general reasons why one might be led to intentionalism.

We have already encountered several of these reasons, so our discussion will be brief at places. The first four reasons arise from more philosophical or armchair speculations. But there is a fifth reason, which is more direct and empirical, that we have not yet developed.

1. Robust deception

Some (e.g., Davidson) think that intentions are needed to distinguish genuinely deceptive cases from other forms of motivated irrationality like wishful thinking. This is not to say that intentional self-deception is more common than Mele-style self-enhancement and other forms of hot biasing. Rather, it is just to claim that the latter is not truly self-*deceptive*. Such deflated self-deception might not even be purposive.

2. Selectivity

Motivation, fortunately, does not always give rise to irrationality. It would be disastrous if our wishes always skewed our beliefs:

> Mary desired to believe that John loved her regardless of whether it was true, and that made it (practically) rational to favor that belief. In contrast, pleasant though it might have been to believe that my brakes were functioning normally, I had no desire to believe it regardless of whether it was true, and thus I had no (practically) rational motivation to favor believing it. (Talbott, 1995: 62)

Notice how wishes strategically influence belief. Few of us self-deceive in high stakes situations (car brakes), or at least in urgent high stakes situations. This relates to Bermudez's selectivity problem: Why do desires sometimes skew belief and sometimes not? An intention to believe, he claimed, can distinguish between these two cases. Mele's PEDMIN theory, among other possibilities, offers a alternative, deflationary explanation. It is very costly to have false beliefs about the safety of one's brakes; false beliefs about one's looks or competency (within reason) are not so costly.

3. Unity

Many deflationary accounts have a hard time accounting for negative self-deception, as the person is not motivated for the world to be that way and it is unnatural to describe them as "wishing" to so believe. Deflationists could provide different accounts for positive and negative self-deception. Such disjunctive theories might be true, but unity, simplicity, and beauty are generally considered to be theoretical virtues. Intentionalists offer such unity: Both the positively and negatively self-deceived are intending (attempting, etc.) to produce belief. Desire-to-believe theories, which posit a mere desire with the same content as the proposed intention, fare better than those which posit world-directed motives. The desire-to-believe theorists *do* offer a unified motivationalist theory: Both the positively and negatively self-deceived are motivated by a desire to believe, just like intentionalists posit a unifying intention to produce the belief. But again, one could reasonably object that, in many cases of negative self-deception, there is not even a desire to so believe (e.g., in one's ineptitude or a spouse's infidelity). Also note how the gap between intentionalism and desire-to-believe motivationalism, as advocated by Nelkin and Funkhouser, can be quite narrow.

4. Responsibility

Self-deception is normally a non-clinical condition, and it is common to hold people responsible (blameworthy) for it. While other forms of epistemic sloppiness can also be blameworthy, some think that the self-deceived deserve a different kind of condemnation – one more appropriate for liars than for those who are merely poor, sloppy, or wishful thinkers. (We will examine the issue of responsibility in some detail in Chapter 6.) Invoking intentions makes it easier to hold the self-deceived responsible for their condition. The idea is that the self-deceived do not merely succumb to a deception, but they actively made an effort to bring it on themselves. Generally speaking, the more robust the agency behind the deception, the more plausible attributions of responsibility become. Further, the self-deceived do not have a deficit of reasoning (sometimes, in a perverse sense, they even seem to have an abundance of it), so they are perfectly competent to detect and correct their condition.

While intentionalism might make it easier to assign responsibility for self-deception, it is not the only way. People can be responsible for their negligence, even when (as is often the case) it is for something that they did not intend to do. Mele himself thinks that people often are responsible for their self-deception, as it was within their power to be aware of these biases and make corrections. While we do not intentionally bias ourselves, he thinks that we at least can have non-trivial control over it. Self-deception

INTENTIONALISM AND DIVIDED MIND ACCOUNTS   143

is a kind of epistemic negligence. He finds support for this view in studies that show people to be less biased when instructed to engage in symmetrical evidential search, search for both pros and cons, and so on (Mele, 2001: 103). Alternatively, perhaps we should revise the judgment that self-deceivers are blameworthy. By discovering the mechanisms that give rise to a phenomenon, we could discover that it is beyond what we can reasonably expect someone to control.

5. Direct case: testing for effort, deliberation, decisions, control, and the like

Mele often says that it is unnecessary to posit intentional self-deception, as the phenomena can be explained exclusively in motivational terms. That may or may not be true. But even if intentions are unnecessary (in theory) to explain self-deception, why not test for them directly if we have the ability to do so? Pointing out that something is unnecessary is an indirect way to argue against a claim, but it is not conclusive – it is not necessary that men have nipples, but they do. Of course, it is also possible that Mele is simply wrong and intentions are necessary to explain some self-deception. Indeed, if there is some intentional self-deception, we simply might not have a subtle enough understanding of the phenomenon to appreciate why the intentions are necessary.

As we have noted, the philosophical community is not in total agreement when it comes to understanding intentional action and intentions. Intentions are associated with many markers that go beyond mere activity: deliberation, decision, effort, sustained control, etc. And there are methods to psychologically test for at least some of these. Von Hippel and Trivers (2011) attend to two psychological measures that they think can be used to separate self-deception from less agentially involved forms of bias. The first measure is cognitive load. Imposing cognitive load is a widely accepted means to test if a psychological process is effortful, drawing on working memory in particular. What if we find that self-deception fades under cognitive load, as in the Valdesolo and DeSteno (2008) moral hypocrisy studies? This would not decisively show that self-deception is intentional, but it would support that it is at least not automatic. This suggests some level of agential involvement. The second measure is self-affirmation, which is worth investigating as a manipulation to test for effort or other markers of intentional action. The idea is that when we affirm our values or sense of self, or if we have our esteem boosted by success on some task, we are then less likely to be biased in self-serving ways. The standard interpretation is that this is because we are no longer motivated to augment or defend our sense of self. But the Gur and Sackeim (1979) self-confrontion studies show us that the relationship between self-esteem and self-serving bias can be more complicated. In their studies, manipulations of self-esteem produced different kinds of bias, but positive manipulation did not eliminate it.

But do these studies go beyond supporting motivationalism? Von Hippel and Trivers think so:

> Such an effect for self-affirmation not only provides evidence for the role of motivation in the information-processing bias but also indicates that the person had the potential to process the information in a less biased or unbiased fashion. In this manner, self-affirmation manipulations can test our self-deception criterion that the person is aware of the welcome information but at the same time also had potential awareness of the unwelcome information. (Von Hippel and Trivers, 2011: 8)

This also suggests that the self-deceived are responsible for their self-deception, as they have the ability (in some sense, at least) to control it. But again, theorists like Mele will allow that a person can be responsible for their self-deception even while claiming that it is not intentional. We could also object to the inference to the conclusion that the person had the potential to be less biased, thinking of the Gur and Sackeim (1979) studies as a test case. The fact that the skin always gets it (voice identification) right does not entail that the person could have gotten it right as well.

§4.1.3 Connection to divided minds

Accepting intentionalism often leads one to divide the mind as well. This brings us back to our static and, especially, dynamic problems once again. Recall Bernard Williams's argument (§2.1.2) that we cannot simply decide to believe something in "full consciousness" and succeed. Our awareness that we are intending to believe something undermines its success, presenting a problem for intentionalist accounts of self-deception. The natural remedy is to hide the intention – make it unconscious or at least in another pocket of consciousness. In this way, the attempt is not in full consciousness. The self-deceiver is divided to at least some extent, and in its more extreme forms the divisions come to resemble the kinds of agency that we find with interpersonal deception.

INTENTIONALISM AND DIVIDED MIND ACCOUNTS   145

If the dynamic problem is not sufficient to lead intentionalists to divide the mind, a specific form of the static problem could do the trick. Some intentionalists, such as Donald Davidson, hold that the self-deceived must possess the true belief and intend to acquire the false belief. The idea is that the true belief, combined with their preferences, generates the intention to self-deceive. If self-deception requires sustaining this duplicity, then it too might demand divisions. The rationale here is not much different than that behind the dynamic problem: Just as one cannot generate a false belief within a unified mind in radical disregard of rational or evidential considerations, so too one cannot hold contradictory beliefs within a unified mind as that would defy the minimal standards of rationality. Many intentionalists, however, will deny that self-deception requires true belief or even the possession of evidence sufficient to make the self-deceptive doxastic state irrational. So, the dynamic problem is the factor more likely to lead intentionalists to also be divisionists.

While intentionalism is normally associated with some kind of divided mind account, W.J. Talbott (1995) has argued that this is not necessary. His main claim is that intentional self-deception can arise in an "ideally coherent," undivided self. His claim, however, is immediately qualified. Talbott admits that the self-deceived *are* divided in various ways, and their self-deception is to be explained in terms of these divisions. Talbott says that it is obvious that the mind contains divisions between different kinds of memory system (short-term and long-term), faculties or modules, conscious and unconscious processing, and the like. In what sense, then, is his not a divided mind account? Recognizing these familiar divisions and utilizing them in formulating an account of self-deception is *not* enough to make one a "divisionist," Talbott claims. Instead, the interesting issue is whether, in order to explain self-deception, we must draw additional divisions beyond what we posit to explain non-self-deceptive phenomena. Talbott thinks not.

Can intentional self-deception be accommodated with these familiar psychological tools? That depends on how we understand the intention driving self-deception. On this point, Talbott is less demanding than some other intentionalists. He holds that self-deception is the intentional biasing of belief-relevant processes (e.g., attention to evidence) due to a desire to believe a proposition regardless of its truth. The belief itself is not directly, intentionally acquired – just the biasing is intentional. This intention is supposed to be necessary in order to distinguish self-deception, which is strategic, from wishful thinking, which is not. The biases that Talbott describes as intentional are often very similar to the processes that Mele describes in deflationary terms. Some of the activities he describes are clearly intentional – e.g., cutting off or guiding evidence search. But is the intention *deceptive*? Talbott (1995: 42, 51–52) thinks the self-deceiving are intentionally distorting their cognitive process – for example, by intentionally distorting evidence search and diverting attention. Biases of memory and reason are harder to envision as intentional, but he still thinks that they can be. The emphasis on strategy and deceptive tactics is supposed to elevate self-deception from mere purposive behavior to outright intentional action. Talbott goes so far as to claim that one can be intentionally biased with respect to beliefs about one's own mind. But the self-deceived must hide from themselves the belief that they are biased *because of* their desire. This is a failure of self-knowledge.

All of this is supposed to be executed within an individual who is not *unusually* divided. To soften us up to the ease with which such intentions can be executed by normal people, he reminds us that Gricean accounts of communication (along with other common forms of coordinated action) make use of robust, unconscious intentions.[3] Even if they do not accept Grice's theory of communication, philosophers tend to think that it is legitimate to appeal to those kinds of intention (e.g., intentions to produce beliefs in the audience). But we do not need to consider rarefied philosophical examples to see the point. Talbott says that familiar everyday activities like singing a duet, painting a house with another person, or running a "give-and-go" play in basketball are driven by unconscious intentions (Talbott, 1995: 63). (Perhaps it is noteworthy that all his other examples of unconscious intention involve coordinated *social* activity.) Here and elsewhere he exploits the fact that there are inaccessible memories, subpersonal processes, unconscious states (i.e., mental states of which the person is ignorant or unaware), and the mind otherwise is not transparent to itself. The success of the self-deceptive enterprise depends on these kinds of vulnerability.

How successful is Talbott at showing that intentional self-deception can occur within the single-minded? His conclusion should be taken with a grain of salt, as Talbott's argument hinges on both watering down the concept of intention (e.g., making it unconscious and, more significantly, perhaps conflating it with mere purposiveness) and exploiting many so-called "innocent divisions." It may be that neither the motivationalist nor the divisionist is too disturbed by this case. Talbott seems to *accept* the divisions that are paradigmatic of divided mind theorists, especially those grounded in the conscious/ unconscious and transparent/opaque distinctions. Most divided mind theorists posit only "innocent divisions" (although Mele denies even these) – few divided mind theorists think of the divisions as anything as robust as multiple personalities vying within a person. Davidson, for example, has a watered down psychological partitioning – he posits a "metaphorical" divide whenever propositional attitudes fail to rationally cohere (to some vague degree) – that seems compatible with Talbott's view. Talbott's view also seems to agree with many of the currently popular divided mind accounts, such as those discussed shortly that draw on robust unconscious powers. This is because the recent psychological literature on the unconscious emphasizes that these powers are in no way unique to self-deception, thereby meeting Talbott's "innocent divisions" standard. But then again, Freud himself emphasized the ubiquity of robust divisions in everyday life, and his view seems like a paradigm of a divided mind account. If Talbott is objecting only to special subsystems that are devoted to intentional deception, it may be that a view like that of David Pears (discussed in §4.2.2) is his only target.

§4.2 Divided mind accounts

Talbott's advisory that we not trivialize the divided mind thesis is well taken. Of course there are divisions in the mind in some sense: different component parts, working memory and long-term memory, automatic and controlled processes, etc. But is there an additional or distinctive kind of partitioning in the self-deceived? Are they perhaps even divided into subunits that act as their own agents with their own agendas?

§4.2.1 Conscious and unconscious

The most well-known division deployed to explain self-deception is probably that between conscious and unconscious psychological phenomena. This was made famous, both in academia and popular culture, by Sigmund Freud. A recent resurgence of neo-Freudianism,[4] in the form of strong advocacy of unconscious processes, offers even more tools for explaining self-deception. There are both moderate and robust invocations of unconscious processing to account for self-deception.

Moderate unconscious mind accounts

What is the unconscious? It is probably not best to think of it as a realm or mental space, like the unconscious quarters of the mind. Rather, we should think of particular psychological states or processes – lust for the man next door; a reckoning of the costs to repair the car – as being unconscious or not. Consciousness, and the lack of it, is an attribute of mental states or processes. But what is the nature of this attribute? This is one of the most perilous questions in all of philosophy, and many varieties of consciousness have been distinguished – access consciousness, phenomenal consciousness, narrative consciousness, and so on.[5] I will single out one particular sense that seems to be most relevant to the problems of self-deception and which is also commonly employed in experimental psychology. Namely, consciousness is *awareness* of a mental state, attitude, or process; unconsciousness is a lack of such awareness. Experimental psychologists might operationalize this awareness in terms of what is reportable by the subject (although this is fallible), but there are also less direct means to test for it. Awareness consciousness allows for a *degreed* notion of consciousness, as one can be more or less aware of a mental state. Further, awareness of a mental state can be more or less difficult to achieve, allowing us to also make sense of there being a *depth* to consciousness. States that are very inaccessible are often described as being "buried" in the unconscious; other thoughts are only superficially unconscious. Unconscious states can become conscious in various ways, including by having behavioral or other evidence pointed out by a third party, the necessity of a high stakes situation, or a project of introspection.

This understanding of consciousness as awareness connects it with self-knowledge. Unconscious mental states are those that the person does not know, in a very thin sense of knowledge, that they possess. But it is actually a bit more complicated than this. Psychologists speak of the unconscious not just when we lack awareness of a mental state, but also when we are unaware of the ways in which a mental state (of which we might actually be aware) affects us. For example, Julie Huang and John Bargh write:

> A process is described here as unconscious even if a person is able to report the presence of a stimulus and respond to it (e.g., in an experiment, one is judging stockings presented in an array, deems the right-most choice of highest quality, and provides reasons why) but lacks awareness regarding the causes and processes underlying the effect (e.g., that one may have been biased by a position effect on evaluation that favored the right-most stocking independent of quality-related factors. (Huang and Bargh, 2014: 124)

Here we find ignorance of a psychological process involving a conscious perception. It is only the operation of the process – the bias – that is unconscious.

INTENTIONALISM AND DIVIDED MIND ACCOUNTS   149

Even deflationists like Mele allow that extensive unconscious psycholog-ical processing can contribute to self-deception in the form of reasoning biases. So, this is not enough to underlie a non-deflationary division. By a "moderate" unconscious mind account, then, I mean something a bit more. These moderate accounts invoke the unconscious in order to address, in a straightforward manner, the static or dynamic problems of self-deception. (I am not claiming a rigorous or extremely principled divide with this usage. This is just stipulated.) Deflationary accounts, in contrast, avoid these problems by deflating the phenomena (e.g., eliminating dual belief and deep conflict; denying that self-deception is intentional and perhaps even purposive) so as to render unconscious machinations unnecessary. The most prominent static problems are those relating to belief, specifically for those who demand dual beliefs (by taking the interpersonal analogy seriously) or at least recognize deep conflict. It is hard, if not impossible, to maintain straightforwardly contradictory beliefs in a unified conscious-ness. Even mixed belief-like attitudes (e.g., partial belief; cognitive, affec-tive, and behavioral conflict, etc.) can be difficult to maintain within a unified consciousness.

One remedy is to have one of these beliefs, or some of these conflicting belief-like attitudes, be unconscious. This is the view developed by Robert Audi (1982), who emphasizes doxastic and emotional conflict as paradig-matic of self-deception. This conflict is all supposedly driven by a want (e.g., to believe that not-p or for the world to be such that not-p) that exerts itself in both consciousness and unconsciousness. In the conscious mind, it causes the person to avow that not-p. But it also causes the true belief that p to remain unconscious. Audi then advances three necessary and jointly sufficient conditions for paradigmatic, if not all, self-deception:

1   The person unconsciously has the true belief that p.
2   The person is disposed to sincerely avow that not-p.
3   The person has a want that has two functions:
     a   It keeps the true belief repressed in the unconscious.
     b   It disposes the person to avow that not-p even in the face of con-trary evidence. (adapted from Audi, 1982: 137)

This account does not require dual belief. While avowals are normally good indicators of belief, they are supposed to be misleading in these cases. These self-deceptive avowals are misleading not because the person is lying as they speak; rather, their avowals are sincere. They simply are not aware of what they believe, and the true belief is retained in the unconscious. This inconsistency between the genuine, unconscious, true belief and the sincere avowal of the falsehood is the conflict underlying the static problem as Audi sees it. By invoking the unconscious, he aims to show how it is possible to maintain the sincerity of the avowals without falling into either lying or outright delusion.

But why does Audi think that the self-deceived really possess the true belief? He gives examples that depict the self-deceived as lacking the conviction of their avowed belief and acting contrary to it. One of his main examples involves a woman, Ann, who is in self-deceptive denial regarding her terminal cancer (Audi, 1982: 134–135). While she speaks of recovery, there is supposed to be evidence of a contrary belief. This evidence includes: Her talk of recovery is stated either too weakly or too strongly, she experiences emotions like anxiety and depression that belie her avowals, and she behaves in some ways so as to accommodate the truth (e.g., makes funeral arrangements). Audi repeats the maxim that "actions speak louder than words" (1982: 139; 1985, 173) to justify attributing the true belief and withholding belief in the avowed false proposition. But it is not clear which actions speak loudest, and a character like Ann has actions that do not align wholeheartedly behind one belief. Although Audi does not develop this point, evidence avoidance behavior might be most revealing of genuine belief, as evidence sensitivity is a hallmark of belief. Recourse could also be made to the person's behavior in high stakes situations, under the premise that important action speaks loudest of all.

How does Audi think that unconscious beliefs function? They are supposed to function very much like their conscious analogues when it comes to affecting action, emotion, and practical reasoning. To explain why in cases of self-deception the person instead avows something inconsistent with their unconscious belief, Audi posits a motive (want) that trumps the unconscious belief's normal operation and prevents it from generating its customary effects in the realms of thought and assertion. The unconscious belief does have some conscious effects, but the person will not be aware of its influence and will not attribute this belief to themselves without undergoing some serious self-scrutiny or receiving outside correction (if then). Preserving the interpersonal analogy to at least some extent, Audi holds that the self-deceived must retain some sense of the truth. He has been one of the earliest and most forceful advocates of the deception/delusion distinction; self-deception, unlike self-delusion, requires sustained conflict. If the unconscious true belief is lost and replaced with wholehearted false belief instead, then there is falsehood (delusion) but no longer any deception. As we have seen, this is a significant point of disagreement with Mele and other deflationists. For Audi, self-deception requires that the true belief remain hidden from conscious awareness. At the level of consciousness there is a "virtual belief" or a higher order belief failure: the self-deceived have a false second-order belief about what they believe, an illusion of belief. But at the first-order level, Audi thinks that self-deceivers are largely rational and possess the true belief (Audi, 1985: 177; also see Funkhouser, 2005: 305–309). This failure of self-knowledge does not exist for the self-deluded.

This is one way to deal with the static problem involving belief, but what about the want or desire that drives both the repression and the avowal? Is the want also unconscious, and must it be in order for it to be effective? Audi (1982: 151–152) argues, with convincing examples, that the want itself could be either conscious or unconscious. An intention to deceive, if it is to be effective in the moment, would almost surely have to be unconscious, but Audi is not an intentionalist. Mere motives can produce certain biasing effects and initiate repression even when these motives are consciously experienced. I am consciously aware that I want my daughter to succeed at school, and this is what (self-deceptively?) biases my evaluation of her performance and causes me to repress contrary knowledge. Nevertheless, it seems that there must be something here that is unconscious. Namely, I lack awareness of how that desire influences my judgment, memory, and self-knowledge. A question to consider in regards to the dynamic problem is whether such desires can effectively produce the biasing effect even when we are aware of, not only the desires themselves, but also the distorting effects they produce on our reasoning. Likely so, as unwarranted associations can resist even conscious awareness – e.g., placebos can still be effective even when people know that they are taking a mere placebo. Self-deception, like a placebo, goes beyond the normal and rational functioning of thought, exploiting the brutely mechanical powers of mental states. Awareness of such bias is not the norm, however, so the question might be of more academic than practical interest (see Figure 4.1).

We might challenge the prominent role that Audi gives to avowals. On his view, it seems that the whole point of self-deception is to generate misleading, although sincere, avowals. Avowals are normally directed at an audience, at least if these are understood as speech acts. Research shows that frequent avowal is one of the strongest grounds for attributing belief to another, even outweighing the utterer's non-linguistic behavior

152 INTENTIONALISM AND DIVIDED MIND ACCOUNTS

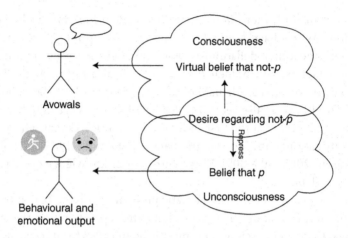

Figure 4.1 Audi's divided mind (conscious/unconscious) account

(Rose, Buckwalter, and Turri: 2014). This suggests a social function for self-deception: We self-deceive to generate avowals that lead others to attribute a mistaken belief to us. Yet this point is not emphasized by Audi, who sees self-deception as satisfying more personal and less social desires. However, it may be that the avowal is also directed at the self, manipulating the self-deceiver to self-attribute the belief that not-p. This fits with Audi's overall picture of self-deception as a failure of self-knowledge, but, if this remains the focus, it might be better to appeal to less social psychological activity and behavior in place of avowal. If we go in that direction, we might consider embracing Bach's (1981) claim that the self-deceived aim to induce the thought that not-p and downplay the role of avowals.

While Audi (1982: 152) claims that the unconscious determines much of our behavior, he does not go into details as to how this is achieved. He is explicit that his interests are more in the state of self-deception than the dynamics that lead there. In part, this is because he takes self-deception to be an ahistorical concept (1997: 104). By this, he means that it does not matter how one gets into the self-deceptive state so long as the person simultaneously is disposed to avow something while unconsciously believing the contrary, where both the avowal and the unconscious state of the belief are explained by a concurrent want. Obviously, there is a story to tell about how the want achieves these ends. It may be that the true belief cannot be successfully kept under wraps in the unconscious while making sincere avowals to the contrary unless there is quite sophisticated unconscious scheming (e.g., evidence avoidance and rationalization) operating in the background. Some more recent work in psychology and philosophy provides us with tools to explain how this is possible.

Robust unconscious mind accounts

Moderate unconscious mind accounts do not insist that the unconscious has deceptive or reasoning powers that approximate the sophistication of the conscious mind. Rather, they hold that the unconscious has just enough powers to avoid the paradoxes of self-deception. Robust unconscious mind accounts, on the other hand, get more into the dynamics of self-deception. Central to their case is a commitment to unconscious processes approximating conscious processes in their sophistication (e.g., ability to pursue goals in the face of changing evidence and context). A recent but also very controversial research programme in psychology argues for such a sophisticated unconscious, both in terms of motivating and executing deception among other controlled processes (Bargh and Morsella, 2008; Hassin, Bargh, and Zimerman, 2009). On robust unconscious accounts the motivation or intention to self-deceive can be unconscious, along with the execution of a sophisticated deceptive ruse that rivals its conscious analogues. This general idea has been applied to self-deception, most prominently, by von Hippel and Trivers (2011, especially §5).

While there are vigorous disagreements over the extent of the role that the unconscious plays in our lives, there has been a neo-Freudian turn toward acknowledging that it is significant. One corollary of this is that we often lack knowledge of our true motives and beliefs. From an evolutionary perspective, it is obvious that unconscious processing preceded conscious processing, with the latter somehow being built from or added to the former. This means that we should expect similarities in how conscious and unconscious processes unfold. Indeed, creatures without consciousness (like a jellyfish) can engage in at least simple goal-directed behavior and can also join with others in producing coordinated action. Neuroscientific evidence confirms that executive control can occur outside of awareness, that the same brain structures are involved in motivating and controlling both conscious and unconscious goal pursuit, and that conscious intentions and action-guiding representations are located in distinct parts of the brain (Huang and Bargh, 2014). In short, there is a lot of sophisticated processing of information and goal pursuit going on behind the scenes (unconscious) that we are either completely oblivious to or misattribute to consciousness.

Funkhouser and Barrett (2016) argue for a notion of *robust self-deception* that draws on these powers of the unconscious. Similar to Audi, they think that doxastic tension appears in many common examples of self-deception, with truth retained in the unconscious and falsity promulgated by the conscious mind. (Whereas Audi thinks that this tension is essential to paradigmatic self-deception, they argue for the weaker claim that it appears in some cases of self-deception.) Robust self-deception is supposed to contrast with the deflationary form of self-deception common in many of Mele's examples. Funkhouser and Barrett claim that there is very little deception in these examples (e.g., the university professors who think they are better than average), with the operation of a hot bias really being no more deceptive than the operation of a cold bias. They require three additional ingredients to transform these hot biases into robust self-deception: 1) *strategic* goal pursuit, 2) *flexibility* across changing situations, and 3) *retention of the truth* (Funkhouser and Barrett, 2016: 683). They argue, along the lines of Huang and Bargh (2014), that the unconscious can satisfy these conditions to a degree that at least approximates conscious goal pursuit.

Several different unconscious processes can provide evidence for robust self-deception.

UNCONSCIOUS EVIDENCE AVOIDANCE

Some self-deception is guided by processes that seem to reveal unconscious possession of the truth and purposive efforts to repress that truth. (This was Audi's point, as well.) These forms of self-deception are supposed to be more deceptive than mere hot biases because they better fit the interpersonal analogy in which one party possesses the truth and manipulates another party so that it is not aware of that truth. As an example, Funkhouser and Barrett (2016) consider a man and a woman on a dating site who unconsciously manipulate their user profiles and pictures to cover their less flattering features. (Of course, others do these manipulations consciously.) They could quite strategically take selfies at angles that disguise their hairline or body size, redirect conversation on that first date, and otherwise present a misleading picture of themselves in a strategic and flexible manner that is executed unconsciously so as to deceive their date. These same unconscious processes could also be turned inward for the sake of self-deception. Funkhouser and Barrett argue that if the redirection, avoidance, and other forms of evidence manipulation are precisely targeted, this shows that there is also retention of the truth. The (self-)deceiver knows precisely what to avoid.

INTENTIONALISM AND DIVIDED MIND ACCOUNTS   155

Notice how evidence avoidance biases differ from biases to seek out favorable evidence. It is hard to see how one could consciously avoid confronting *particular* bits of evidence and succeed at self-deception *in the moment*, at least if that evidence is particularly strong. It is important that we add "in the moment" here, because one could succeed later on by forgetting that conscious plan. If the man consciously covers up his hairline with a ballcap in order to hide the evidence of baldness, he might succeed at deceiving others, but he cannot plausibly convince himself in that moment that he is not bald. He is aware of the very fact that he is trying to hide from himself – the classic dynamic problem. Perhaps this manipulation can help him eventually forget that he is bald, but not while the evidence avoidance is consciously before his mind. In this example, there is not much of a distinction between the evidence (seeing the baldness) and the fact itself. When there is greater distance between the evidence and the facts it ostensibly supports (say, it is open to multiple interpretations), there are more possibilities for rationalization and conscious confrontation of the evidence. Extremists and conspiracy theorists can always find a way to rationalize away any datum as "fake news," just another part of the conspiracy, and so on. One could also consciously avoid general categories of evidence without knowing (even unconsciously) the specific details of what one would find there. One might avoid questioning witnesses (e.g., those who were with their son and could report whether he was doing drugs) or consulting sources (e.g., "liberal" mainstream news) without knowing the particular evidence they would find there. But Funkhouser and Barrett emphasize that other avoidance behavior is so specific that it reveals (unconscious) knowledge, or at least non-trivial suspicion, of the truth. Think of someone who avoids checking their bank balance because they unconsciously know that it is much too low. Resistance to correction, especially if it appears to be *ad hoc*, can be another indicator that a more robust deceptive project is at work (Rorty, 1988: 14).

Biases for favorable evidence are different, and it is much more plausible that they can succeed even when they occur consciously. This is because as one seeks out evidence for a proposition they want to believe, they need not simultaneously be aware of any facts that undermine that belief. The confirmation bias can play out before the conscious mind, as in the kind of project that Pascal recommended for his wagerer (e.g., associate only with believers). The eventual believer might find herself fortunate to have been influenced into the correct belief. Of course, biases for favorable evidence can occur and operate unconsciously as well, and they very well might be more successful when unconscious. But unconscious evidence avoidance biases are an even stronger indicator of unconscious true belief, suggesting greater manipulation and more deception than what we find with a merely biased evidence search. This evidence repression also aligns with the fact that self-deceivers are largely rational individuals who appreciate the force of evidence, which is why they go to such great pains to manipulate it.

UNCONSCIOUS MEMORY AND ATTENTION BIASES

Biased memory search can occur without possession of the truth. As Mele pointed out, it could occur for straightforwardly hedonic (rather than overly tactical) reasons – e.g, it just feels good to think about your son's successes. Memory biases do not necessarily display robust self-deception, but some of them do. As with evidence search more generally, memory avoidance is more robustly deceptive than is a bias for seeking (epistemically or hedonically) favored memories, especially if the avoidance targets specific memories. The memory must be repressed because the person appreciates, at some level, where it leads.

There is evidence that our attention can be unconsciously directed toward things for the sake of goal pursuit, and our attention can be unconsciously directed *away* from things that do not fit with our goals. Jiang et al. (2006) exposed study participants to "invisible" nude figures (i.e., images that did not reach consciousness), which nevertheless caught the participants' attention as measured by their accuracy in reporting later visible stimuli occurring at the very same location. But there were fascinating differences in performance depending on the sexual orientation of the participant and the sex of the nude image. For heterosexual men and homosexual women, invisible female nudes improved report accuracy. And for heterosexual women and homosexual men, invisible male nudes improved report accuracy. It is exactly as if they were unconsciously drawn to the images they would like to see. Most interesting of all, however, when the images did not match the participant's sexual preference, there was a decline in report accuracy. In these cases, the participant's attention was "repelled" by the image that ran counter to their sexual goals (Jiang et al., 2006: 17050). Their attention is not indiscriminately drawn to alluring images, but it is either drawn or repelled according to how the image meshes with their sexual goals. And this is all done below the level of conscious awareness. This study suggests rich possibilities for unconscious redirection of attention so as to avoid evidence that contradicts our preferred beliefs or goals in a variety of self-deceptive domains.

INTENTIONALISM AND DIVIDED MIND ACCOUNTS   157

UNCONSCIOUS INTERPRETATION AND RATIONALIZATION

Von Hippel and Trivers (2011: 10) discuss a fascinating study that they interpret as displaying rationalization that is plausibly unconscious. Snyder et al. (1979) conducted a study in which people had to choose to sit in one of two rooms with a television playing. There were two chairs in front of each television, with one occupied and the other empty. In one room, a handicapped person occupied the chair, in the other room, it was a non-handicapped person. The interesting effect was produced by varying the movie shown on the television. If the televisions were showing the same movie, then most (58%) of the participants chose to sit next to the handicapped person. However, if the televisions were playing different movies the results were quite different – 83% sat next to the non-handicapped person instead! Why the difference? The hypothesis endorsed by Snyder et al., and accepted by von Hippel and Trivers, is that when different movies are playing the participants have a rationale that they can offer to explain their choice – they are not avoiding the handicapped person, they simply prefer the other movie. That is, they want to hide the real motive for their choice, but there is no socially desirable alternative justification when the same movie is shown on both televisions. Funkhouser and Barrett (2017) claim that this rationalization occurs unconsciously, as the result of the study is surprising and it is implausible that so many people would spontaneously come up with this same conscious rationalization (not knowing, at the time of their choice, that they would have to explain it later). If we who read the study did not consciously think of this rationalization right away, why think that the participants did? This also suggests that the unconscious can be shrewder than the conscious mind. Further, the subjects did not report any motive to avoid the handicapped or an effort to rationalize. But this could be due to the effects of socially desirable responding.

This study should certainly be taken with a grain of salt. The sample size was small, and in recent years we have seen that many psychological studies (in social psychology, especially) have failed to replicate. But a study like this, which can be improved on and altered in various ways, at least points us at ways to test whether unconscious rationalization occurs.

UNCONSCIOUS DESIRES AND MOTIVES

All people have unconscious desires and motives. Environmental cues can trigger these motives, initiating unconscious goal pursuit. For example, most people have sex-based motives to self-present in certain ways in front of those they find attractive. One of these ways concerns how they speak.

Heterosexual men tend to lower their voice pitch when talking with women they find attractive, while women tend to speak with a higher pitch when speaking to males they find attractive (Fraccaro et al., 2011; Hughes, Farley, and Rhodes, 2010; Leongomez, et al., 2014). Of course most of these people are consciously aware, in a general sense, if not on the particular occasion, that they have sexual desires. But they often do not know when they are activated, and it is highly unlikely that they are consciously aware that they are manipulating their pitch in these ways. This example is particularly apt for our purposes in that this seems to be unconsciously (or non-consciously) motivated deception. The manipulation is strategic in that women tend to prefer lower pitched male voices, and vice versa for men. And it is also flexible in that the voices are altered only in these select circumstances. If deception can be unconsciously executed against others, there is no obvious barrier to its being executed against oneself. Just as we have natural, unconscious motives to deceptively self-present to others, we might have natural, unconscious motives to deceptively defend a favorable self-image or overly optimistic future.

The neo-Freudian advocates of the unconscious give us some tools to advance the debate over self-deception. The psychological literature here is both immense and unsettled. Audi's philosophical account was a good start at a divided mind account, but more needed to be said about how such a self-deceptive state can be achieved and maintained. Some unconscious deception (activity) seems necessary to repress a belief in the unconscious and regulate its influence. The unconscious processes just discussed could offer a partial explanation, but they are highly controversial. For a skeptical examination of the studies discussed here, see Paul Doody (2017). Doody argues that all such studies depict psychological processes that either fail to be strategic and flexible (and, hence, robustly deceptive), or else there is insufficient evidence that they are unconsciously generated. There is also unclarity as to whether these supposedly robust unconscious mental processes are effortful, intentional, and controllable. These are all marks of agential involvement and responsibility.

§4.2.2 Distinct functional units

Freudians and neo-Freudians have the luxury of separating the Deceiver and Victim roles, placing one with the conscious mind and the other with the unconscious. This is not the only way to partition the mind and these roles, however. Others have argued that both the dynamic and static problems of self-deception can be avoided by positing partitions within the conscious mind, such that a belief that p and an intention to believe that not-p reside in a mental partition segregated from the belief that not-p which they sustain. The self-deceived can be divided into distinct functioning agents or systems, not necessarily marked by a difference in conscious awareness. We saw this back in §2.2 with Davidson's partitioned mind account of self-deception, driven more by the necessity that blatant irrationality cannot reside in the same mental system. Starting in the 1980s, David Pears (1984, 1991) developed a divided mind account of self-deception that has strong affinities with Davidson's account, but subtle differences as well. This project was part of a larger attempt to map the terrain of *akrasia* (i.e., loss of control not due to compulsion) and motivated irrationality.

David Pears's book *Motivated Irrationality* was one of the earlier works by a first-rate, established analytic philosopher to construct a philosophy of mind and action by engaging with the relatively new discoveries of cognitive and social psychology. (He heavily cites the Nisbett and Ross (1980) collection, for example.) Whereas Freud tended to think that all deviations from rationality were due to either incompetence or wishes (hot biases), Pears drew attention to cold biases (what he called "perversions of reason") as a third category. Indeed, Pears thought that Freud's theory actually works better to explain the operation of cold biases than hot biases, because the effects of a cold bias are generally overcome once they are pointed out. (He might very well be wrong about the easy correctability of cold biases.) Hence, they must remain unconscious to be effective. But a hot bias can be effective even when the person is consciously aware of the wish. Indeed, most hot biases that lead to self-deception and other forms of motivated irrationality are not buried deep in a largely inaccessible unconsciousness as Freud imagined. Rather, our wishes frequently reside near consciousness. Still, we are normally unaware of the effects that these wishes have on the beliefs that we form. In short, Pears (1984: 72–76) argued that consciousness does not eliminate irrationality (although it often makes it more difficult), so unconsciousness is not necessary for it.

Davidson's alternative way of dividing the mind – what Pears calls the "functional theory" – is wholly driven by considerations of rationality. For this reason, it might seem like merely an *ad hoc* treatment of irrationality. As Pears describes it:

> If one of his desires or beliefs fails to interact in a rational way with any element in the main system, it is assigned to a sub-system. (Pears, 1984: 83)

160 INTENTIONALISM AND DIVIDED MIND ACCOUNTS

Pears objects to this Davidsonian philosophy of mind by noting that if this were all there were to partitioning, then it lacks empirical content and is merely stipulative: Partitions are *defined* into existence simply whenever there is lack of rational engagement. Fortunately, Pears thinks that explanatory power can be found elsewhere, specifically with the interactions between the main system and the subsystem.

Davidson held that the subsystem is an internally rational system that intends to deceive the main system. This posit has explanatory power only in cases of hot biasing, for which there actually is a wish that establishes such a goal and intention. There is no such wish in cases of cold biasing, so the partitioning really does seem to lack explanatory value. As Pears elaborates on this suggestion, the subsystem should be understood as an agent in its own right:

> [A] person really consists of two separate systems. One would be the main system, which controls his daily life and includes the favoured but irrational belief and the information that makes it irrational; and the other would be a sub-system, which includes the cautionary belief, that, given his information, it was irrational to form the favoured belief. The point of the hypothesis is that the cautionary belief would have prevented the formation of the irrational belief if only it too had belonged to the main system, but, unfortunately, it could not intervene, because it was confined to the sub-system. (Pears, 1984: 67–68)

The divisions between these systems is supposed to be independent of the division between conscious and unconscious states – the states in the subsystem could be conscious, and the main system can contain unconscious elements. That being said, Pears greatly respected the power of the unconscious (belief, perception, wish, etc.) to generate thought and action. Indeed, he anticipated many of the insights of the neo-Freudian psychologists who tout the powers of a largely automatic, unconscious mind:

> Consciousness strikes us as omni-competent and all our achievements seem to be its achievements. But if we really think that, we are simply overlooking the successes of inbuilt automatisms and effortless preconscious tricks. (Pears, 1984: 83)

Pears drew heavily on the unconscious powers of the mind to both motivate and execute self-deception, although he also allowed that some of this could be performed consciously. On his account, the motive is a wish to instill a belief, placing Pears with the desire-to-believe theorists as is typical of intentionalists. His talk of "wish" shows that his primary focus is on positive self-deception. Still, he recognizes cases of negative self-deception driven by negative emotions like jealousy or fear. These also serve a positive function, according to Pears, primarily aiming at getting us to be more cautious and careful. Still, he tends to think that in the negative cases there is less of a deceptive ruse and that the deception is more tropistic ("nature takes over") (Pears, 1984: 42–44). He also does not consider belief produced by brutely causal belief distorters (e.g., drugs) to be truly self-deceptive. Rather, truly deceptive means fall into three broad categories: acting as-if, filtering evidential input, and biasing the processing of information once received (Pears, 1984: 59–61).

To achieve its wish, the subsystem must also have some knowledge of the main system's beliefs and desires, without sharing its own states with the main system. This raises worries similar to those Sartre raised against Freud's Censor. If the subsystem becomes aware of the main system's beliefs and evidence, then how can it avoid acquiring the unwelcome belief itself? The mere *awareness* of the main system's beliefs and related informational content seems to threaten the internal rationality of the subsystem – and the need for internal rationality is what motivated positing the subsystem in the first place! Pears has a couple of responses. First, Pears claims that the subsystem is not interested in the external world. In effect, the main system is its environment, and its business is to monitor it. This is why its wish is to instill a belief rather than to change the world. Second, it is possible for the subsystem to be aware of the main system's evidential position without accepting that evidence itself (Pears, 1984: 92, 101) (see Figure 4.2). We should keep in mind that the systems have their own goals and information, and the relationship between the two systems is not symmetrical. While the subsystem is aware of the main systems's beliefs, the main system must remain in the dark concerning the subsystem's intentions and evidential position.

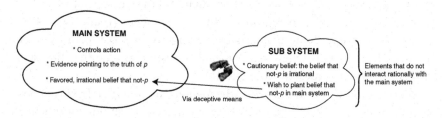

Figure 4.2 Pears' systems model of self-deception

162   INTENTIONALISM AND DIVIDED MIND ACCOUNTS

Pears, like Davidson and Freud, developed his divided mind theory, at least in part, in order to account for the intentionalism of self-deception. He did consider and rebut alternative, deflationary proposals such as Johnston's (1988) tropistic account. Pears framed the issue in a way similar to how we have presented it here: how much agential involvement is necessary for self-deception? He points out that this likely varies considerably for different kinds of self-deception. Johnston very well might be correct that there are certain kinds of wishful thinking for which a simple tropism is sufficient to explain the occurrence (maybe Mele's examples of self-enhancement are like this as well). Pears is happy to concede that much (Pears, 1991: 394). But he says that there are also cases of self-deception with "complex structure," which cannot be accounted for merely in terms of mental tropisms:

> Suppose that someone cannot face a regrettable but obvious fact about his own character, and that over many years his behaviour and avowed interpretations of the evidence are exactly what is needed in order to preserve his non-recognition of the fault. In a case like this the moves required to neutralise each new piece of evidence, or to avoid confrontation with it, are complicated, and if they are not going to count as intentional adaptations, they must, at least, be the result of some parallel, and equally effective kind of processing of the information in each new threatening situation. The alternative view – that the sustained pattern of evasive behaviour and forced interpretation is coincidental – really would be incredible. (Pears, 1991: 398)

With these examples, Pears is getting at what we have been calling "deep conflict" cases. But rather than focusing on the output (e.g., a conflicted belief), Pears is attending to the complexity of the self-deceptive process. This example perfectly fits the description of Funkhouser and Barrett's robust self-deception: There is strategic and flexible (i.e., across many situations) avoidance of the evidence. Pears believed that the operative subsystem in such cases is a "pared down" intentional agent (Pears, 1991: 404). But he is probably being uncharitable or targeting a straw man by interpreting the alternative view (e.g., mental tropisms) as claiming that such evasive behavior is merely "coincidental."

Pears's account goes well beyond the mental partitions that Davidson posited in order to allow for the attribution of irrational (contradictory) beliefs. Pears was also interested in accounting for the dynamics of self-deception,

INTENTIONALISM AND DIVIDED MIND ACCOUNTS   163

and this led him to hypothesize full-blooded subagents with their own agendas.[6] Davidson insisted that self-deception must be intentional, and on his version this demanded dual belief and mental division. But it was not clear how the intentional deception is achieved and how the partitions relate to one another. His orientation was also somewhat reversed from that of Pears. Whereas Davidson saw discomfort with the unfavored belief generating and sustaining a partition that holds a contradictory belief, Pears posited a pre-exisiting autonomous agent (subsystem) that manipulates the main system. Pears's proposal for the philosophy of mind underlying self-deception is certainly speculative, but it can be empirically tested. Davidson, in contrast, took mental partitioning to be an *a priori* necessity if there are to be blatantly irrational beliefs.

§4.3 Temporally divided selves

"Self-deception" can refer to either a process or a state. Emphasizing the process of self-deception, some intentionalists have argued that the static and dynamic problems can be avoided by noting the changing cognitive states of self-deceivers who either forget their original intentions or find their resultant belief states to be fortuitously in line with their original intentions (Bermudez, 2000). In these ways, some have argued that complex divisions – unconscious minds or scheming subagents – within a single self-deceiver are neither necessary nor commonplace. The patient reader might have suspected that much less exotic divisions underlie self-deception: The person simply has one set of beliefs, motives, evidence and awareness at one time, but another set of beliefs, motives, evidence and awareness at a later time. The static and dynamic problems are resolved by *temporally dividing the self*. This is yet another way to sacrifice the self and make self-deception more like interpersonal deception. However, its advocates will point out that it is not really any sacrifice at all, as substantial changes in doxastic, motivational, evidential, and awareness states are commonplace. Still, the move undercuts the unity of the person to some extent.

Even a staunch deflationist like Mele recognizes that some self-deception is explained in this way:

> Ike, a forgetful prankster skilled at imitating others' handwriting, has intentionally deceived friends by secretly making false entries in their diaries. Ike has just decided to deceive himself by making a false entry in his own diary. Cognizant of his forgetfulness, he writes under today's date,

> "I was particularly brilliant in class today," and counts on eventually for-
> getting that what he wrote is false. Weeks later, when reviewing his diary,
> Ike reads this sentence and acquires the belief that he was brilliant in class
> on the specified day. (Mele, 1997: 99)

Theorists can easily handle both the static and dynamic problems when the self-deception is spread out like this. We can see how the person can have contradictory beliefs at different times and even intentionally deceive themselves by forgetting the intention. Mele simply denies that most self-deception is so intentional or exploits our forgetfulness concerning a self-deceptive project.

Jose Luis Bermudez (2000), an unabashed intentionalist, argues that these psychological changes over time are much more commonplace than Mele suggests, and they also take different forms than Mele's more extreme Ike case. Bermudez argues that seeing self-deception as tem-porally extended can be a way to address both the static and dynamic problems, consistent with the demands of intentionalism. First, he claims that the intention need only be to acquire a belief regardless of its truth. The person need not further possess the true belief or even think that the desired belief is false. Second, it is quite possible to act intention-ally without remembering or being aware of this intention. It is not that the intention is deeply repressed in some Freudian unconscious. The cases he imagines are much more pedestrian – such as when I sign on to some university committee with the intention of advancing my career, although I am not aware that I am acting on this intention (Bermudez, 2000: 314). When something is a long-term process, like career advance-ment or self-deception can be, we often lose awareness of the intentions that nevertheless drive our actions. This is a more watered down account of intention than what many action theorists will accept. It is not so much that the intention is forgotten, as in the Ike example, but rather that it operates in the background. Third, due to biased evidence search, redirection of attention, and rationalization, our later selves can come to think that the evidence actually supports that belief that we intended to acquire. Given this change in evidence or our perception of the evidence, we could even maintain the desired belief through retrospective aware-ness of our original intention and motives.

Roy Sorensen (1985) argued that the static problem of self-deception – namely, the apparent dual belief requirement that comes with treating the self-deceived as both Deceiver and Victim – is avoided when we realize that self-deception, like many other phenomena, is what he calls a *scattered event*. A scattered event is one that is extended or spread out in time, much like the United States is an extended and spread out place. If self-deception is a scattered event, then the self-deceiver can without paradox believe one thing at the beginning of the event and another thing at the end of event, similar to how the United States can be beautiful in Alaska and otherwise in Oklahoma. The key move is to distinguish merely connected events from scattered events, with the latter having some kind of unity. Sorensen compares self-deception to events like an assassination in which the victim dies hours after the shooting. These are processes that extend through time, and there is no one moment at which the killing takes place or the self-deception occurs. The mistake is to think that there must be some time at which the self-deceived believe both propositions. But instead, he claims:

> So one can be simultaneously the deceiver and the deceived even though one cannot simultaneously believe and not believe the same proposition. (Sorensen, 1985: 69)

This is because the scattered events that count as self-deceiving and being self-deceived overlap.

This metaphysical maneuver might help us avoid the most flagrant logical or psychological static problem of dual belief, but what about the dynamic problem? Scattered events allow us, in a bookkeeping sense, to describe the self-deceived without contradiction. But a metaphysical treatment only goes so far; some kind of psychological theorizing is also needed to explain how the transition from belief to disbelief can occur. Bermudez attempts to fill this gap left by Sorensen's treatment by also appealing to the temporal dimension of self-deception, all while accepting the demands of intentionalism. One of his main ideas is that intentionalists can handle the dynamic problem – how an intention to acquire a belief regardless of its truth could possibly succeed – by having that intention fade from memory over time (perhaps even being completely gone by the time the false belief is acquired) or working in the background without the self-deceiver's knowledge. If the intention fades away over time but the deception is achieved and sustained after this point, then one could object that it is a stretch to say that the self-deception was intentionally induced. Things were done intentionally, perhaps, to lead to the deception. But the deception would then be successful only when there is no longer any intention to acquire a belief regardless of its truth. It was instead produced through "autonomous means" as Johnston (1988) puts it. Bermudez does say that an intention can persist and operate in the background without the person's knowledge. This may happen in non-deceptive cases as well (e.g., the career advancer), but, in those cases, it is not problematic how the intention could be efficacious. If the background intention is instead to produce a belief that we have insufficient reason to accept (and perhaps very good reason to reject), there are clearly obstacles to its satisfaction. It is not enough to say that intentions can operate without our knowledge. It must also be shown how intentions can operate without our knowledge so as to thwart our better judgment and truth-tracking mechanisms. This requires cognitive sophistication beyond what we find with more commonplace background intentions. This point is emphasized by an intentionalist like Pears who talks about cases of "sustained self-deception with a complex structure" (Pears, 1991: 400), in which the intention to mislead must be regularly operative so as to protect the main system from threatening information. He even says that the subsystem must be aware of its deceptive intentions and reasons for doing so. This is not necessary for many other kinds of successful background intention.

Neither does the Sorensen scattered events maneuver or Bermudez's temporal extension point handle all the static problems. There is not just the static problem of how one can both believe a proposition (*qua* Deceiver) and not believe a proposition (*qua* Victim). That can sometimes be handled by spreading the different psychological states over time as they recommend. There is also the philosophical/psychological problem of how best to describe the belief states of many self-deceivers at a given time. Deep conflict theorists will argue that there are many times (some will even say that this always occurs) at which self-deceivers bear the marks of what is normally sufficient for attributing each of two contradictory beliefs to them. This does not mean that the person truly has the dual beliefs, but it demands a more sophisticated treatment of the nature of belief.

§4.4 Other intentionalist and dual belief views

The theses of intentionalism, divided minds, and dual belief interconnect in various ways. Davidson represents one trajectory: By conceptual necessity, self-deception requires an intention to deceive and dual belief (to distinguish it from wishful thinking), and these factors require a divided

INTENTIONALISM AND DIVIDED MIND ACCOUNTS   167

mind. But not all intentionalists require dual belief or unusually divided minds (e.g., Bermudez and Talbott). Others might argue that intentionalism demands a divided mind in order to handle the dynamic problem, and this at least allows for the possibility of dual beliefs existing in the separate divisions. Finally, one could start with the psychological claim that minds are divided, with this starting point opening one up to the possibility of intentionalism or dual belief.

Those outside of philosophy seem to be even more inclined to accept both intentionalism and dual belief. However, they often have accounts of intention and belief that philosophers will find too anemic. For example, von Hippel and Trivers (a psychologist and biologist, respectively) claim to accept intentionalism:

> If someone else managed to miss the point, let us state it clearly – we certainly believe that self-deception is intentional, in the sense that the organism itself intends to produce the bias, although the intention could be entirely unconscious. That is, humans have been favored by natural selection to self-deceive for its facilitative effect on the deception of others. (von Hippel and Trivers, 2011: 42)

But this last sentence is not at all what philosophers mean by intention. The fact that something has been naturally selected shows it to be purposive, but this is different from its being intentional. Intentions are additional psychological states. Males who lower their voice pitch in the presence of attractive females are doing this purposefully (as this behavior was presumably naturally selected), but it does not follow that they are doing it intentionally. Von Hippel and Trivers (2011: 2) do not further insist on a dual belief requirement, although they allow that self-deceivers sometimes possess dual beliefs.

Some prominent accounts from psychology insist on the conceptual constraint of dual belief. We saw this with Gur and Sackeim (1979), who held that self-deception requires the simultaneous holding of contradictory beliefs. But the vast majority of philosophers would deny that a skin conductance response is sufficient grounds for a belief attribution. In large part, this is because philosophers tend to give greater weight to holistic rational and behavioral considerations for belief attributions. But if the skin responses were sufficient for belief, this would show that dual belief does not require a divided mind. More recently, Steven Pinker (2011) has argued that self-deception requires "dual representations," one accurate and the other inaccurate. Interestingly, he refrains from calling them beliefs, but that is how he describes them as functioning. His reason for insisting on dual representations is conceptual: It is necessary to distinguish self-deception from errors and biases. Of course, deflationists think that this distinction can be accounted for in purely motivational terms. But Pinker will likely retort that motivated biases are still merely biases, and that "real deception" requires greater psychological complexity and (perhaps) agential involvement. In contrast, we have seen that some intentionalists deny that dual representations are necessary.

Other psychologists deny the dual belief view, using "self-deception" to refer to a single-minded state. Paulhus (1986), for example, uses "'self-deception" to refer to positively biased responses that are actually believed to be true. This does not require dual belief, even though Paulhus (1986) claims to be working within the Gur and Sackeim conceptual framework. Such self-deception is contrasted with impression management, which is a conscious effort to manipulate how one appears to others (e.g., on a first date or job interview). Paulhus developed questionnaire tests for so-called *self-deceptive enhancement* and *self-deceptive denial*, which he combined into what he called the Balanced Inventory of Desirable Responding (BIDR) test (Paulhus, 1991). These tests asked questions that were likely to evoke inaccurate but nevertheless sincere answers that enhance the positive and deny the negative – e.g., "I always know why I like things" or "I could never enjoy being cruel." Skewed, favorable answers were taken to be indicative of self-deceptive belief. But there is no reason to think that the contrary true belief is also known by the participants. Of course, one could reasonably challenge whether these answers reflect sincere but inaccurate beliefs in the first place.

Some philosophers have held that self-deception requires the simultaneous possession of contradictory beliefs (e.g., Demos and Davidson). In order to show how this is possible, they then tend to offer an unorthodox understanding of belief or divide the self. Still others will deny that self-deception is possible, as such dual beliefs simply cannot obtain. But it is more common for philosophers to deny the necesssity of simultaneous contradictory beliefs. This can either take the form of an outright denial: The self-deceived can be quite single-minded. Or it can take the form of a qualified denial: The self-deceived appear to have both beliefs, but they only have (at most) one. The latter is the view of Bach and Audi, who accept apparent dual belief but insist that the one belief is only an

INTENTIONALISM AND DIVIDED MIND ACCOUNTS   169

illusion. We have seen that some psychologists, keen to find methods for determining belief, will be more inclined to attribute the reported or avowed belief.

Summary

- Intentions involve effort and other forms of agential involvement. The selectivity, robustness, and responsibility of self-deception might demand something intention like. There could be psychological tests for effort, control, and other markers of intentional action in self-deception. Intentional self-deception also might require a divided mind, as Davidson posited.
- Self-deception might require an unconscious recognition of the truth. It is likely that there is some unconscious processing that at least contributes to acquiring and retaining the deceptive state. Some psychologists and philosophers have claimed that unconscious processing can be just as sophisticated as conscious processing when it comes to enacting such a deceptive project.
- The conscious/unconscious is not the only division that could undergird robust self-deception. Pears has argued for self-deceptive modules that are agents in their own right. This might correlate with unconscious processing, but the distinctions do not perfectly align. Pears also attributes more agency to the self-deceived than many others are comfortable with.
- Temporal divisions also can be invoked to explain robust self-deception. The self-deceived might not maintain contact with their intentions to deceive. Memory deterioration and brutely causal belief distorters can also enable self-deception over time.

Recommended reading

There is a large philosophical literature on the nature of intentional action, and Anscombe (1957) and Davidson (1980) are good places to enter this terrain.

The best primary sources for reading about intentionalist theories of self-deception are Pears (1984) and Davidson (2004).

Huang and Bargh (2014) and the accompanying commentaries are an excellent introduction to the provocative psychological debates over robust unconscious processing.

Bermudez (2000) offers a very good, short defense of intentionalism that emphasizes the temporal dimension of deception.

Notes

1 To get a flavor for the subtleties of these debates, read the *Stanford Encyclopedia of Philosophy* entry on action: https://plato.stanford.edu/entries/action/

2 For more detailed discussion of these issues, turn to Anscombe (1957), Davidson (1980), Frankfurt (1988), and Bratman (1999).

3 Grice (1957) offered a theory of speaker meaning according to which the meaning of a speaker's words is determined by what she intends for the audience to come to believe as a result of her utterance.

4 I will use the term "neo-Freudian" to refer to more recent experimental psychologists who emphasize robust unconscious powers. Sometimes the word is used to refer to the immediate successors of Freud, but that is not my intention.

5 For a good introduction to these matters, see the *Stanford Encyclopedia of Philosophy* entry on consciousness (https://plato.stanford.edu/entries/consciousness/) or Rocco Gennaro's book *Consciousness* in the Routledge *New Problems of Philosophy* series.

6 Amelie Rorty (1988) offers another, albeit less developed, theory of self-deception as involving multiple, independent subsystems.

5

REVISIONARY ACCOUNTS
BELIEF AND PURPOSE

5.1 **Revising belief**
5.2 **Biological accounts: non-psychological purposiveness**
5.3 **Signaling accounts**
5.4 **Social influences on self-deception**

We have just analyzed views that attempt to salvage an understanding of self-deception on the model of interpersonal deception, according to which it is intentional or involves significant mental divisions. Now we will turn to accounts that focus on the belief states and purposefulness of self-deception, revising traditional understandings of its underlying psychology. These proposals fall under the *sacrifice belief* or *sacrifice deception* (*intentional or purposive manipulation*) headings described in §2.1. Under the former heading, we will examine nuanced accounts of belief that attempt to make better sense of the appearance of dual belief or the irrationality distinctive of self-deception. Then, we consider revisionary accounts of the motives for self-deception. Some of these proposals are better thought of as *revising* belief or intention rather than as *sacrificing* them. In particular, there are those who argue that the motives for self-deception can lie outside the psychology of the self-deceived, driven by biological forces or the intentions of others.

§5.1 Revising belief

We saw in §3.5.4 that theorists have deep disagreements as to what typical self-deceivers believe, with virtually every option in play. This suggests one of two things: 1) either they do not share the same understanding of what it is to be self-deceived, or 2) our philosophical and psychological understanding of belief is woefully deficient or contentious. This section focuses more on the second issue. Part of what makes self-deception so interesting is that it involves violations of one's own standards of rationality, challenging us to reconceive or at least clarify the concept of belief and the boundaries of its application. This has led some philosophers to revise or supplement common folk psychological explanations. Many philosophers take beliefs, alongside desires, to be the most basic representational states – we represent the world as being a certain way, we want the world to be a certain way, and these combine to move us to action. But we also know that a simple belief-desire psychology is a gross simplification of the human mind. Ordinary descriptions of people's behavior and state of mind make use of many finer distinctions. In addition to acting on their beliefs, we also speak of people acting on their convictions, hopes, fears, doubts, suspicions, thoughts, intuitions, speculations, hypotheses, imagination, pretense, or faith. Perhaps, then, the self-deceived are better described in subtler terms than outright belief.

At a minimum, belief has these attributes:

> *Representational*: Beliefs represent the world as being a certain way. They are true or false according to whether those representations are accurate.
>
> *Personal Attitude*: Beliefs reflect the entire person's perspective on the world, as opposed to a non-agential sub-system's representation of the world. Our eyes or visual sub-system might "think" that one line in the Müller-Lyer illusion is longer than the other, but if we are aware of the illusion we do not believe this. Belief is more of an all-things-considered judgment.[1]
>
> *Rationality*: Beliefs must cohere, meeting at least a minimal standard of rationality. Since beliefs are supposed to represent how the person views the world, certain combinations of beliefs cannot be tolerated because they do not represent a coherent picture of the world. This means that belief is at least relatively holistic – they are to be attributed in clusters rather than on a case-by-case basis.

REVISIONARY ACCOUNTS: BELIEF AND PURPOSE   173

Connections: Our beliefs have connections to other psychological states
and behavior. Beliefs combine with desires to generate intentional action.
Beliefs generate emotional responses.

Self-deception introduces complications, if not outright violations, along
each attribute. It is by no means clear what the self-deceived represent as
true. Different parts or subsystems of the person (conscious/unconscious,
emotional/rational, behavioral/cognitive) might represent the world in
different ways. The person is not properly responsive to the evidence or
rationality. And they display some of the appropriate belief connections,
but not others (e.g., they avow a proposition, but they do not act on it).
These points are all interconnected. The issue, once again, is that of doxastic tension or deep conflict. What is the proper remedy? In the following
subsections, we will consider treatments that descend to subpersonal states,
articulate notions of partial belief, or offer substitutes for belief. Each of
these proposals denies at all least one of the belief ascriptions (belief that p
or that not-p) and offers something else in its place.

§5.1.1 *Subdoxastic attitudes*

The mental and behavioral conflict experienced by the self-deceived, while
having the appearance of being due to contradictory beliefs, might actually be due to conflict between belief and subdoxastic states (or conflict
among subdoxastic states themselves). Beliefs are personal states or attitudes, reflecting the point of view of the entire person. A subpersonal
state is a state that is instantiated below the personal level. Subdoxastic
states are belief-like states – say, representations of the truth of p – that
are subpersonal, often the output of cognitive subsystems designed for
special purposes. So, these substitutes for belief meet the Representational
demands, but do not meet Personal Attitude. As we will see, they are also
limited in Rationality and Connections.

Stephen Stich (1978) offers an authoritative statement of the distinction
between beliefs and subdoxastic states. Both beliefs and subdoxastic states
are representational states involved in information processing, but Stich
describes subdoxastic states as comparatively deficient in two ways. First,
our beliefs are accessible to conscious awareness, unless there is some
mechanism in place to block that access. The ability to access and report
our beliefs is supposed to be the norm and default, but this is not true of
subdoxastic states. Second, our beliefs tend to be inferentially integrated.

We can take a belief and use it as a premise in many posssible inferences, potentially connecting it with countless beliefs, desires, and actions. But subdoxastic states are much more limited, often confined to a particular task. A couple of Stich's (1978) examples illustrate these properties: implicit grammatical knowledge and detecting pupil dilation. People are able to discern whether a sentence is grammatical or not by applying rules that are not accessible to consciousness and that do not integrate with other bits of knowledge (it is the output of a system devoted purely to language comprehension). People have this knowledge, but not in the form of beliefs. For the other example, it has been shown that men are able to detect pupil dilation in women and make judgments of attractiveness on that basis, but without conscious awarenesss or integration. In one study, men were shown two nearly identical photographs of the same female, differing only in that the pupils were retouched so as to be enlarged in one photograph. Without being able to explain why, men tended to find the woman with larger pupils more attractive. Something in them was tracking this difference in pupil size (subdoxastic), but they were not consciously aware of this and the ability is used to make only limited inferences (say, about attractiveness).

One could claim that some of the self-deceived's distinctive thoughts, emotions, behaviors, and other responses can be explained, not by beliefs, but by such subdoxastic states instead. Mele takes this approach with regard to the Gur and Sackeim study with participants who had skin conductance responses indicating familiarity with their recorded voice while verbally denying recognition. Mele (1997: 96) suggests that the skin responses could be produced by a subdoxastic state, not genuine belief. One could generalize the point such that each of the following responses, typical of self-deceptive conflict, is attributed to a subdoxastic state: the resentment experienced by a wife self-deceived about her husband's infidelity, the evidence avoidance of a mother self-deceived about her son's drug use, or the guilt occasionally felt by a man who is negatively self-deceived that his wife has been unfaithful.

This subdoxastic route is an alternative and rival to unconscious belief explanations, such as those advanced by Robert Audi. Audi's case of Ann the illness denier is a difficult case to assess because, as with many cases of deep conflict, it lies on the border between subdoxastic states and belief proper. Audi says that Ann has the unconscious true belief because her avowals lack total conviction, she experiences anxiety and depression, and she acts in certain ways (e.g., makes funeral arrangements) that suggest she knows the truth. But if these are inaccessible to consciousness and there is a failure of inferential integration, then these might be the product of subdoxastic states instead. Someone like Stich might counter that Audi is correct to posit genuine unconscious beliefs rather than subdoxastic states, since there are self-deceptive motives that establish obstacles that explain why the belief is inaccessible to consciousness. If the motive to self-deceive went away, presumably the true belief would become conscious. Further, even without losing the self-deceptive motive, the belief can be made accessible to consciousness through introspection or therapy.

We just considered attempts to attribute truth-oriented subdoxastic states combined with false belief or virtual (conscious) belief, but there are other ways of accounting for deep conflict in terms of personal and subpersonal discord. One could argue that the self-deceived have the true belief that p, but have a subdoxastic state that not-p, which generates the tension. One could think of thoughts and avowals as being driven, not by beliefs, but by such subdoxastic states. Or, one could argue that the self-deceived have no determinate beliefs, but simply have conflicting subdoxastic states instead (Funkhouser, 2009). This strategy of psychological descent can be applied to motives as well, as in Johnston's (1988) argument that rather than being an intentional action self-deception is driven by a subintentional mental tropism. Revisionary accounts that appeal to subpersonal states and processes gain plausibility because self-deception, as a failure of rationality, resists handy explanation in terms of intentional action (which is rationalizing) and outright belief.

It can be tempting to resort to subdoxastic states when striking irrationality – such as a failure of inferential integration – is involved. But those who are not extremists about the norm of rationality will recognize that the realm of belief can contain such deficiencies as well. We have reason to think that we are dealing with beliefs, rather than something subdoxastic, to the extent that the representational states in question are responsive to a wider body of evidence and are sensitive to changes in context. These are ways of showing that the representation is not inferentially encapsulated or special purpose. This seems to be true of many of the underlying representational states in self-deception – evidence is pursued and avoided very strategically across diverse epistemic contexts, emotions are elicited as subtle bits of evidence come in (rather than as a simple response to a stimulus), and so on. Whether the representational states are belief-like or subdoxastic has practical therapeutic consequences as well. The former should be amenable to rational scrutiny, whereas the latter might need a more mechanical approach aimed at changing habits.

§5.1.2 *Partial or indeterminate belief*

There are other ways to account for conflict without leaving the realm of belief and without attributing any (full) belief either. While not primarily driven by concerns about self-deception, Eric Schwitzgebel (2001, 2002) has developed a theory of belief that is tailored for deep conflict cases. On his view, belief is a multitrack dispositional state that allows for various forms of what he calls "in-between believing" in addition to handling the stereotypical cases of unqualified belief. His dispositional account of belief is not the only way to account for the idea of partial belief, but it is an especially plausible and influential account that has clear application to self-deception. This proposal, like the next two we will consider, offers states or attitudes that meet Representational and Personal, but are weaker than belief on Rationality and Connections.

Dispositions are conditional properties – tendencies to produce certain manifestations under certain triggering conditions, other things being equal. Fragility, for example, is a dispositional property understood as the tendency to break (manifestation) when dropped onto a hard surface, struck, etc. (triggering condition). But this holds only *ceteris paribus*: If you have a protective case on your fragile smartphone, it might not break when dropped. Schwitzgebel says that belief is a multitrack dispositional state, meaning that there are many dispositional properties associated with any individual belief. He divides these dispositions into three broad categories: phenomenal, cognitive, and behavioral. A person who believes that her flight has been canceled feels anger (phenomenal), starts thinking of new travel plans (cognitive), and heads to the ticket counter to speak to a representative (behavioral). While each response is completely understandable and even to be expected, none of these manifestations is absolutely guaranteed by the triggering condition of a canceled flight. If she had strict deadlines that made a later flight unacceptable, then she might not have bothered to speak to the representative or even start thinking about alternative travel plans; if she had taken her anti-anxiety pills, maybe she would not have even experienced anger.

Countless background conditions must be in place to allow for these manifestations, and it is practically (if not also theoretically) impossible to specify them all. Nevertheless, we still have a good sense of how we expect believers to act in particular situations. These dispositions collectively make up a stereotype for each belief, but believers need not possess all the stereotypical dispositions in order to genuinely possess the belief. For example, our traveler would still believe that her flight has

REVISIONARY ACCOUNTS: BELIEF AND PURPOSE   177

been canceled even if she had she not experienced anger. Some disposi-tions are more central to the stereotype and, therefore, should be given more weight in determining belief. Different philosophers of mind have emphasized the importance of different dispositions – e.g., behaviorists give greater weight to the behavioral dispositions of belief. Schwitzgebel thinks that there is no hope, however, for a rigorous weighting of these different dispositions so as to generate necessary and sufficient conditions, or some operational definition, for belief. The vagueness and context sensitivity of belief is ineliminable. Those who possess some middling amount of the relevant dispositions are in a state of "in-between" belief – neither accurately described as believing that p nor believing that not-p.

There are many interesting cases in which the dispositions for belief do not bundle together as we would customarily expect of a wholehearted believer. Only some of these are cases of self-deception, and others belong to the "nearby phenomena" discussed in §2.7, such as ambivalence, vac-illation, hypocrisy, confabulation, imagination, or pretense. Many cases of non-stereotypical or in-between belief are not necessarily driven by a motive – for example, when an impartial juror is ambivalent as to whether a defendant is guilty. But here is one of Schwitzgebel's examples that man-ifests the motivated deep conflict that we have seen so frequently empha-sized as characteristic of self-deception:

> Geraldine's teenage son Adam smokes marijuana. Usually Geraldine is unwilling to admit this to herself, and sometimes she adamantly denies it. Eating lunch with a friend, Geraldine can deplore her friend's parent-ing because of his daughter's drug use while denying in all sincerity that Adam has any similar problems. Yet she feels afraid and suspicious when Adam slouches home late at night with bloodshot eyes, and when she accuses him of smoking pot, she sees through his denials. In a certain kind of mood, she would tell her therapist that she thinks Adam smokes marijuana, but in another kind of mood she would genuinely recant such a confession. When Geraldine's husband voices concern about Adam's behavior, Geraldine sincerely comes to her son's defense. What does Geraldine believe on the subject? Someone insisting on a simple "Yes she believes that he smokes marijuana" or "No, she doesn't" will be hard-pressed. (Schwitzgebel, 2002: 260–261)

Geraldine is self-deceived or self-deceiving, and the best account of her doxastic state might be that it is genuinely indeterminate what she believes.[2]

178 REVISIONARY ACCOUNTS: BELIEF AND PURPOSE

This view is developed in Funkhouser (2009), which argues for an even broader dispositional base for belief (including physiological responses and perception). Conflicting dispositions – say, to avow one thing but act on another (among many other possible forms the conflict can take) – might even be typical of self-deception. Both Schwitzgebel and Funkhouser claim that psychological descent – reverting to talk of the specific dispositions rather than belief *simpliciter* – is the proper remedy. This is not to say that all cases of self-deception involve indeterminate or partial belief, but Funkhouser (2009) argues that there is a significant class of deep conflict cases that do.

It is important to see how this view goes well beyond merely pointing out that belief comes in degrees. Remember that Lynch (2012) tries to account for the tension found in some varieties of self-deception by making recourse to motivated and unwarranted degrees of confidence. But an unreasonably low or high degree of confidence need not involve any inconsistency across the different categories of dispositions. Someone with a low degree of confidence in a proposition can have the appropriate phenomenal, cognitive, and behavioral dispositions (e.g., they feel, think, and act weakly or with uncertainty). Schwitzgebel is pointing out that there can be inconsistency across the dispositions, such that no definitive level of confidence could possibly be assigned. This is not just an epistemic point about our inability to determine what the person believes. Rather, the claim is that even if we knew all the dispositional facts, there would still be cases in which there is no discernible fact of the matter as to what the person believes. There are many different "dimensions" of belief, understood as different dispositions or categories of dispositions. The psychological space for partial and even indeterminate belief is immense and varied.

§5.1.3 Thought, acceptance, imagination, and pretense

There are other personal level representational states that depict something as true, although these states do not rise to the level of belief. Some of these states are said to fall short of belief because they are not governed by rationality or, perhaps relatedly, do not strongly guide behavior.

Kent Bach's (1981, 1997) proposal that the self-deceived have the occurent *thought* that not-p (or simply avoid having the thought that p), while believing that p, is typical of such views. Whereas thoughts are consciously occurring events, beliefs are persisting dispositional states that need not even bubble over into thought. Our beliefs typically dispose us to have the corresponding thoughts, but in self-deception a motive generates an essential mismatch. Bach holds that the underlying belief-relevant dispositions of the self-deceived align with true believers, although they repeatedly avoid having the corresponding true thoughts. The self-deceived husband believes that his wife is unfaithful, yet he repeatedly avoids entertaining this thought and might positively think otherwise. This accounts for the apparent irrationality of the self-deceived: Thoughts are not constrained by rationality, and they need not integrate with beliefs (or even with other thoughts) (Bach, 1981: 356). In this sense, a thought is neither rational nor irrational. The irrationality of self-deception must then reside with the role that thoughts are allowed to play for the self-deceived or in their lack of self-knowledge concerning what they believe.

Whereas Bach thought that the self-deceived acquire the phenomenology (thought) of a true believer but without actual belief, others have argued that they acquire some of the typical dispositions of a true believer without actual belief. L. Jonathan Cohen (1992) advances a complicated and unorthodox theory that falls into the latter category. Cohen argued for a more idiosyncratic understanding of belief, which he then contrasted with an attitude he called *acceptance*. According to Cohen, we accept many things that we do not believe. To accept a proposition in his sense of the term is to be committed to using it as a premise in both theoretical and practical reasoning.[3] I decide to board an airplane, say, accepting that it is a very safe form of transportation – I have a policy whereby I am willing to act on that premise. This is quite a bit different than the role that thought plays for Bach. Now how does this relate to belief? As with Bach and most contemporary philosophers, Cohen held that belief is a dispositional state. But unlike most others, he denied that belief consisted in dispositions to speak or act in certain ways. This is where many will part ways with his account, as it is common to see a commitment to use a proposition in theoretical and practical reasoning as constituting (if not wholly, at least to a significant degree) belief. Instead, he claimed that belief is a disposition to *feel* that something is true (Cohen, 1992: 8).

We typically accept what we believe (in Cohen's sense). That is, we are willing to reason with what we feel is true. And we also tend to believe what we accept. But Cohen emphasized that people can fully accept a proposition, such that it guides their thoughts and actions, without actually believing it. For example, a military planner might accept that the enemy will counter with a flanking maneuver but not believe this. The military planner accepts this by necessity: he must accept some particular response so as to plan accordingly. Or a research scientist accepts a certain hypothesis regarding the epidemiology of diabetes, because she is part of a team researching a particular prevention strategy. As we can see, there are often quite practical reasons to accept something that might not have adequate epistemic justification. These are what we might call working assumptions, but for Cohen they are a bit stronger than that – acceptance is like a policy or commitment (Cohen, 1992: 12).

Cohen saw that this framework could be applied to the problem of self-deception. On his view, the self-deceived believe the true proposition, meaning that they do have a disposition to feel its truth. But he claims that this disposition is not activated. This is perfectly coherent and possible, as dispositions in general can remain unactivated (e.g., a material can still be malleable even if it is never actually bent). Cohen recognized that he needed an explanation for how this occurs, and here he resorts to repression and the unconscious. So, his account must draw on other resources besides just the acceptance/belief distinction, and it still must reckon with the dynamic problem of how such repression can occur. His account respects the conflict of self-deception in that, while the self-deceived believe the truth, they accept what is false. The self-deceived will think and act on premises that, were they to think about them, they would be disposed to feel as false.

There are a few objections or concerns to raise against this account. First, it is not clear that the self-deceived genuinely accept the falsehood, at least in deep conflict cases. Acceptance is supposed to demand something like a policy or commitment, but the deeply conflicted likely do not accept the falsehood in high stakes situations. Further, their strategic avoidance behavior could show that maintaining the self-deception requires that they not accept the falsehood. If we accept something, then we think it is safe or at least prudent to act on it, but the self-deceived often do not reach this level of confidence. Second, if they do accept the falsehood in this stronger sense, then many of us would be inclined to describe the self-deceived as fully believing the falsehood (i.e., as being self-deluded). If this is correct, many of us will resist Cohen's separation of acceptance and belief (at least in this case). If someone has a serious commitment to using a proposition as a premise in theoretical and practical reasoning, this objection argues, then they *do* believe it. But Cohen's treatment of the static problem requires that the former obtains without the latter. Regardless, such strong acceptance of the falsehood is unlikely to coexist with a disposition to feel the truth. Third, he still needs to draw on fairly robust unconscious powers to explain the repression of the true belief. If we are to grant these powers, it is not clear that a sharp distinction between acceptance and belief is necessary any more to handle the static puzzle. We could just resort to solutions like those discussed in Chapter 4.

The idea of non-belief acceptance is a good one, although we might disagree with Cohen's understanding of it and utilize it in other ways. The self-deceived have some kind of insincerity and are plausibly described as acting on things that they do not really believe. If the self-deceived are motivated to ignore or distort the truth, they might be best described as not being in the belief game at all. That is, perhaps they neither seek nor attain a false belief. Tamar Gendler (2007) emphasizes the reality insensitivity of the self-deceived, arguing that they are *imagining* or *pretending* rather than genuinely reaching an irrational belief or belief-like state. On her view, the difference between pretense and belief is not merely one of degree, but it is a difference in kind. Gendler argues that the essential difference between pretense and belief concerns the aim, function, or *telos* of each: Belief essentially aims at the truth (reality sensitive), whereas pretense does not (reality insensitive).[4] Aiming does not mean that you always hit your target, of course, so she allows for beliefs that miss the mark. Beliefs can certainly be false, and they can even be biased. Still, on her view believers are attempting (in some sense of that term) to get at the truth. For this reason, they must be sensitive to evidential and rational considerations – they cannot be willfully or otherwise indifferent to these.

It is often quite natural to describe the self-deceived as merely imagining or pretending that the object of their deception is true, especially if we emphasize deep conflict cases (as Gendler does). This can be made to fit both positive and negative cases. The hopeful young woman is only pretending that she already is a professional success; the insecure husband is only pretending that his wife has been unfaithful. The idea is that they both genuinely believe the truth. These are supposed to be cases of mere pretense, rather than belief, because the subjects are not getting themselves into that state through reality-sensitive means. Further, they retain behavioral dispositions (e.g., avoidance behavior and behavior in high stakes situations) indicative of having the true belief. Still, the pretense secures many of the superficial features of belief. As Gendler has emphasized, the imagination can mimic belief when it comes to producing thought, emotion, and action. Something that we merely pretend to be true can still connect logically with other propositions (think of a supposition in a *reductio ad absurdum*), cause us to feel strong emotions (think of literature, film, and plays), and even move us to act (think of a child's game of make-believe or an adult's theatrical performance) (Gendler, 2003, 2006). In these ways, self-deception as pretense might meet the person's psychological needs and easily be mistaken for the operations of belief.

In earlier work, Ariela Lazar (1999) argued that the imagination sometimes strongly guides the self-deceived, but, unlike Gendler, she saw this as a reason to think that imagination can rise to the level of belief. Discussing the fantasies of Madame Bovary as an example, she claims that the imagination can give rise to fantasies that she takes to be "representative of reality." This is clearly a different view than Gendler's, which erects a wall (i.e., a truth *telos*) between imagination and belief. Lazar claims that these fantasies could even be beliefs, but they are labeled "fantasies," because they are so detached from evidential considerations. Nevertheless, Lazar makes clear that belief need not be rational; neither must a belief be consistent with the bulk of our other beliefs. For this reason, she does not see a sharp line dividing imagination from belief. Indeed, she thinks that self-deceptive fantasies influence thought and behavior in the very same way as do beliefs (Lazar, 1999: 285–286). This allows Lazar to claim that the self-deceptive state is irrational – as it is a representation of reality – whereas Gendler sees it as a reality-insensitive state that is not governed by the norm of rationality.

While pretense does not aim at the truth and is not itself governed by rational and evidential standards, there is still a sense in which Gendler claims that self-deception as pretense is irrational. As we have seen, on her view the self-deceived do not have an irrational belief. Neither is the pretense itself irrational, as it is not supposed to be constrained by evidential considerations – it is reality insensitive. Instead, the irrationality lies with the extent to which the self-deceived let the pretense take over their lives:

> Moreover, the account accords well with the sense that self-deception is often an irrational condition: after all, one canonical characterization of irrationality is that it is a state where something imaginary inappropriately comes to play the cognitive role of something real. (Gendler, 2007: 234)

This is not a form of theoretical irrationality, however. Presumably, the self-deceptive pretense just is not prudent or healthy – it is not rational to *behave* in this way. While Gendler holds that the self-deceived over-extend a pretense, a "precarious" balance must be maintained in order for it to properly remain self-deception rather than sliding into either recognition of reality or delusional disconnection. A similar point can be made about Bach's thought-based and Audi's avowal-based accounts: The self-deceived cannot lose contact with reality.

There are limitations to pretense, then. Gendler claims that the self-deceived have "a *topic-specific* reason for wanting to occupy herself with thoughts of not-P, and (perhaps independently, perhaps consequently) for letting her actions reflect an apparent belief to that effect" (Gendler, 2007: 242). This is not the same thing as wanting the belief itself – notice how she instead talks of "thoughts" and "apparent belief." In fact, the self-deceived, as non-pathological individuals, still have a standing motive for their actions to be guided by reality-sensitive attitudes. Gendler describes two possible means whereby this standing motive can override the self-deceived's topic-specific reason to self-deceive. First, there is *evidential override*, in which the evidence for the truth is so overwhelming that it is impossible for her to allow the pretense to continue to direct her thoughts and actions. Here Gendler reminds us that the self-deceived often resort to evidence avoidance tactics in order to maintain their state of mind. Second, the self-deceived can find themselves in a higher stakes situation that renders the motive to self-deceive a *trumped incentive*. In her example, a seriously ill person can no longer afford to self-deceive when medicine that can restore her to health becomes available (Gendler, 2007: 244–245). In regards to both of these factors, Gendler contrasts cases of self-deception (deep conflict) with outright self-delusion. The self-deluded, as full believers in the falsehood, will not avoid evidence and are willing to act on their false belief even in important contexts.

We might challenge her treatment of the irrationality of self-deception and the issue of evidential override. It is certainly correct that the more obvious the evidence for p becomes, the harder it is to maintain the self-deception that not-p. But it is not generally true that it is harder to *pretend* that not-p in the face of overwhelming evidence for p. I have no difficulty pretending to be a frog even though the evidence against it is obvious to me. The very fact that self-deception is sensitive to evidence in the way that evidential override illustrates seems to undermine the claim that self-deception is pretense, given that the latter is supposed to be reality insensitive.[5] Indeed, we could argue:

Premise 1: Self-deception is reality sensitive. Successful self-deception requires selective acquisition, attention, or interpretation of the evidence. Indeed, this is symptomatic of self-deception.

184   REVISIONARY ACCOUNTS: BELIEF AND PURPOSE

Premise 2: Pretense is not reality sensitive. We can non-defectively pretend that not-p in the face of evidence that we recognize as overwhelmingly supporting p.

Conclusion: Therefore, self-deception is not pretense.

Gendler is likely correct that the self-deceived are typically motivated to maintain certain thoughts or appearances. But this argument suggests that their illusion is not best characterized as an act of pretense.

We can also appeal to the norms that we apply to the self-deceived. We tend to accuse them of violating norms of theoretical reasoning, as on Mele's theory in which they are guilty of hot or cold biases. This would be appropriate only if the self-deceived were still in the belief game, so to speak, rather than engaging in a pretense. Those who are pretending are not engaged in biased reasoning, as they are not reasoning at all. Instead of alleging a theoretical irrationality, Gendler claims that it is inappropriate to act on reality-insensitive attitudes when the behavior is relatively important. It is certainly inappropriate to seriously act out of one's imagination when the stakes are high, but the self-deceived do not do that – only the self-deluded do. What about less extreme circumstances, the relatively safe spaces in which most people engage in self-deception? We might wonder if it is even inappropriate, or in any way practically irrational, to self-deceive in low stakes situations in which it might be an adaptive response.

Gendler's theory does a good job of getting at the idea that the self-deceived want to think of the world as being a certain way but also maintain a connection to reality. And the fact – if indeed it is a fact – that the self-deceived abandon their ruse in high stakes situations fits well with her claim that the self-deceived are merely engaged in a pretense. Self-deception, like pretense, seems to require a safe space. For this very reason, Lynch (2012) thinks that these are better described as cases of escapism rather than of self-deception. Yet in other ways the self-deceived act out their not-p thoughts beyond what we would expect of a mere pretender. A father who is merely pretending that his son is not doing drugs with Blaine (while believing otherwise) would not allow his son to go out with Blaine. Yet, the self-deceived father does allow his son to go out with Blaine even though an impartial cognitive peer would recognize how unwise that is. Indeed, a mere pretense would likely be disappointing to someone motivated to self-deceive. Further, we are normally aware of acts of pretense: Someone is merely pretending, at least typically, only if they are aware that their thoughts and activity are not representative of reality. But the self-deceived do not want that awareness, so it is unlikely that they are pretending.

REVISIONARY ACCOUNTS: BELIEF AND PURPOSE 185

Notice how much the phenomenon that Gendler describes differs from Mele's paradigm examples of self-deception. Mele's examples are not mere pretenses (no deep conflict) – the university professors are not merely pretending that they are better than average; the author is not merely pretending that his paper should have been accepted for publication. It is not so much that these theorists have competing theories for the same phenomenon. Rather, they appear to be offering theories for different phenomena. Lynch's (2012, 2016) recommendation seems apt: We should distinguish between merely hiding from the truth (escapism, pretense, willful ignorance) and actually believing a falsehood. Our earlier discussion might also show that there are even more possibilities between these two well-defined extremes.

§5.1.4 *Suspicion, anxiety, and fear*

Sophie Archer (2013) argues that the self-deceived hold neither the belief that p nor the belief that not-p. One might think that this is the same view that Schwitzgebel, Lynch, and Funkhouser espoused with their partial or indeterminate beliefs. But her view is different in that she says that the self-deceived are neither in-between believers nor indeterminate believers. Instead, they determinately and flatly possess neither belief (nondoxasticism). As an example, she considers Audi's case of Ann, the illness denier, whom he describes as unconsciously having the true belief. Archer counters with an alternative explanation:

> Ann is *anxious* about the state of her health and *suspects* that things are worse than she is currently aware, and that she may find out that something she *fears* is the case. (Archer, 2013: 272)

So far this is just an argument against the necessity of positing unconscious belief – it does not establish that the self-deceived never possess the unwelcome belief. She also rejects attributing the welcome belief, both for the reasons Audi himself gives and because Ann seems to be merely acting as-if or pretending that what she wants to believe is true.

Suspicion, doubt, and uncertainty are conceptually close to belief, and one might object that these notions are not sufficiently distinct for them to count as nondoxastic options. Doubts are to be pursued or at least taken seriously, and they have epistemic value in a way that anxiety and fear do not. Suspicions and doubts are reactions to evidence or requests for further evidence. For these reasons, one might think that suspicion and doubt

REVISIONARY ACCOUNTS: BELIEF AND PURPOSE

are something like low-degree beliefs. Archer and Mele reject this move, denying that they rise to the level of belief at all. Others have held that very specific forms of evidence avoidance (e.g., not checking the bank balance until after payday) or targeted emotional responses (e.g., resentment after he spent the evening having dinner with Jane, but not when he did so with Jill) indicate not just suspicion or low-degree belief, but a normal level of (perhaps unconscious) belief.

In contrast with suspicion and doubt, anxiety and fear are often divorced from evidential considerations – I might fear flying without having any real doubts about its safety. As such, explanations of evidence avoidance and other behavior that conflicts with avowals in terms of anxiety or fear are true alternatives to belief-like explanations. Of course, anxiety and fear can also influence our beliefs, as Johnston and Barnes have argued.

Archer's position is unusual in that it denies both beliefs. It is more common to find these negative psychological states invoked by those who attribute the false belief to self-deceivers. These alternative psychological states are supposed to explain the appearance of true belief. Mele, for example, thinks that the self-deceived possess the false belief and need not manifest any internal conflict. But if they do appear somewhat conflicted – say, they avoid situations that can present unfavorable evidence – then this can be explained by mere suspicion rather than outright belief (Mele, 2001: 71–72, 79–80). Negative states like anxiety and fear are plausible substitutes for the true belief only when we are dealing with positive self-deception. It does not sound right to say that the man who is negatively self-deceived about his wife's fidelity has fear or anxiety that she is faithful, for example. (Those emotions are much better candidates to replace the *false* belief in negative self-deception.) Even though he says she is unfaithful, he nevertheless has some conflict that shows he is not wholehearted in this belief. What non-belief-like state could play that role, in place of fear or anxiety, for negative self-deception?

§5.2 Biological accounts: non-psychological purposiveness

Let's shift now from discussing revisionary accounts of the belief states of the self-deceived to discussing revisionary treatments of motives. The logic of self-deception has been studied from the perspectives of many different disciplines: Philosophy, psychology, biology, and even economics have all contributed. The models and logics offered from these various disciplines can all be used to support specific psychological mechanisms and functions for self-deception. In this section, we will turn to biology for insight. Philosophical discussions of self-deception have focused on the issue of psychological intention or purposiveness, but there are many examples of deception in nature that have non-psychological explanations (e.g., natural selection). This raises the interesting possibility that some such deception could also be turned on the self on purpose, but absent a psychological intention to self-deceive. So, maybe there can be purposive self-deception in humans and other animals that is not necessarily captured by the folk psychological categories of intention, desire, and belief.

David Livingstone Smith (2014) argues in this very way. His starting point is to note that deception is not a uniquely human phenomenon, and it is prevalent throughout the animal world. Smith's prime example is the mirror orchid, which mimics female wasps so as to draw male wasps from flower to flower for the purpose of pollination. But why count this as genuine deception? More generally, what separates genuine deceptiveness from something that is merely misleading? (Recall Figures 2.2 and 2.4.) His answer is that the former is purposive or functional, whereas the latter is not. Mirror orchids are deceptive because they have the purpose of exploiting the male wasp's functional tendency to view such patterns and scents as indicating potential mates. We attribute this purposiveness to contemporary mirror orchids because their ancestral orchids differentially reproduced in virtue of this ability to lure male wasps. On the side of the male wasps, the victims of this deception, they have representational systems that have the function of detecting potential mates. The orchids are deceptive, then, because they have patterns and scents with the function of undermining the functional, representational system of the male wasps (Smith, 2014: 190). Note the necessity of purposive or functional systems on the part of both Deceiver and Victim.

That is an interesting theory of deception, but how can it be applied to self-deception? On Smith's view, self-deception is simply this very same model of deception as applied to the self. While he does not accept the interpersonal model of deception, Smith does embrace the interorganism model deception. Just as mirror orchids have attributes with the function of exploiting another organism's purposive representational system, a single individual could have two purposive mechanisms that are in deceptive conflict. Self-deception occurs when a single organism has one mechanism that functions to correctly represent reality (e.g., a belief-forming mechanism) and another mechanism that functions to undermine that representational mechanism. Biases within a single mechanism are not sufficient to generate self-deception. It is further essential that the second mechanism not merely causes the former to misfire; rather, it must have the function (say, acquired from natural selection) to do so. These mechanisms can be relatively simple. The former representational mechanisms need not be so robust as to generate full-fledged beliefs (e.g., it likely does not in the case of wasps). And the latter mechanisms need not be interpreted as having *intentions* to undermine the former; it just has the function of so-doing. For this reason, Smith calls his view the *teleofunctional non-intentionalist theory of self-deception*.

This is a revisionary account of self-deception in that it offers a novel alternative to the motives and intentions that populate the dominant, rival conceptions. But even more radically, this theory jettisons folk psychological requirements altogether. The alternatives to folk psychological requirements are much more rudimentary mechanisms that need only be representational (on the part of the Victim) and purposive distorters (on the part of the Deceiver). But even this minimal conception affords Smith the ability to distinguish self-deception from the mere operation of a hot bias or wishful thinking. Many hot biases and cases of wishful thinking are not purposive – at least, they do not have the purpose of distorting belief. As Smith puts it, when a person fails to believe as she wishes the world to be, she has not thereby failed at achieving one of her goals. But self-deception is an attempt to get things wrong for a purpose: The *point* is to get things wrong, just as the point of a mirror orchid's patterns and scents is to trick wasps. Here Smith's more rudimentary toolkit gives him a surprising advantage over a deflationist like Mele. As we have seen, many have objected to Mele that his theory includes phenomena that are not truly deceptive (e.g., hot biases, wishful thinking, no-conflict cases) as self-deception. Smith is able to avoid this objection without committing himself to psychological intentions.

Smith offers one biological account of self-deception, but by far the most well-known biological account is that developed by Robert Trivers. While he has actually argued for many different functions that self-deception could have evolved to serve, he argues that one reason is "central" or "primary" (Trivers, 2011: 3; von Hippel and Trivers, 2011: 4). He first proposed the idea in the Foreword to Richard Dawkins's *The Selfish Gene*:

> For example, if (as Dawkins argues) deceit is fundamental in animal communication, then there must be strong selection to spot deception and this ought, in turn, to select for a degree of self-deception, rendering some

> facts and motives unconscious so as not to betray – by the subtle signs
> of self-knowledge – the deception being practiced. Thus, the conventional
> view that natural selection favors nervous systems which produce ever
> more accurate images of the world must be a very naïve view of mental
> evolution. (Trivers, 1976/2006, Foreword: xxvi)

The idea is that self-deception has the purpose of better deceiving *others*. Further, this is a *biological* purpose or function established by natural selection. In these ways, the account is revisionary when it comes to the motives and intentions for self-deception. There need not be any *psychological* motivation in the form of a desire or intention underlying the deception, just psychological tendencies that were naturally selected for their ability to manipulate others. He thinks this warrants calling the self-deception intentional. It may be that these tendencies are appropriately describable as desires, or that accompanying desires to self-deceive were selected for, but that is not essential to the theory.

Trivers is not particularly troubled by attempts to analyze self-deception, and he attempts to "sidestep" the static problem altogether by stipulating that: 1) the self is the conscious mind, 2) in self-deception the conscious mind "stores" false information, and 3) the unconscious mind may or may not store the true information (Trivers, 2011: 9). These are obviously significant stipulations. He declares that doxastic conflict is not necessary, but it may exist between conscious and unconscious representations. He thus allows for simple biases to count as self-deception, so long as these biases were naturally selected so that they count as deception rather than mere mistakes. In cases in which there is doxastic conflict, he describes robustly unconscious processes underlying the conflict.

The Trivers logic that self-deception has an other-deception function is pretty simple. We often benefit from spreading or advertising deceptive beliefs to others. (We will discuss these supposed benefits in §7.3.) In particular, we will tend to benefit from spreading overly positive representations of ourselves – think of the 94% of university professors who thought they were better than the average professor. But it is costly to do this as a conscious, intentional act of deception. These costs include the increased chances of getting caught due to the fact that intentional deception (e.g., lying) imposes cognitive load and comes with various cues that can give the game away (e.g., "tells" such as nervousness or avoiding eye contact). They also include the negative repurcussions that come with being caught as a liar. This logic pushes against psychological intentions to self-deceive as well, to the extent that such intentions make self-deception effortful. Trivers argues that this pressure to withhold awareness of the truth (say, about one's competency) leads to the truth being banished from the conscious mind, residing merely in the unconscious mind if not lost altogether.

Trivers has been consistent in claiming that a facility for deception detection and punishment provides the evolutionary pressure for self-deception. There would be no need for self-deception, at least for the sake of better deceiving others, if we could just lie with impunity. His theory assumes or predicts that people are decent lie detectors, incentivizing either more cold-blooded means of lying or alternative forms of deception. Unfortunately for his theory, experimental studies have shown that we are not particularly good lie detectors, faring only slightly above chance levels (Vrij, 2011). Trivers is well aware of this, but he makes the unusual move of attempting to support his evolutionary hypothesis by arguing that the empirical case for poor lie detection is inaccurate, primarily due to the limitations of the laboratory setting (von Hippel and Trivers, 2011: 2–4). This line of argument seems hopeful at best. Even if self-deception were incentivized because it eliminates the tells of deception, we must still weigh the costs to self that come with possessing false information that can (mis)guide its own behavior as well as that of others. Further, if self-deception were for the sake of other-deception, then we should expect it to disproportionately occur for information sought by others and in contexts that afford us opportunities to manipulate others. We do not yet have evidence to support these claims (Van Leeuwen, 2007b: 334–335).

Assuming, as Trivers claims, that self-deception exists so as to eliminate the tells of intentional or effortful deception, what predictions should we make concerning the mental structure of the self-deceived? One might expect single-mindedness (what we earlier described as self-delusion), as duplicity supposedly reveals our deception by imposing cognitive load, nervousness, and suppression. If we are biased so as to better manipulate others, it seems that we would be most convincing when we possess unqualified belief. It is surprising, then, that von Hippel and Trivers (2011) go out of their way to establish the non-unitary nature of the mind and the sophisticated powers of the unconscious that often diverge from conscious thoughts and intentions. If we allow for both conscious and unconscious representations, there are four possibilities for how information is stored in the mind (ignoring the cases in which no representation is stored). These are depicted in Figure 5.1. Options A and D represent single-minded truth and falsity, respectively. With option A, the person is in full possession of the truth, making other-deception possible only by a conscious effort to lie. This requires the conscious mind to hold both a truth and false representation, and this is the very kind of cognitive load that Trivers thinks we are incentivized to avoid. Options C and D are better for other-deception, as there is falsity in the conscious mind. This means that the conscious mind (the self, on Trivers's view) can just be itself, making deception easier as there is no need for dual representations within the conscious mind and the deception will likely come across as sincere. C-type cases are similar to the Bach/Audi conflict cases, whereas D-type cases are more like Mele's examples of outright self-delusion. It seems that option D, in particular, would be optimal when it comes to being convincing for the sake of other-deception. This is because no part of the person represents the world otherwise. In C-type cases, in contrast, there would be the risk of an unconscious representation affecting speech, action, or emotion so as to betray the self. While Trivers certainly allows for D-type cases, he also goes out of his way to make the case for conflicted cases fitting C. But the Trivers logic would predict a trend toward D instead. (Neither does it seem that conflict – retention of the truth in the unconscious – is an unavoidable psychological constraint. Although, perhaps some stronger connection to the truth is prudentially valuable for guiding the person's own actions.) B-type cases are included for completeness, although Trivers does not attend to them when discussing self-deception's supposed other-deception function. Nevertheless, they are very possible. A person could consciously know the truth while having unconscious mechanisms that represent things otherwise (much like someone can know that their partner has been faithful, but yet have unconscious representations depicting things otherwise). This would make other-deception even more difficult than with the C-type cases, as dual representations in the conscious mind (truth and falsity) are generally thought to be more taxing than the merely one false representation needed on option C in order to deceive others (see Figure 5.1).

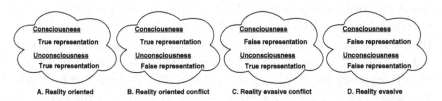

Figure 5.1 Representations in the conscious and unconscious mind

In conclusion, there are a couple of worries about their emphasis on robustly unconscious processes. First, are we so sure that this unconscious activity does not generate tells of its own? Von Hippel and Trivers emphasize robust unconscious activity, of the kind we discussed in §4.2.1, which may sometimes be effortful (Huang and Bargh, 2014). Even if not imposing cognitive load, it can still induce nervousness, emotions, or otherwise percolate into observable behavior. Second, even if it can be pulled off, this psychological complexity is gratuitous given the presumed goal of deceiving others. Self-delusion would be better than deep conflict – the person would be better off getting the information out of mind altogether. The other-deception hypothesis might explain biases, but it does not motivate or explain deep conflict cases.

In light of these various objections, Neil Van Leeuwen (2007b) argues that self-deception is not an adaptation but instead is what evolutionary biologists call a *spandrel*. A spandrel is not itself a biological adaptation, but rather a by-product of structures (that might themselves be adaptations). For example, human chins were not selected for a particular function, but, rather, exist as a by-product of the jaw. In a similar way, Van Leeuwen argues that self-deception is not a specific module that was selected for, but rather it is a capacity that emerges due to five features of the mind: a motive to avoid discomfort, selective attention to the evidence, inertia in our web of belief, a simplicity bias, and awareness of self-fulfilling beliefs (339–340). These mental features may or may not be adaptations themselves. But in various combinations, Van Leeuwen argues that they give rise to self-deception just as jaws give rise to chins. For example, attending to certain evidence is painful, so we selectively avoid that evidence. As a consequence of these independent facts about the mind, we are led to self-deception. There is a true story about how we acquired each of these five mental features, but there is no separate story to be told about why we have the capacity to self-deceive. It is simply a by-product of these other features working in combination.

Whether or not self-deception itself is an adaptation, some incentivized biases are likely biological and allow for explanation in terms of natural selection. This is especially true for biases that have a very close connection to reproductive success: perceived sexual interest in potential mates, risk assessment, social status, health, etc. Other incentivized biases are clearly culturally acquired – a father self-deceptively thinks that his son is an outstanding baseball player. But even in many of these cultural cases the bias can be classified as biological as well. The issue is one of granularity.

REVISIONARY ACCOUNTS: BELIEF AND PURPOSE   193

Described as a bias favoring baseball talent in one's offspring, it seems inappropriate to describe it as the product of biological natural selection. But if it is described at a coarser grain – say, as a bias favoring athletic fitness in one's offspring – then it is plausible to ascribe it to biology. Natural selection can also be found with cultural evolution and individual learning, and the goals of a society or individual are often not those of biology. Even natural selection explanations need not reduce to biology.

§5.3 Signaling accounts

Deception goes hand-in-hand with communication. When a communicative system is in place, there are almost always incentives to lie or otherwise mislead. Human communicative systems – including language – undoubtedly grew out of simpler systems, such as the more rudimentary varieties of animal signals. Over the last few decades a rich literature on signals – animal signals, as well as signals in human culture (e.g., formal education, religious rituals) – has emerged. Signaling theory has given special attention to the mechanisms that are supposed to promote honest signaling, the conditions under which deception is possible, and the limits to deceptive signaling. Communication, apart from idle conversation, is ultimately for the sake of manipulation in a neutral sense of that term – we are trying to get people to do things. Research on signaling and communication, then, is likely relevant to self-deception. Self-deception could possibly be a form of dishonest signaling or communication – to the self or others – that is performed for the manipulative effects it induces.

§5.3.1 Self-signaling

Danica Mijovic-Prelec and Drazen Prelec (2010) offer a psychological model of self-deception that is heavily influenced by economic models of signaling. Like Smith, they are looking to offer an alternative to traditional intentionalism and Mele-style deflationism. Their proposal is also driven by helpful psychological distinctions concerning belief, continuing the recent trend of offering more sophisticated treatments of belief-like attitudes in the spirit of the others we discussed in §5.1. They distinguish three kinds of belief relevant to self-deception: deep belief, stated belief, and experiential belief. Deep beliefs are the dispositions driving action (including verbal behavior), stated beliefs are avowals and similar actions, and experiential beliefs are the emotional experiences that follow such avowals.

Their theory is that self-deception is a form of self-signaling. Self-signaling refers to the manipulations induced by communications to ourselves about a personal feature that is hidden to us. So, on their view, self-deception is always about some personal characteristic:

> Self-signalling presumes the existence of an underlying characteristic that is (i) personally important, (ii) introspectively inaccessible, and (iii) potentially revealed through actions. (Mijovic-Prelec and Prelec, 2010: 230)

In the case of self-deception, they claim that the deep belief is the personally important characteristic that is introspectively inaccessible but can be revealed through actions. This model makes significant claims about mental architecture and self-knowledge. First, it assumes that the object of self-deception is hidden from introspective access. We do not have privileged first-person access to the deep beliefs that generate our actions. Instead, they embrace the self-perception theory of Bem (1972) and hold that we know our own minds in a way very similar to how we know the minds of others. Relatedly, we can deceive ourselves in ways very similar to how we can deceive others. Second, they posit a radical bifurcation in the mind underlying our psychological opacity. In their vocabulary, there is an *actor* module and a distinct *interpreter* module. The actor module generates our actions (including verbal behavior), and the interpreter module attributes mental states to the self on the basis of the observed behavior. But there is a shocking disconnect between ourselves as actors and self-aware agents:

> This argues for the structural separation of modules responsible for action selection and those responsible for interpreting and rewarding those actions. It also argues for denying internal information to the interpretational mechanisms. (Mijovic-Prelec and Prelec, 2010: 238)

Why would the actor module strategically mislead the interpreter about its actual characteristics? Their favored answer seems to be that this is done for the sake of psychological comfort or experiential belief. Mijovic-Prelec and Prelec are very influenced by the Quattrone and Tversky study (discussed in §3.4) in which participants make efforts to avoid an unfavorable diagnosis. Recall that this was the study in which subjects apparently manipulated their tolerance to cold water in order to receive a more favorable medical diagnosis. Mijovic-Prelec and Prelec see this as being the standard form of self-deception – the self-deceived seek good news even at some cost to the pursuit of their long-term goals. The construct of *diagnostic* utility is supposed to get at the value people find in believing that they possess a personally important characteristic. They conducted an experiment that they interpret as illustrating this phenomenon. Their study participants were biased toward receiving favorable diagnostic news even at some relatively minor cost to long-term success at an unimportant classifying task with a monetary reward. But in their experiment, the potential long-term gain was not significant, and they perhaps underestimated the role that superstitious or magical thinking could play for such participants.

While at different places they say that self-deception is always about the self's personal "characteristics" or "motives," this is misleading. They also recognize familiar forms of self-deception that concern the characteristics of others – e.g., whether a spouse has been faithful (Mijovic-Prelec and Prelec, 2010: 230, 237). It is better, I would recommend, to see their self-signaling theory as taking self-deception to involve, in a sense, a false second-order belief or simple ignorance regarding deep belief. This fits well with the distinctions they emphasize between the three levels of belief and their claim that diagnostic utility drives self-deception. In their terminology, the person has stated and experiential beliefs that contradict their deep belief. But these deep beliefs could be about anything.

There are also some serious difficulties facing their psychological proposal. Avowals are supposedly generated by deep beliefs, yet a distinct interpreter module is supposed to self-attribute beliefs. So if a third party inquired about the person's beliefs, the deep belief would be the module responsible for the answer. Yet if the person herself wants to know what she believes, a distinct interpreter mechanism is supposed to provide this answer. One wonders why Mother Nature would not give us more direct access to our deep beliefs, or at least the ability to answer ourselves in the same way that we answer others. Further, there are questions about how to reconcile this retrospective opacity with the apparent access we have to motives prior to action, as when we reflect or deliberate about how to act.

§5.3.2 *Other-signaling*

Whereas Mijovic-Prelec and Prelec focus on self-deception for the sake of personal manipulation, it is also possible to see beliefs and belief-relevant activities (e.g., avowals, behavior, or emotional expression) as serving socially communicative functions that aim at manipulating others. In effect, we have already seen this with Robert Trivers's theory of self-deception as being in the service of other-deception. While Trivers does not explicitly embrace and develop the signaling framework in connection to self-deception, his proposal fits with much work on animal signaling and he acknowledges its relevance (von Hippel and Trivers, 2011: Authors' Response). Whether one emphasizes self-signaling or other-signaling depends on whether one attends to the personal or social functions and benefits of self-deception.

The idea behind the other-signaling hypothesis is that just as there is diagnostic value in signaling a deep belief to the self, there can be social value in signaling a deep belief to others. Roughly, a signal is something that is designed or selected to communicate information to be detected by a receiver in order to modify that receiver's behavior (Funkhouser, 2017: 811–812). For example, a peacock's tail feather seems designed to be detected by peahens and to manipulate their behavior. It is so long and colorful *because* peahens selectively attend to it. Funkhouser (2017) argues that beliefs can also function as social signals. People are designed with mindreading mechanisms that are specifically designed for attributing beliefs to others. This opens up the possibility of beliefs being strategically altered because of how they affect others once read by them. For example, if other people will detect my self-assessments and treat me differently based on what I believe and report about myself, then I am incentivized to have overly positive views of myself and broadcast them to others. I need not consciously strategize this plan, but biases in this direction could be naturally selected because they have this positive effect. The other-signaling proposal is a thesis about the etiology of certain biases and beliefs, as well a claim about their function and benefits. This same characterization of signaling can be applied to self-signaling, with some introspective mechanism or mechanism for interpreting one's own behavior playing the role of mindreader (think of Mijovic-Prelec and Prelec's interpreter module).

Much work has been devoted to studying how much dishonest signaling a given environment and signaling system can sustain. Honest signaling is the norm as receivers are incentivized to discount or ignore misleading signals. But how can a signal be "known" to be honest? One of the main mechanisms to ensure honest signaling is the handicap principle or the theory of costly signaling (Zahavi and Zahavi, 1997). Signals that are costly to produce or difficult to fake are more likely to be truthful – e.g., a peacock's tail feather is an honest signal because only biologically fit peacocks have the resources to produce a long and colorful tail feather. Similarly, some have argued that patriotic displays and religious practices or beliefs are costly signals because it is risky to enlist in the military or it is costly to attend church every week and tithe (Soler, 2012). If these are truly signals, then they were designed or selected – by biology, culture, or individual learning – so as to be detected by others and have them treat us better or simply trust us more.

The logic behind the other-signaling hypothesis is not exactly the same as Trivers's stated logic. For Trivers, the pressure to self-deceive primarily comes from the costs of lying. This can apply to other-signaling as well: It is harder to effectively signal a belief that one does not actually possess, and one is likely to be punished more if caught in such an effortful deception. But the primary pressure for the other-signaling hypothesis has nothing to do with the costs of lying. The logic is that one socially benefits from having a certain belief that others can detect, so for that reason alone it is selected. This logic holds independent of the truth or rationality of the belief, so it can provide an additional incentive for certain true beliefs to be selected. But as true beliefs are likely to be selected for other reasons (e.g., they further goal pursuit), it is more likely that we will discover signaling at work for beliefs that do not seem justified or especially helpful for the person's private interests.

A signaling function can be acquired through biological natural selection, analoguous to the selection of a peacock's tail feather. This would most likely explain only quite general biases that are both universal and which produce beliefs that further reproductive success (e.g., self-enhancement and in-group biases) (Funkhouser, 2017). Like most claims in evolutionary psychology, this speculation is quite controversial. But self-deception for the sake of other-signaling can also emerge due to motives acquired within a lifetime rather than through biological inheritance. A man might self-deceive into thinking that his wife has been faithful because his peers have taught him that a woman's infidelity is always due to some weakness on the man's part. He self-deceives in order to signal his masculinity to his peers.

§5.4 Social influences on self-deception

Social factors play a large role in our mental lives, so it should not be surprising that biases and deception can be triggered by our social and cultural environment. This is an area, as applied to self-deception, that is ripe for future research. While self-deception is deception of the self by the self, other people can also factor into this process. Robert Trivers has done more than anyone else to emphasize the social dimensions of self-deception.

He is most known for arguing that others often serve as the audience for our self-deception, and we self-deceive in order to manipulate them. But Trivers argues that the influence can go in the other direction as well: Others can manipulate us into self-deception.

Trivers describes a kind of *imposed self-deception* in which others provide us with a motivation or incentive to self-deceive. They might also contribute to manipulating evidence, but they cannot do all the work – it must still be self-deception rather than outright other-deception. His primary examples of imposed self-deception draw on his work as a biologist who did much work on the logic of recurring animal conflicts, such as those between parents and their offspring. Parents and offspring have imperfect (.5) relatedness. So, parents could be incentivized to shape their children to have cognitive and behavioral tendencies that further the parents' interests over the child's interests. This quite general fact about parent–offspring relations can lead to widespread childrearing practices like putting the collective good of the family above those of the individual child. This can induce self-deception regarding the value of altruism and one's own family members (Trivers, 2000/2002: 281).

Besides these rather abstract biological considerations, others can impose self-deception simply by putting us in a situation that compels self-deception as a coping mechanism. A woman who was abused as a child rationalizes why her mother physically assaulted her, and she worries about the mother's well-being (Trivers, 2000/2002: 282). It is understandable that a child would want parental love and support, even to the point of deceiving herself so as to create this illusion. Such imposed self-deception often furthers the abuser's interests. In the extreme, this is seen with Stockholm Syndrome, in which the victims self-deceive to cope with their situation, their deception furthering the agenda of the kidnappers or abusers (e.g., the hostage is more willing to please, less likely to escape, actively defends the kidnappers, and so on). But other times, the imposed self-deception might simply be a defensive, adaptive response on the part of the victim for her benefit alone. The tortured person might create a self-deceptive fantasy about their future life or make a game of their miserable conditions. This need not benefit the torturer in any way – it simply is a desperate attempt to make the best of a horrible situation. It is not just negative situations that can impose self-deception on us, as favorable treatment can also induce self-deceptive rationalization. Suppose you live in a socio-economic-political environment that is fundamentally exploitative of others, but you are one of the 1% who greatly benefits from this unjust arrangement. You might then self-deceive about the morality of your actions or the fairness of this arrangement. Your family, peers, and social institutions could help prod you in this direction.

In addition to these Trivers' cases, I recommend adding a second category of self-deception that is initiated by others – what we can call *baited self-deception*. In these cases, the victim has a standing motive or tendency to believe something, and others act so as to exploit that vulnerability. The person is baited or lured into a self-deception, but the person already had the motive and then does most of the heavy lifting once the motive has been triggered and perhaps directed by another. Think of a good sleight of hand magician who knows how to let you deceive yourself. The worlds of advertising and online informational content offer good examples of this as well. Commercials do not have to outright deceive you in order to manipulate you, often against your own best interests. Instead, they can present certain imagery or lifestyles that activate biases that you already possess. The luxury car commercial need not actively deceive you into thinking that the car is a good purchase for someone with your modest financial means. It can instead present you with an image or idea (e.g., the "American Dream") which causes you to self-deceive that you can afford it, which is what you wanted to believe all along. A social media site is not necessarily deceiving you as it keeps referring you to articles similar to those that you have clicked in the past. These articles tap into your prejudices, and the steady onslaught of such content furthers your deception on some social-political or simply factual topic (e.g., climate change). The social media site might not care at all about what you believe and have no intention to deceive you. But it has a referral system in place that *de facto* triggers you to further your own self-deception by catering to your standing prejudices. Advertisers, conmen, lovers, propagandists, and online content providers have learned that they can be quite effective without resorting to the hard sell.

There might not be any sharp lines to draw between imposed, baited, and wholly self-initiated self-deception. One might be tempted to say that every case of self-deception is, in some watered down sense, "imposed" on the person by their human nature, family, or social environment. But I would caution against going that far, as we likely have wide agreement on paradigmatic examples of each of those three kinds of self-deception. Still, there probably is no bright line separating them.

Others not only initiate our self-deception, they can also enable it. *Enabled self-deception* is self-deception that, while not necessarily intiated by others, is furthered or encouraged by them either implicitly or explicitly. They might deliberately direct you toward evidence that supports what you want to believe, or you might seek to associate with people who are receptive to your favored belief (although they do not intend to mislead you). Your friends reassure you that your son is not doing drugs, although they do not believe it; your friends further your political self-deception because they genuinely have those same political beliefs. Again, you must still be carrying out most of the deceptive work in order for this to count as self-deception rather than other-deception.

In what is known as *collective self-deception*, others can even participate in self-deception with you. This can refer to either the sum of many similar self-deceptions among members of a group, or it can refer to the singular self-deception of some collective organization (Deweese-Boyd, 2017: §7). As an example of the former, some have claimed that religion is "the opiate of the masses." By this, they might mean that religious people self-deceive so as to comfort themselves with pleasurable thoughts. The claim is simply that this one kind of self-deception is commonplace among the mass of people because they tend to share the same kind of beliefs, biases, desires, and so on. This kind of collective self-deception does not pose any distinctive philosophical or psychological problems, at least as far as self-deception goes. There is not some one thing – "the masses" – whose self-deception we must account for according to some group-mind psychology. The mechanisms are the same as what we find with solitary self-deception, although the fact that others are engaged in the same self-deception will likely make it easier to succeed (Ruddick, 1988). This is because of the influence of peer pressure and the more significant evidence distortion that can arise with multiple participants. Yet if the community's evidence and influence becomes too distorted, it might shift from collective self-deception to outright other-deception.

Some claim that self-deception can also occur within a single collective or institution, in addition to these summative or plural forms. A university might be said to be self-deceived regarding its academic standing, or a country might self-deceive about its human rights record. If this is supposed to be something different than the self-deception of the individual employers or citizens, this is probably due to official statements, policies, and procedures of the university or country. It seems that these institutions would need to have something playing the role beliefs, motives, and the like so as to at least meet the minimal standard of motivated irrationality. For this reason, some will think that the description of the university or country as self-deceived is only metaphorical. Can it be literally true that a university, country, or other institution possesses psychological states? But perhaps self-deception can be characterized without invoking psychological states, as David Livingstone Smith's biology-based account allows. An institution can have mechanisms designed to accurately represent the facts (say, an intelligence service) and a different mechanism designed to distort how those facts are presented to that very same institution (say, a propaganda wing or state department). If there is such singularly collective self-deception, the issue of responsibility becomes more complicated. The entire institution might be blameworthy, but there could be culpable failures at the individual level as well.

Summary

- In order to resolve the Basic Problem, some revise the resultant state that makes one count as self-deceived. Rather than being outright belief, the resultant state might instead be subdoxastic or partial belief. Or it might be a different kind of attitude altogether: thought, acceptance, pretense, fear, or anxiety. This move can solve the static problem (no dual belief) and also mitigate the dynamic problem by aiming at something short of belief.
- There are also revisionary accounts of motives and intentions. David Livingstone Smith offers an account in terms of representational systems with functions to represent and misrepresent, without requiring any specific psychological motivation. Robert Trivers offers what he touts as an intentionalist theory, where the intention is a function that results from natural selection. In his case, the primary function of self-deception is to further the deception of others. Others claim that some self-deception serves a signaling function, either to the self or to others.
- Self-deception can originate with others who either impose it on us or bait us into it. We can also be collectively self-deceived, and perhaps a collective institution can itself be self-deceived.

Recommended reading

Schwitzgebel (2001) is a short introduction to in-between belief. He further develops his dispositional theory of belief in Schwitzgebel (2002). Gendler (2007) makes a strong case for self-deception as runaway imagination or pretense. She also makes a convincing case for the self-deception/self-delusion distinction.

David Livingstone Smith (2014) articulates a highly original biological (teleofunctional) account of self-deception. Mijovic-Prelec and Prelec (2010) offer a very technical economic model of self-deception as self-signaling, combined with an experimental study.

Trivers (2011) is a highly readable presentation of his theory of self-deception. It also offers many examples of imposed and collective self-deception.

Notes

1 It should be noted that this holistic, conservative approach to belief is rejected by some. For example, Gilbert et al. (1990) and Mandelbaum (2014) claim that we default to belief when presented with a proposition to entertain. The idea is that disbelief takes work, but belief does not. This makes belief seem to be the product of a non-agential subsystem. As these theorists emphasize, this is very much a non-standard (although perhaps empirically supported) view of belief.

2 Schwitzgebel (2002: 261) actually claims that Geraldine is only partially self-deceived, since there are (non-high stakes?) contexts in which she would acknowledge the truth. But he later (264) says that self-deception is a case of genuine in-between belief.

3 Michael Bratman (1992) articulates a very influential account of acceptance that differs somewhat from that offered by Cohen. He does not explicitly apply his account to self-deception, but we can easily imagine such applications given that he says that acceptance can be guided by practical considerations, is under voluntary control, and is not bound by holistic considerations of rationality. Bratman, unlike Cohen, also emphasizes the context relativity of acceptance. For both, however, acceptance can guide action in robust ways.

4 The aim, function, or *telos* of belief can be determined in various ways: conscious intention, enculturation (habituation and education), or the natural selection of belief-forming mechanisms (Velleman, 2000: 252–255). Velleman has since backed away from this account, but see Steglich-Petersen (2006: 514–515) for a more recent statement and defense.

5 Michel and Newen (2010: 736–737) and Porcher (2014: 305–308), in slightly different ways, also object to Gendler on this point: Self-deceivers seem to be in the belief game.

6

RESPONSIBILITY FOR SELF-DECEPTION

6.1 The ethics of belief
6.2 Self-knowledge
6.3 Rationality and responsibility
6.4 Does context matter?

Up until now we have focused on characterizing self-deception and showing how it is executed. We now turn to reasons why it might be objectionable and its practitioners held acccountable. Two reasons are of particular importance to philosophers: Self-deception is a failure of self-knowledge, and self-deception is a failure of rationality. If the self-deceived can know and control these failures, then they might be responsible – in particular, blameworthy – for their condition.

§6.1 The ethics of belief

The most well-known discussion of "The Ethics of Belief" is by W.K. Clifford (1879), who wrote a widely anthologized article with that very title. Interestingly, Clifford opens his article by telling a story of self-deception.

204 RESPONSIBILITY FOR SELF-DECEPTION

The owner of an emigrant ship had many doubts about his ship's fitness – it was old, needed many repairs, and others had warned him that it was not seaworthy. Yet these thoughts were unpleasant to him, as repairs would be expensive and a delay would cost him passenger fees. So the shipowner made an effort to block the unwelcome thoughts from his mind, and he focused on the fact that the ship had safely made the voyage many times before. He also put his faith in God. Through these means he acquired "a sincere and comfortable conviction that his vessel was thoroughly safe and seaworthy." Unfortunately, his conviction was unjustified, and the ship sank in the middle of the ocean.

This seems to be a clear case of self-deception, and Clifford claims that the shipowner is ethically or morally responsible for it. This moral responsibility is supposed to hold independent of three factors that he singles out: the sincerity of the belief, the consequences of acting on it, and even its truth. The fact that the shipowner sincerely held the belief that the ship was safe in no way mitigates his responsibility, as "he had no right to believe on such evidence as was before him." Neither is the guilt dependent on the negative consequences (ship sinking) or even the falsity of the resultant belief. Clifford says that even if the ship had made it across the ocean safely or if the ship had, in fact, been seaworthy, the shipowner was believing immorally, because the evidence indicated otherwise. In these regards, Clifford is an exemplar of the evidentialist position that people are obligated – in Clifford's case, morally obligated – to believe as the evidence indicates.

Beliefs, not only actions, are morally important because there is a necessary connection between belief and action, all beliefs eventually affect our actions and other beliefs in various ways, and our beliefs are part of a "common property" that can be transmitted to others. Because of the importance of belief, Clifford concludes that it is always morally wrong to believe on insufficient evidence, suppress doubts, and avoid investigation. Since these are the typical and perhaps even essential behaviors of the self-deceived, the condition is immoral. Morality is fundamentally about how we treat others, and Clifford thought that self-deception is immoral because it adversely affects others:

> Belief, that sacred faculty which prompts the decisions of our will, and knits into harmonious working all the compacted energies of our being, is ours not for ourselves but for humanity. It is rightly used on truths which have been established by long experience and waiting toil, and which have stood in the fierce light of free and fearless questioning. Then it helps to

bind men together, and to strengthen and direct their common action. It is descecrated when given to unproved and unquestioned statements, for the solace and private pleasure of the believer; to add a tinsel of splendour to the plain straight road of our life and display a bright mirage beyond it; or even to drown the common sorrows of our kind by a self-deception which allows them not only to cast down, but also to degrade us. (Clifford, 1879: 182–183)

Given its social dimension, self-deception is supposed to be closely related to sins such as theft, fraud, lying, and cheating.

Note well that Clifford is concerned with attributions of *moral* responsibility. But there are other dimensions along which people and their behavior can be evaluated and responsibility assigned. This applies to belief as well. (See Chignell, 2018: §2 for discussion.) Actions can be evaluated for their *prudence* – e.g., if one does not eat one's green vegetables, then one is to be blamed for being imprudent. This kind of blame is not necessarily a moral condemnation, and it could be that certain beliefs or belief-forming processes are imprudent but not immoral. *Epistemic* evaluation – say, for rationality – is another dimension of evaluation. A certain inference might be irrational, and a pupil can be blamed for making it. But it is unlikely that this is an expression of moral disapproval. We know that self-deception is, minimally, motivated irrationality, so it will have a negative epistemic evaluation. But it is not so clear that this means the person should even be epistemically blamed for the failure. Not all mistakes are culpable mistakes.

Some philosophers resist assigning praise or blame to believers along these various dimensions because they accept some form of *doxastic involuntarism* – the thesis that belief is not under voluntary control. The opposing thesis, *doxastic voluntarism*, comes in stronger and weaker forms. It can be *direct* in the sense that beliefs can be acquired at will, just by choosing to so believe. This is what we saw Bernard Williams argue against (§2.1.2), on the grounds that belief must instead be responsive to reason and evidence. The weaker form of doxastic voluntarism is *indirect*, holding that we can control our beliefs by initiating a process that will eventually alter them. Those who are on the intentionalist side of the spectrum typically argue that this is how self-deceivers are able to overcome the dynamic challenges. They initiate a process of biased evidence search, rationalization, selective socializing, and the like. If, instead of resulting in belief, self-deception produces only selective thought, avowal, or pretense, then it seems that these are things that could be directly willed. The issue of control is important because many think that there is a necessary connection between voluntariness, control, and related concepts, on the one hand, and responsibility, on the other. Others, such as Pamela Hieronymi (2008), argue that while belief is involuntary, people still bear responsibility for their beliefs.[1]

Philosophers widely accept that belief is heavily constrained by evidence. But it is probably going too far to say that the evidence forces one belief on us. Quine (1951) argued that any belief could be saved in light of any observations, as long as the person is willing to make enough rational adjustments elsewhere. In this sense, at least, we are not completely passive to experience, and there might be wiggle room to control belief. In an extreme form, we see this with conspiracy theorists. A flat earther might be presented with the same evidence that we possess, but he interprets it in a different way. He claims that pictures from outerspace have been fabricated, which commits him to nefarious auxiliary beliefs about NASA. (He makes similar moves to explain eclipses, the seasons, world travel, etc.) The flat earther also has some positive evidence for his view – the Earth looks flat, and it does not feel like we are on a spinning ball. Note that he does not simply choose to believe that the earth is flat and leave it at that. Rather, he makes rationally appropriate adjustments – knowing exactly what pieces of evidence to discredit as fraudulent and other bits to emphasize – in order to protect his belief.[2] More commonly, life gives us a mixed bag of evidence from which reasonable people can disagree. Some of us see good reason to be optimistic about the future productivity of the new hire, others of us less so; some of us see the order we find in the world as supporting belief in an intelligent designer, others do not. We tend to tolerate these opposing beliefs derived from the same set of evidence. Some of the self-deceived are more like the conspiracy theorist who must make radical adjustments and auxiliary assumptions, but most probably exploit the flexibility closer to the reasonable disagreement end of the spectrum. Regardless, there is at least logical and psychological space for a person to have some say in what they come to believe. This also might suggest that there is more to rational or wise belief than just the logician's notion of rationality. While the conspiracy theorist could be completely logical and consistent, there is something wrong with his judgment. And while people can sometimes make great efforts to accommodate recalcitrant data, there is no guarantee that their emotions and behavior will agree to fall in line. We see this often with the self-deceived. The father always has a story to tell to explain away the son's shortcomings, but he still cannot help but feel disappointment.

RESPONSIBILITY FOR SELF-DECEPTION   207

While belief is probably not under direct voluntary control, many beliefs are due to cognitive and behavioral habits that can be controlled to at least some extent. Among these habits, attention has been given to cognitive and motivational biases as especially important to self-deception. A general principle for assigning responsibility is that, speaking a little loosely and holding other things equal, a person is more responsible for an outcome to the extent that she is involved, as an agent, in bringing it about. I am not responsible for my naturally dark hair color as I did nothing to bring it about – I was just born that way. Erin is responsible for her guitar-playing skill, however, as she practiced hard to develop it. There are many in between cases, and no case will ever reach the level of total responsibility as every earthly outcome is at least partially determined by factors beyond the person's control (e.g., natural aptitude, opportunity, non-defective functioning, etc.). We saw back with Figure 2.4 that beliefs can be produced by habits or factors that manifest varying degrees of agential involvement. Correspondingly, there are likely varying degrees of responsibility for beliefs formed in these ways: cold biases, merely hot biases, purposive biases, and intentional biases. It seems a bit much to blame someone for falling prey to the biases that come with the availability heuristic – say, when they overestimate a certain health risk because of the ease with which confirming instances come to mind. In fact, this may be a nearly universal side-effect of the proper functioning of our shared cognitive architecture. Contrast this with an intentional effort to seek misleading evidence or otherwise distort one's reasoning in a purposive manner, such as Pascal's wagerer or a father who goes out of his way to avoid confronting the truth about his son. It is much more plausible to hold these people responsible. For these reasons, deflationary accounts have a harder time than do intentionalist accounts when it comes to assigning responsibility.

But the issue is by no means simple, and two factors are especially important. First, are people even aware of the biases or factors that drive their self-deception? Second, is there anything they can do to control them? There is a long tradition in philosophy, traceable to Aristotle, which demands these two necessary conditions for (moral) responsibility: knowledge and control (Fischer and Ravizza, 1998: 12–13). But are these conditions met by the biased and self-deceived? While people often have a general idea that they have biases favoring their children and themselves, many are clueless about the systematic effects of cold and hot biases. People are usually surprised to hear the results of the heuristics and biases literature, for example. This ignorance mitigates responsibility unless we think that people *should* know about these biases. But it is unreasonable to expect most people to be aware of these psychological facts. (Perhaps improved education – both formal and informal – will make this a more reasonable demand in the coming years.) Nevertheless, those of us in the know can establish curricula and practices to train people to overcome these psychological tendencies, and perhaps people could be blamed if they fail to follow that instruction.

What about those cases in which self-deception is conceived as a purposive or perhaps even intentional activity? It might seem more plausible that these people would know about their biases. But non-deflationists (e.g., Freud, Pears) tend to go out of their way to hide the purposes from the conscious mind so as to avoid the dynamic problems. If the conscious mind or main system is oblivious to these purposes, then it again becomes less plausible that they are blamewothy for the effects. Perhaps educated people do have an obligation to be reflective, but there are limits to our ability to access our own minds.

Neil Levy (2014) examines our responsibility for unconscious biases that are quite similar to the hot biases that deflationists take to be largely constitutive of self-deception. Levy claims that, to the extent they are inaccessible to consciousness, people are not responsible for these biases. As an example he discusses Uhlmann and Cohen's (2005) study in which participants were tasked with evaluating two candidates – one male, one female – for the position of police chief. In some versions, the male candidate was streetwise but not formally educated, while the female candidate was formally educated but not streetwise. In other versions, this was reversed. In both cases, participants tended to favor the male candidate. When asked to justify their answer, participants cited the attribute (streetwise or formal education) that the male candidate possessed, in spite of the fact that the female candidate had this attribute just as often. It seems that a bias backed by rationalization is at work. But the participants might not be consciously sexist. As Levy correctly points out, for many men and women these sexist associations are only implicit. Levy's (2014: 94–95) position is that if the person would resist this implicit sexism were he aware of it, then he is not responsible for it. These might not be cases of self-deception, in part because participants might lack a motive to favor the male candidates. But when a motive is present, its influence on producing bias will often be unconscious as well. So, Levy would hold that such self-deceivers are not responsible for their condition.

RESPONSIBILITY FOR SELF-DECEPTION   209

What about the second point, concerning control over self-deception? Once people become aware of these biases, it is possible to overcome or at least dampen many of them. I can remind myself that I am partial to my children and try to assume the position of an objective observer instead. But the effects often still linger. Daniel Kahneman warns of the tenacious influences of anchors like initial offers in negotiations. Even if people are aware that the anchor is irrelevant, it still influences judgment (recall the redwood tree example from §1.2). What are we to do, then? He recommends just walking away and refusing to participate in negotiations when unreasonable first offers are made (Kahneman, 2011: 126). There are other belief-forming factors that we can control once we become aware of them. Self-deception often involves machinations beyond mere bias, and there are several ways this can be irresponsible behavior: deliberately skewed evidence search, a lack of care when evaluating evidence, close-mindedness to the criticisms of others, and so on. We will discuss some of these shortly (§6.3).

Belief is a dynamic and ongoing process, and we can be responsible for more than just the initial acquisition of a belief. A child raised in a racist household might not be responsible for the racist beliefs she acquired through her parent's brainwashing, but she very well could be responsible for retaining those beliefs in adulthood. Even if an adult is not responsible for believing the fake news he has been fed, he could be blamed for deciding to actually act on it if the stakes are high and the belief is socially disapproved (e.g., shooting up a pizza parlor on the basis of a conspiracy theory). This is a fine line, though, as belief seems to entail some fairly robust behavioral dispositions. It might be that the person is responsible for the belief as well, and acting on it is a further characteristic for which they are responsible. Robert Audi (1982: 148) makes a threefold distinction paralleling these points for self-deception: the self-deceived could be morally responsible for getting into self-deception, remaining in it, or acting out of it.

In this section, we have focused on the ethics of belief, but the ethical issues surrounding self-deception are actually broader. As we saw in our earlier chapters, several philosophers think that the self-deceived do not acquire the false or unjustified belief. But parallel ethical issues can arise for their alternative psychological states: Is it ethical to think, avow, or pretend contrary to one's beliefs? Many will think that we have an obligation to face reality, and this obligation could be violated without outright acquiring the illusory belief.

§6.2 Self-knowledge

Self-deception has been judged to be a failure of self-knowledge in two different senses. First, some hold that the self-deceived always have a deceptively skewed view of their own personal characteristics. They might not know their own athleticism, intelligence, moral character, and so on. This makes self-deception about the self in a very straightforward sense, and the positive cases fall under the category of self-enhancing and otherwise self-serving biases. Second, some deep conflict theorists think that the self-deceived do not know what they truly believe or think about some matter; they have hidden their beliefs or thoughts from themselves (Bach, Audi, Funkhouser, Gendler, Fernandez). Indeed, this mental opacity is sometimes thought to be essential to self-deception, with the deception collapsing if accurate self-knowledge is ever attained. But it is important to realize that these hidden thoughts could be about anything – they are not necessarily about personal characteristics. For example, someone might self-deceive about racial equality. They could pay lip service to the idea that the races are on equal footing, but, unconsciously, they might think otherwise. The implicit racism does not concern one of their personal characteristics, but this is still a failure of self-knowledge so long as they do not know what they really think (associate, endorse, etc.).

Each of these failures of self-knowledge can occur without the others. I might self-deceptively believe that I am very athletic when I am not, and I need not have any hidden beliefs or thoughts to the contrary. The implicit racist example goes in the other direction. (If you think the implicit racism is in a sense about a personal characteristic – we all belong to a race, after all – then replace it with something clearly non-personal. A person can self-deceive about the existence of God, a partner's fidelity, whether people ever walked on the moon, and so on.) Those who advocate for the second kind of failure of self-knowledge are insisting on some conflict or inconsistency arising in an at least partially opaque mind. In contrast, we are supposing that I am single-mindedly deluded about my athleticism. It certainly is possible, however, for these two kinds of self-knowledge failure to co-exist – I might exaggerate the degree of my charity, but deep down I know that I am selfish. Each failure of self-knowledge could be blameworthy for distinct reasons – the former for its partiality, the latter for its lack of reflection.

While I have recommended distinguishing these two failures of self-knowledge, Richard Holton (2001) argues that self-deception is always *about* the self because it always involves false beliefs about the self. His position collapses the supposed distinction between the two failures of self-knowledge. In defense of his claim, he argues that we self-deceive about *subject matters*, as opposed to individual beliefs. There is likely truth in this. The self-deceptive father does not believe simply that his son has not been doing drugs, but also that he is a "good kid" in other regards as well. The motives for self-deception might not be directed at a single proposition either, but rather at a cluster (subject matter). Holton claims that even with self-deception that is ostensibly not about the self – say, the husband's self-deception about his wife's fidelity – there is a false self-referential belief:

> I think that it is very likely that we will very soon stumble upon some areas where he is making a mistake about himself: he thinks he is giving both sides a fair hearing, weighing the evidence equally, when he is not. He will be mistaken about whether he is living up to his own belief-forming standards. (Holton, 2001: 60)

But why think that the self-deceived are this reflective? It is doubtful that most self-deceivers give such thought to how their beliefs and thoughts stand against their own epistemic standards. The self-deceived cuckold need not think that he has given a fair weighing of the evidence for and against his wife's fidelity. He is likely not to give that a thought at all. Further, in a very intuitive sense, the cuckold is deceived about his wife's fidelity, not his own belief-forming standards. Even if it were the case that he must have a false belief about his belief-forming standards as a necessary condition for self-deception, it is not clear that this would warrant describing it as self-deception about the self.

These failures of self-knowledge have been described in terms of the person's beliefs, but people are often unaware of other, lower level psychological attitudes that affect their behavior, emotions, and thought. The last couple decades have seen an explosion of research that theorizes and measures *implicit attitudes*. Implicit attitudes are often thought of as associations occuring outside of conscious awareness that have behavioral and other effects.[3] They are typically conceived as automatic responses that, unlike beliefs, are altered only by creating new habits rather than through rational adjustment. While implicit attitudes can generate behavior, their effects are more circumscribed as these attitudes reflect limited associations in contrast with the more holistic nature of belief (which is also, at least typically, accessible to consciousness). Implicit biases like racist or sexist associations are common examples, although implicit attitudes can be positive as well. Mere awareness of racist or sexist stereotypes can cause psychological associations (e.g., "black" and "crime"; "woman" and "cooking") that are disavowed at the level of conscious judgment.[4]

Discord among conscious beliefs and implicit attitudes might also be common for the self-deceived. They might consciously think and perhaps even believe that they are highly qualified professionals yet have implicit attitudes to the contrary. These implicit attitudes can percolate into behavior and emotion (causing avoidance behavior and anxiety), betraying their avowed optimism. This is another form that deep conflict can take, doing justice to doxastic tension without positing dual beliefs. These attitudes are different, however, from the unconscious true beliefs that a theorist like Audi thinks the self-deceived actively repress. Implicit attitudes are weaker states: They are typically not understood as full beliefs, and they are not actively repressed either. If they are not consciously accessible, rationally adjustable, or deliberately acquired or repressed, then it is less plausible that people are responsible for them. (Having said that, see Mandelbaum 2016 for argument that they are rationally adjustable belief states.) Regardless, it is customary to see self-deceptive falsehood as existing more in the controlled conscious mind than in the automatic unconsious mind. If the self-deceived are in any way accountable for their implicit attitudes, more often than not this will be to their credit, as these are more likely to contain remnants of the truth.

The history of philosophy has seen some prominent moral philosophers argue that self-deception is a morally worrisome failure of self-knowledge. In the 18th Century, Bishop Joseph Butler argued that the self-deceived tend to display both kinds of self-knowledge failure, especially as it concerns our moral character. Butler held that the root cause of vice is selfishness, and this is the driving force in our self-deceit as well:

> [V]ice in general consists in having an unreasonable and too great regard to ourselves, in comparison of others ... But whereas, in common and ordinary wickedness, this unreasonableness, this partiality and selfishness relates only, or chiefly, to the temper and passions; in the characters we are now considering, it reaches to the understanding, and influences the very judgement. (Butler, 1729/2017: 86–87)

As an astute moral psychologist, Butler recognized the pervasive effects of both hot biases and robust unconscious processing.

RESPONSIBILITY FOR SELF-DECEPTION   213

Selfishness provides the motive for partial thought, but how is self-ignorance actually achieved? We can extract three key elements to Butler's account. First, there is a lack of reflection and attention to personal characteristics. As Butler describes it, this behavior is intentional yet unconscious:

> It is as easy to close the eyes of the mind, as those of the body: and the former is more frequently done with wilfulness, and yet not attended to, than the latter; the actions of the mind being more quick and transient, than those of the senses. (Butler, 1729/2017: 89)

Second, while there is a general lack of reflection, Butler admits that the self-deceived often do have suspicions. These are not just suspicions about the truth of the self-deceptive proposition itself, but also about related pieces of evidence or behavior that should be "unknown or forgotten for ever." Robustly deceptive acts are sometimes necessary to quell these suspicions. He focuses on moral traits, describing the deception in the strongly intentionalist terms favored by Davidson:

> Yet you see his behaviour: he seeks indulgences for plain wickedness; which not being able to obtain, he glosses over that same wickedness, dresses it up in a new form, in order to make it pass off more easily with himself. That is, he deliberately contrives to deceive and impose upon himself, in a matter which he knew to be of the utmost importance. (Butler, 1729/2017: 65)

The self-deceived establish whatever evidential wiggle room they can – their suspicions are general and conscious, but the particular details underlying them are kept hidden. Third, there are not clear-cut and absolute rules for applying moral maxims. Self-deception about one's moral worth can be achieved by taking advantage of this ambiguity and tolerance for exceptions. There is no simple algorithm for determining moral worth, allowing plenty of opportunity for self-deceptive rationalization.

Butler thought that we are culpable for self-deception, in general, because it is a failure of both reason and reflection. These are the themes with which we opened our book. At its core, we are blameworthy for a partiality borne of selfishness:

> But if there be any such thing in mankind, as putting half-deceits upon themselves; which there plainly is, either by avoiding reflection, or (if they

do reflect) by religious equivocation, subterfuges, and palliating matters to themselves; by these means conscience may be laid asleep, and they may go on in a course of wickedness with less disturbance. (Butler, 1729/2017: 64)

We see that apart from the intrinsic badness of deception and selfishness in general, self-deception about our moral nature is especially problematic. It leads us to commit more immoral actions: We rationalize away morally questionable behavior, and we deceive ourselves about our defective character. In these ways, we fail to take corrective measures to change our sinful habits.

A short while later, Adam Smith (1759/1982) argued that our desire to think well of ourselves causes us to be unduly partial when retrospectively analyzing the morality of our actions. As with Butler, Smith claimed that this motivates us to take purposive steps to avoid facing undesirable truths about our own moral behavior. But the moral conscience's perspective, according to Smith, is supposed to be that of an *impartial* spectator, so such self-deceit is especially problematic. The damage done by self-deception is supposed to be extreme:

This self-deceit, this fatal weakness of mankind, is the source of half the disorders of human life. If we saw ourselves in the light in which others see us, or in which they would see us if they knew all, a reformation would generally be unavoidable. We could not otherwise endure the sight. (Smith, 1759/1982: 158–159)

Smith thought that the remedy is to appeal to the general moral rules that we have formulated as a response to observing the moral behavior of others. These general rules can serve as checks on the passions and our self-love, both of which induce partiality that can have inordinate influence in a given moment:

If he should allow himself to be so far transported by passions as to violate this rule, yet, even in this case, he cannot throw off altogether the awe and respect with which he has been accustomed to regard it. At the very time of acting, at the moment in which passion mounts the highest, he hesitates and trembles at the thought of what he is about to do: he is secretly conscious to himself that he is breaking through those measures of conduct which, in all his cool hours, he had resolved never to infringe. (Smith, 1759/1982: 161)

RESPONSIBILITY FOR SELF-DECEPTION 215

Our responsibility for self-deceit resides with this struggle.

There is a tradition of Christian philosophers in particular identifying self-deceptive self-ignorance as a source of immorality. Immanuel Kant, like Bishop Butler, falls into this category. In his typical manner, Kant emphasizes not so much the pride that comes with acting in accord with our conscience, but the relief that comes with doing right and avoiding punishment or a sense of guilt. Our consciences induce anxiety about the possibility of improper behavior, and they primarily drive us to alleviate anxiety by behaving properly (Kant, 1797/1996: 190–191). As many (e.g., Johnston and Barnes) have noted since Kant, self-deception often arises when there is a felt need to alleviate anxiety. So, self-deception concerning our conscience is predictable. To caution against this, Kant interprets the Delphic maxim to know thyself as applying specifically to our moral character:

> This command is "*know* (scrutinize, fathom) *yourself*," not in terms of your natural perfection (your fitness or unfitness for all sorts of discretionary or even commanded ends) but rather in terms of your moral perfection in relation to your duty. That is, know your heart – whether it is good or evil, whether the source of your actions is pure or impure. (Kant, 1797/1996: 191)

Kant notes that we have selfish desires ("wishes") to have a pure heart, and these lead to partiality. But we have a moral duty to issue impartial self assessments. As Kant describes it, this quest for moral self-knowledge is no picnic:

> Moral cognition of oneself, which seeks to penetrate into the depths (the abyss) of one's heart which are quite difficult to fathom, is the beginning of all human wisdom. For in the case of a human being, the ultimate wisdom, which consists in a harmony of a human being's will with its final end, requires him first to remove the obstacle within (an evil will actually present in him) and then to develop the original predisposition to a good will within him, which can never be lost. (Only the descent into the hell of self-cognition can pave the way to godliness.) (Kant, 1797/1996: 191)

Self-knowledge is not fun, but it is the moral thing to do.

Stephen Darwall (1988) argues that moral philosophers like Butler, Smith, and Kant give pride of place to self-deception because of the role that conscience plays in their moral theories. Their theories share a concern with constituting a good character. Darwall claims that self-deception is not intrinsically problematic for a consequentialist or even duty-based theorist (unless they add a special duty not to self-deceive). But it is especially problematic for character-based accounts of morality – constitutionalist accounts in particular – since self-deception compromises that very character. If we have a moral obligation to be guided by our own best judgment (conscience), then we have a moral obligation not to pervert that judgment. Our best judgment should be impartial, which self-deceivers are not. Worse yet, self-deceivers sometimes purposefully generate fictitious moral judgments. This is a culpable undermining of the core of one's morality – the task of creating a self with integrity – as understood by certain character-based moral theorists (Darwall, 1988: 424).

It is not just conscience-focused moral philosophers who assign negative responsibility for self-deception. It is also the major "sin" according to existentialist philosophers who prize authenticity and admonish bad faith. Like the moral philosophers before them, the existentialists focus on those types of self-deception that undermine their fundamental values. For existentialists, this will be self-deception about one's very being. The most well-known development of this existentialist thought is Sartre's notion of bad faith, although the seeds can be found with Kierkegaard. For Sartre, we exist as fundamentally creative beings. He famously held that, as a consequence of our radical freedom, people are radically responsible for their mental lives. Bad faith is no exception, and it is especially problematic because it opposes the basic ontological truth that each of us is a being-for-itself rather than a concrete given. Sartrean bad faith is just one form that self-deception can take, but existentialists will likely think that people are responsible for the other forms as well (e.g., the jealous husband, the biased father). This is because existentialists emphasize radical responsibility and tend to downplay the roles of the unconscious and external factors in our mental lives. Fundamentally, self-deception is an ethically culpable failure of self-knowledge.

§6.3 Rationality and responsibility

Even if there is not a failure of self-knowledge, the self-deceived at least fail to meet epistemic norms. But people are not always responsible, even epistemically responsible, for their epistemic shortcomings. There are honest mistakes of reasoning that people should not be blamed for making, like overestimates due to anchoring. Generally speaking, more deflationary accounts of self-deception will put the irrationality and responsibility for self-deception on par with what we find with other mistakes due to hot and cold biases. Sometimes there is heightened accountability because there is an expectation of vigilance or at least the avoidance of negligence (e.g., do not be influenced by partiality when deciding whom to hire), but many other times there will be none. Intentionalist and purposive (effortful) accounts make epistemic responsibility more likely, at least if these intentions and purposes can be known. It would be an epistemic sin to knowingly go against reason and the evidence.

Although we are sometimes responsible for our cognitive mistakes, Neil Levy (2004) argues that if a couple of widely accepted claims about the mind are true, then there is no responsibility for self-deception as such. These claims are the denial of the Cartesian thesis of the transparency of the mind and the denial of intentionalism. The former claim is now an established scientific fact, and it was even known by the likes of Bishop Butler, if not by Plato and many other predecessors. A lot of processing occurs outside of awareness, and we harbor many unconscious drives and associations. Even the conscious mind is not fully transparent to itself, especially across time. The second is a less well-known claim specific to self-deception. Traditional views that assigned moral responsibility for self-deception, like Butler's, thought of it in intentionalist terms. Levy argues that if this intentionalism is abandoned, then so, too, should moral and epistemic responsibility. Levy, along with most deflationists, also denies the dual belief requirement that often accompanies intentionalism, so it is not the case that the self-deceived are hiding from a known truth.

Yet, Levy points out that many deflationists still blame the self-deceived. He singles out Johnston and Barnes, who accuse the self-deceived of culpable "epistemic cowardice," all the while claiming that the process is subintentional. Levy concedes that the self-deceived can be held accountable for deliberately using autonomous means (i.e., brutely causal belief distortion) to alter their beliefs. But this is not the norm. Levy's primary target is, instead, the Mele-style deflationist who equates self-deception with certain kinds of hot bias. Since most people are not aware of these biases or their remedies, we generally are not responsible for them. Levy claims that responsibility arises only when special efforts are expected, and this occurs only when the subject matter is important and there are some doubts about it. Yet, he claims that these two conditions are rarely both met by the self-deceived. The second claim is singled out, as Levy thinks that the self-deceived rarely have doubts. While this may be true under deflationary accounts of the hot bias variety (think back to Mele's examples from §3.2), we know that many other theorists take nagging doubts or suspicions to be typical, if not necessary. Finally, Levy denies that we are responsible for having the character traits that make us prone to self-deceive, as it is unlikely that we have control over such traits (and control is necessary for responsibility). People are generally ignorant of the fact that they are violating the so-called ethics of belief.

At times Alfred Mele has suggested that self-deceivers are culpable because they can correct and control their hot biases. He points out familiar corrective measures: trying harder to gather evidence for both sides of an issue, encouraging skepticism, and generating a list of pros and cons (Mele, 2001: 103). Kent Bach (1981: 368) also believes that the self-deceived are responsible for their negligence. While not intentionally deceiving themselves, the self-deceived are epistemically careless and not protecting against the distorting influences of desire. But, again, is it reasonable to expect people to be aware of the effects of these desires? People self-identify with photographs of themselves that have been morphed to look more attractive, and well over half of university professors think they are better than average. Many of these enhancements are surely due to desires to be attractive or successful, but it seems a bit of a stretch to blame these people for the biases their desires produce. While these desires might be known, their influence on our beliefs remains unconscious. Why, then, is it any more blameworthy than the operation of a cold bias due to, say, the anchoring heuristic? In both cases, the influence is unconscious, but it can be somewhat regulated when pointed out and special efforts are made.

Jordi Fernandez (2013) continues the theme of negligence, claiming that conflicted self-deceivers are epistemically negligent for not knowing what they believe. (Fernandez acknowledges that his point does not hold for self-deception without conflict, as in most of Mele's examples.) The culpability arises because the self-deceived possess the grounds for the true first-order belief, and these should serve as grounds for the second-order belief as well. "Grounds" are the mental states that normally produce belief – e.g., perception, evidence, testimony. Fernandez accepts a model of self-knowledge according to which grounds reverberate up to higher levels of belief. To find out what you believe, you simply look at what you think is true. So, the self-deceived husband should believe that he believes his wife is unfaithful for the very same reason that he believes ("deep down") that she is unfaithful. Yet, Fernandez claims that the self-deceived fail to have their second-order belief accord with the grounds that they possess. This is supposed to show them to

RESPONSIBILITY FOR SELF-DECEPTION   219

be epistemically negligent. But we might hesitate: There is no guarantee that they can access these grounds without special effort or that the mechanisms evading these grounds can reasonably be controlled by the agent.

Self-deception and biased reasoning can be corrected and controlled to at least some extent in at least some cases. Bishop Butler (1729/2017: 90) recommended a particular heuristic to help overcome self-partiality and its effects on belief. We are to imagine that someone is setting out to defame us, and then ask ourselves what character weaknesses he would focus on. The idea is that those who self-deceive have some suspicions as to what their weaknesses really are. The defamation test is supposed to heighten those suspicions, and this alone can have the effect of undermining the self-deceit. Butler also asks us to take on the perspective of an impartial audience – the jury, so to speak, before whom the defamation case will be presented. We are not to consider what we think is true, but what these impartial jurors will believe is true. Self-deceit is supposed to be vanquished by this combination of raising the stakes and taking an impartial perspective. Extending the impartiality exercise, Butler goes so far as to say that we should apply the Golden Rule to our judgments and thoughts. The idea is that whatever other people should believe of us, we should believe of ourselves. Alternatively, whatever we would believe of another in our position, we should believe of ourselves. The same decision procedure that holds for action ("do unto others ...") should hold for judgment.

Not only can biases and self-deception be treated and controlled through epistemic instruction by philosophers, academic psychologists, statisticians and the like, they are also amenable to therapeutic treatment. Several psychological disorders involve elements of bias and self-deception. For example, those suffering from bulimia nervosa tend to overestimate both the importance of body image and their body size. Indeed, biased and perhaps even self-deceptive thinking are thought to be central to a range of eating disorders:

> The transdiagnostic cognitive behavioral account of the eating disorders extends the original theory of bulimia nervosa to all eating disorders. According to this theory, the overevaluation of shape and weight and their control is central to the maintenance of all eating disorders. Most of the other clinical features can be understood as resulting directly from this psychopathology. It results in dietary restraint and restriction; preoccupation with thoughts about food and eating, weight and shape; the repeated checking of body shape and weight or its avoidance; and the engaging in extreme methods of weight control. (Murphy et al., 2010: 614–615)

These overevaluations can be treated quite effectively through cognitive behavioral therapy, which has been proved to be the most effective treatment for adult patients. One component of cognitive behavioral therapy is the treatment of cognitive biases by changing thought and behavioral practices (Murphy et al., 2010: 617). These non-medicinal treatments could, in theory, be executed by the patient herself, but it is not expected that most people possess this therapeutic knowledge or discipline. Regardless, professional care greatly improves treatment outcomes. So while these biases can be controlled, it does not follow that the patients were in any way responsible for them. The fact that we can control biases and self-deception with professional guidance or great effort does not show that we are responsible for them in ordinary, unsupported circumstances.

It is hard to determine with any precision how much self-awareness and self-scrutiny we should demand of people. Two additional variables are likely significant for deflationary accounts: the intensity of the hot bias and the degree of the deviation from rationality. People are probably less culpable for biases resulting from calm, standing desires that are low in phenomenological intensity (e.g., standing desires to be attractive or successful) than they are for the biasing influences of strongly felt, transitory emotions and desires (e.g., lust for the woman at the bar or anger at a spouse). This might sound counter-intuitive, as people talk about being carried away by powerful emotions, and the law tends to mitigate punishment for crimes committed in the heat of passion (e.g., manslaughter versus first-degree murder). But when the desire or emotion is strongly felt, you are more aware of the desire itself and you should be more aware of its possible influence on your thoughts: "Take a breath and think about it. You know how you get when you're angry." It is harder to practice that mindset for the calm desires that are always present but seldom felt. Stronger emotions and desires also produce even more extreme deviations from rationality – e.g., a sense of embarrassment causing defensiveness about a child's abilities, or accusations of infidelity borne of anger. Whatever its cause, we expect people to be aware of extreme deviations from the evidence.

We have mostly been talking about responsibility for getting into self-deception. The early stages of self-deception can be innocent enough, starting with a small bias favoring a belief. But like a small lie, it can grow or simply become more difficult to maintain without additional measures. In some cases, responsibility might arise only as greater efforts are needed to sustain it. This fits with the general theme that with greater agential involvement comes greater responsibility. As the self-deceptive process unfolds, this can happen in a couple of salient ways. First, over time the evidence can accumulate against the favored belief. Self-deception, like belief more generally, has inertia – we tend to continue believing what we already believed. But at some point it really should be abandoned. It was once not so obvious that his son was using drugs, and the father could easily self-deceive that all was well. But over time only a fool (or self-deceiver) would not see that the son has a drug problem. As the evidence shifts dramatically, so can responsibility. Second, one's cognitive peers can call one out for one's self-deception. We should respect the opinions of others, at least to the point of prompting self-scrutiny and reevaluation, and when we fail to do so we become more involved in an effort to hide from reality. If you have been warned, you become more responsible for your action or condition. When the self-deceiver digs in his heels in response to these factors, his responsibility increases.

Others will wait to assign responsibility for the actions generated by self-deception, but not necessarily for the self-deceptive belief itself. Similar maneuvers are made in other areas, as some argue that actions due to implicit biases can be controlled even if the implicit biases themselves are not under control (Mendoza et al., 2010). This gets complicated however, because not all theorists agree that self-deception results in belief. Take the view that self-deception is either a fantasy or pretense (Lazar, Gendler). There might not be anything wrong with the fantasizing or pretending in itself, but responsibility arises when these illusions influence our real actions. This fits with the general view that accountability arises only for what is public or impacts others. Fantasy and pretense can normally be segregated from serious action, and some self-deceivers are the rare exceptions (perhaps along with schizophrenics, the delusional, and some others). But if self-deception results in outright false belief instead (going well beyond implicit attitudes, as well), then it is a bit more difficult to blame people specifically for acting on their beliefs. Philosophers tend to think that belief, unlike fantasy and pretense, entails fairly robust behavioral dispositions. If so, it seems better to blame people for erroneously believing in the first place (in the spirit of Clifford) rather than blaming them for acting out of the misguided beliefs they have acquired.

The discussion in this chapter has been largely premised on the idea that self-deception is bad, something blameworthy. But, as we will see in Chapter 7, some argue on empirical grounds that it is actually beneficial. There are also traditions in philosophy that see some self-deception as essential or even noble. Plato (*Republic*: 414b–415c) spoke of "noble lies" that we should tell to others, and perhaps there are noble, or at least tolerable, self-deceptive "lies." Ernest Becker (1973) claimed that human greatness is achieved by living under a vital lie that denies our mortality. Perhaps we should live under the illusion that our projects – maybe even human life and morality itself – have greater importance than they really do. If not actually praiseworthy, these self-deceptions might be tolerable coping mechanisms given the meagerness of the human condition.

Philosophers, as lovers of wisdom, might be guilty of fetishizing truth. The truth is our business, but that does not mean that it is always so valuable. (If all you have is a hammer, you see everything as a nail.) While people should not self-deceive so as to justify and permit immorality, this does not mean that motivated ignorance is always bad or that full awareness (especially self-knowledge) is always good. It is at least conceptually possible that self-deception could make one a better parent, spouse, employee, citizen, or person. Self-deception could be a nearly essential requirement, in at least some circumstances, for maintaining motivation, overlooking faults in another and preserving a valued personal relationship, or keeping a good mood so that one is pleasant and healthy. In those circumstances in which it is an essential or good means to further human flourishing, why would we blame or otherwise hold one accountable for a natural coping mechanism? Pragmatist philosopher Ferdinand Schiller (1924) argued that belief should be conceived more as falling under the norms of biology (survival and flourishing) rather than the norms of philosophy (truth). As such, he concluded that some self-deception is an "essential requisite of human life."[5] In effect, it is no more blameworthy than hunger, blinking, or sexual desire.

§6.4 Does context matter?

Responsibility for our biases and self-deception varies with our knowledge and control over them. Perhaps it also varies according to the "heat" of the motivation and the degree of deviation from rationality that it induces. In addition to these four factors (knowledge, control, heat, and irrationality), responsibility for self-deception is likely sensitive to context as well. In some contexts, a person might not be accountable for self-deception at all, as there is no expectation of critical self-scrutiny or impartiality. In other contexts, they might be accountable for their self-deception, but their responsibility is mitigated. Context changes the expected level of epistemic vigilance.

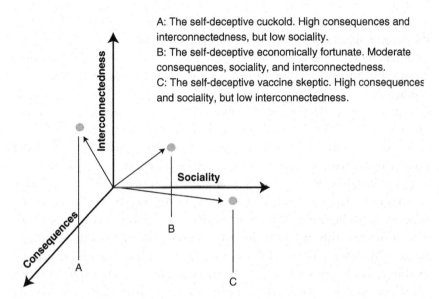

Figure 6.1 Modeling the contextual factors relevant to responsibility

Three variables are especially important as contextual dimensions that affect responsibility: consequences, sociality, and interconnectedness (see Figure 6.1). These three factors tend to heighten the costs and benefits of self-deception, and as the stakes rise so does the responsibility. The idea is that when the stakes are higher we should be more vigilant, so there is a greater likelihood or degree of responsibility for potentially costly self-deception. These contextual dimensions mirror Clifford's reasons for taking belief seriously, although he stated that all beliefs have significant values (at least potentially) along each dimension.

The consequences are the expected results of acting or remaining inactive out of a particular form of self-deception. Examples include the harms of letting your son go out with his trouble-making friends (continued drug use) or of deciding not to go to the doctor (untreated disease). These consequences could befall either the self-deceiver herself or others, as in Clifford's tragic story of the sinking ship. As moral responsibility tends to rise when others are involved, we should be especially interested in the consequences that others could suffer from our self-deception. (Ideally, models of the contextual factors would distinguish personal consequences and consequences for others.) Other things being equal, we should expect greater responsibility as the expected consequences rise. Consequences cannot be known with certainty, so the relevant calculation will be risk times potential harms/benefits.

Next, responsibility tends to rise with the social connections by which the deception can spread. Self-deception is less private when it is transmitted to others by outright testimony, or others perceive our self-deception and acquire it through imitation or other autonomous means. This dimension captures the potential for our self-deception to function as a social signal or contribute to collective self-deception. The social dimension also has the potential to significantly magnify the consequences of self-deception.

Interconnectedness refers to the extent to which the self-deceptive belief influences the person's other beliefs. Just as it is a truism that you cannot stop with just one lie, self-deceptive beliefs typically require auxiliary falsehoods for their sustenance. Depending on the degree to which the evidence is overwhelming (under a normal interpretation) or the person values consistency, this can be limited or extensive. Maintaining this act might require discrediting the motives of others who challenge the self-deception or simply hold opposing views. The more interconnected a self-deceptive belief becomes, the greater the opportunities for further consequences and social transmission as well.

Self-deception that might seem pretty innocuous in itself can be quite damaging due to its consequences, sociality, and interconnections. Suppose that a public figure has a personal disdain for the sitting U.S. President and, out of a motive of jealousy or disdain, biases his thought so that he comes to believe that this President was not actually born in the United States, rendering him an illegitimate President in his mind. So what? What does it matter if he has this silly belief? Who cares what he thinks? Well, maintaining this self-deception requires auxiliary deceptions – the President must be hiding a lot about his past, documents must have been forged, etc. In addition to these interconnections, the self-deception has major consequences due to the social effects of the deception. Other people come to believe the same falsehood, often due to similar motives (collective self-deception). The consequences can be enormous. Racist and xenophobic fears could be fed, and the credibility of the President could be undermined. As Clifford exhorted, even "innocent" self-deception can have disastrous results and lead to a dangerous disregard for the truth. So, perhaps there should be responsibility and vigilance for even ostensibly low stakes self-deception.

That example might sound extreme because the person has significant social influence and wields great power. But everyday people can also contribute to collective self-deception, raising the stakes and culpability for them as well. Think of vaccination skeptics who post on social media, or

RESPONSIBILITY FOR SELF-DECEPTION 225

those who self-deceptively exaggerate the rate at which immigrants commit crimes, spreading their deception to others and the ballot box.

We have been discussing responsibility for episodic self-deception. But even if the content of a particular self-deceptive belief does not strongly interconnect with other beliefs, it can further the development of a self-deceptive habit or character trait. One can acquire a disposition for self-deceptive or biased thinking just as one can acquire a disposition for gullibility or outright dishonesty, as Clifford also noted. In this way, self-deception about intrinsically inconsequential matters can gain greater importance. Do some people have a general tendency to flee from reality in self-deceptive ways? And is this tendency, in at least some cases, acquired from habits that can be altered? Marcia Baron (1988: 438–439) thinks that the badness of self-deception consists in the character traits that it breeds – allowing wishes to shape our lives, furthering close-mindedness, avoiding self-scrutiny. These are more than just incidents, but kinds of people we can become: wishful, close-minded, unreflective thinkers. The wrongness consists in not taking care or responsibility for oneself as a belief-forming agent. Maybe responsibility for such character traits is derivative from responsibility for individual episodes, which may or may not be controllable. Even if the context does not make an episode of self-deception high stakes in itself, its contribution to furthering a potentially harmful character trait should be considered.

Summary

- Some think that we are morally responsible for our beliefs because they generate actions and have public effects. The issue of responsibility is complicated, however, if belief is not under our voluntary control. Some cognitive habits can be controlled, but others operate below consciousness and might not respond to reason (e.g., implicit attitudes).
- Some hold that self-deception is always about the self or that it is a failure of self-knowledge. There are prominent moral philosophers who condemn self-deception as a failure of self-knowledge that allows immorality to fester. It is an empirical question, however, how self-knowledge failures impact human flourishing.
- Self-deception is a kind of irrationality that can sometimes be known and controlled. In these cases, we might be responsible for our irrationality, since we can be more reflective and raise our standards (e.g., Butler's defamation test). Context will be important to assessing responsibility.

Recommended reading

W.K. Clifford's "The Ethics of Belief" is the classic text to start with if you are interested in responsibility for belief.

For a classic criticism of self-deception on moral grounds, read Bishop Butler's Sermon 7 and Sermon 10 from *Fifteen Sermons Preached at the Rolls Chapel*, as well as his "Sermon Preached Before the House of Lords."

Darwall (1988) is a very good discussion of the role that self-deception plays in conscience-based moral theories.

The best book-length philosophical treatment of the ethics of self-deception is probably Mike Martin's *Self-Deception and Morality*. It covers the major areas discussed in this chapter: conscience-based treatments, existentialism and authenticity, knowledge and control over biases, and the vital lies tradition. Neil Levy (2004, 2014) offers insightful and scientifically informed skeptical arguments against our responsibility for various biases and self-deception proper.

Notes

1 For a sophisticated and helpful discussion of the varieties of doxastic control and their relations to responsibility, see William Alston (1988).

2 How should we deal with such a person? Here is some good advice from philosopher Nikk Effingham: http://theconversation.com/how-to-reason-with-flat-earthers-it-may-not-help-though-95160

3 While implicit attitudes were standardly construed as associations, in recent years there has been a flurry of philosophical activity arguing for alternative or supplementary accounts, especially so as to accommodate their propositional content. These include Gendler's (2008) notion of alief, Levy's (2015) patchy endorsements, Machery's (2016) character traits, and Sullivan-Bissett's (2019) unconscious imaginings. Frankish (2016) and Mandelbaum (2016) argue for the more radical claim that these implicit attitudes are outright beliefs.

4 The most well-known test for these associations is the Implicit Association Test (IAT), but there are others. For an introduction to the philosophical issues related to implicit bias, see: https://plato.stanford.edu/entries/implicit-bias/

5 The discussion in Mike Martin (1986: 119–120) drew my attention to Schiller's little known work.

7

FUNCTIONS AND COST-BENEFIT ANALYSIS

7.1 The costs of false belief
7.2 Psychological benefits
7.3 Social benefits
7.4 Biological benefits

Whether or not people should be held responsible for their self-deception, we can assess its worth. In a very practical sense, is it good or bad? And what, if anything, is the function or purpose of self-deception? Many particular acts of self-deception have a proximate goal (e.g., desire satisfaction), but there might also be larger functions that self-deception in general serves. Answering these questions will take us beyond philosophy proper, leading us to psychology, biology, economics, and other human and social sciences. Philosophers of self-deception can learn by interacting with these literatures, gaining insight into how self-deception is shaped by these goods and thereby discovering whether it is even condemnable. In return, philosophers can use their knowledge of the underlying philosophical problems of self-deception to better suggest lines of promising empirical research. By knowing the benefits, if any, of self-deception we can get a good idea of the functions that it serves. Philosophers have traditionally held that self-deception is harmful, but empirical research might reveal that to be a naïve or at least incomplete view.

§7.1 The costs of false belief

Before discussing the potential benefits of self-deception, we should address the quite general costs that we tend to incur when we have false or unsupported beliefs. In this discussion, I will assume that self-deception results in false belief, although strictly speaking, this is not necessarily always the case. People can self-deceive into rationally unsupported beliefs that just so happen to be true. And we have seen that some think that the self-deceived actually retain the true belief and never quite achieve the false. Still, self-deception inclines people toward falsity: Unsupported beliefs and thoughts tend to be false and misleading.

The most general cost is that falsity undermines goal achievement. Our beliefs guide our actions, and they should guide our actions. Beliefs are representations of reality, and we are more likely to achieve successful outcomes if we represent reality correctly (at least to a reasonable approximation). If you want to remain healthy, it is best to have an accurate view of your condition so that you know what treatments to seek. If you want to have a successful career, it is best to have an accurate view of your strengths and the steps necessary to succeed at that profession. Sometimes people do get lucky and benefit from false beliefs. Maybe you would have died from a rare side-effect if you had sought the recommended treatments, or perhaps you do not have an aptitude for business but a wealthy benefactor takes you under his wing anyway. While this commonly happens, conditions are not to be evaluated by their unexpected consequences. Instead, we should evaluate conditions by their probable results. And when we have a false belief or act on something other than a true belief (e.g., a fantasy or pretense), we are acting on information that makes it less likely that we will get what we want.

Ryan McKay and Daniel Dennett (2009) argue this point from the perspective of evolutionary biology. Their question is whether any "misbeliefs" – by which they mean any false belief, such as those that may be produced by self-deception – would have been "systematically adaptive" in our evolutionary past. Of course we have been wired with brains that frequently produce false beliefs, sometimes quite predictably. This has been observed and documented in the heuristics and biases literature, to give just one example. Well-adapted cognitive systems generate falsity in this innocuous

FUNCTIONS AND COST-BENEFIT ANALYSIS 229

sense, but this is not enough to show that we are wired for misbelief. They are questioning whether our brains have been *designed* specifically to produce a false picture of reality as a biological adaptation. Or we could ask whether, within an individual lifetime, some have adapted (learned) to seek falsity. Is falsity ever good (in the systematic sense, not just as an exception), rather than simply tolerable?

Among the cases McKay and Dennett consider are a jealous husband on the lookout for infidelity and animals that skew beliefs about the toxicity of the food in their environment out of caution (error management theory). One could argue that their goals are furthered by having beliefs that skew toward the false – erring on the side of believing the spouse is unfaithful or the berries are poisonous – just because the contrary mistake would be so costly to them. As the jealous husband example shows, these costs can plausibly arise in the context of self-deception. But McKay and Dennett (2009: 500–501) claim that caution can be achieved through simple action policies (absent underlying cognitive, or at least belief-like, states), epistemic vigilance, and doubts that fall short of genuine belief. The only exceptions they allow as possibly adaptive false beliefs are positive illusions, which we will discuss shortly.

On the other side, some have argued that truth (or evidentially supported belief) is not the aim of cognitive systems that have been designed to further the organism's survival and reproduction. Even if beliefs are primarily for the sake of successful goal achievement, there is no conceptual necessity linking true or evidentially supported belief to optimal goal achievement. While such a connection is generally assumed, Stephen Stich (1990) argues that philosophers tend to overvalue truth. Instead, he holds that there is no reason to think that systems designed by natural selection would have a robust alignment toward the truth.

Of course, there are limits to our ability to get at the truth. Natural cognitive systems, like artificial systems, are designed so as to allow for an acceptable level of error. This is normally not because truth is unimportant; rather, it is because better cognitive systems would be too costly or are practically unattainable. Costs include the allocation of energy to develop and maintain a better brain, the search for more evidence, time spent assessing the evidence, etc. In addition, there are necessary and contingent limitations on our very ability to get at the truth regardless of cost – e.g., better solutions might not have presented themselves in design space, the physical laws of optics put a cap on vision accuracy, organic brains are essentially prone to fatigue, etc. In these ways, at least some level of falsity

230 FUNCTIONS AND COST-BENEFIT ANALYSIS

is acceptable or inevitable. But these facts do not acount for self-deceptive falsity. Self-deceivers make an effort to distort their representations away from the truth or, as the deflationists would prefer to put it, simply have a motive that distorts a cognitive system otherwise capable of getting at the truth. It might even be more effortful to self-deceive than to get at the truth, so the falsity is not to be accounted for as a merely tolerable cost. As we saw in the last chapter, we often think it is a treatable condition, so it is not an inevitable result either.

There are common forms of self-deception as well as thematic benefits that they bestow. Common reasons for self-deception include:

> *Feeling good*: It feels good to think that your son is not using drugs. It feels bad to think that you have a serious sickness.
>
> *Staying motivated*: You are more likely to persevere at a task if you overestimate your chances of success.
>
> *Selling yourself to others*: Other people believe your self-enhancing assessments, making them more likely to hire, date, or befriend you.
>
> *Getting along*: You gain social goods and are viewed as a cooperative partner when you self-deceive about patriotic, religious, or other in-group matters.

These reasons and benefits are certainly not mutually exclusive – e.g., by overestimating your chances for career success, you might be gaining all four categories of benefit. Still, these are distinct benefits that can come apart. There are also corresponding costs specific to these forms of false belief. That which makes you feel good can leave you inert or unwilling to take the proper corrective measures. That which motivates you can also lead you to misdirect your energies on a project with little chance of success, leading to disappointment. Your self-enhancement might cause others to eventually be disappointed and feel resentment toward you when they discover the truth. And by deceiving yourself about your in-group's merits you make it less likely that problems will be addressed, and you might be elevating what you take to be the group's interests to your own detriment.

The general cost is that false beliefs tend to frustrate goal achievement, but the extent of these costs varies quite a bit by content and context. Dunning, Heath, and Suls (2004) examined the specific costs of false self-assessments (a very common form of self-deception) for the real world settings of health care, education, and the workplace. Unrealistic optimism about one's health is problematic, as perceived vulnerability is one of the most significant motivators for seeking preventative care. On the other hand, unwarranted pessimism can also explain failures to seek out treatment, this time out of a sense of hopelessness. Concerning education, 68% of students were found to assign themselves higher grades than would their teachers (Dunning, Heath, and Suls, 2004: 85). As with health care, these overestimates rationalize not taking measures that could fix a problem. One of the most important attributes for educational success is knowing what you need to learn, but self-deceptive self-enhancement undermines this. Finally, in the workplace, they note that CEOs in particular tend to be overconfident and unchallenged (we might think of Donald Trump or Elon Musk), potentially causing financial ruin to thousands of employees or investors.

The costs of self-deception on a specific occasion will inevitably depend on many factors. Here, too, recall the dimensions of consequences, sociality, and interconnectedness. In the next few sections, we will discuss the costs and benefits specific to these four common reasons for self-deception – feeling good, staying motivated, selling yourself, and getting along.

§7.2 Psychological benefits

While an accurate picture of reality is often thought to be part of good mental health (if not also a moral requirement), some psychological research has supported the view that modest deviations from accuracy might be adaptive for mental health. These deviations are largely due to the six motivational biases that we discussed back in §1.2: self-enhancement, in-group, self-serving attributions, status quo, optimism, and illusions of control. These biases produce predictable, cross-cultural forms of self-deception (Mezulis et al., 2004). Why does this happen, and is it good or bad for our psychological well-being? Shelley Taylor and Jonathon Brown (1988), in a highly influential review and analysis, argued that these "positive illusions" are adaptive. They focused on three categories of positive illusion directed specifically at the self: self-enhancement, illusions of control, and optimism. The psychological benefits they claim from such biases include boosts to self-esteem and enhanced goal pursuit, although claims to such benefits are controversial (Colvin, Block, and Funder, 1995; Robins and Beer, 2001; Taylor and Brown, 1988). While not all theorists (e.g., intentionalists) would classify these biases as self-deception, the biased beliefs that Taylor and Brown examined are typical of many instances of positive self-deception.

Freud saw self-deception, in the form of repression, as an unconscious defense mechanism put in place to protect us from harsh realities. Such repression is also the source of neuroses and phobias, which are supposed to be treated by lifting the repression. Freud acknowledged, however, that positive reality distortion is often beneficial (Freud, 1966). Supporting this line, contemporary experimental psychology has confirmed that self-deceptive ego protection can aid in mental health, at least insofar as a more accurate self-conception tends to align with lower self-esteem and depression. This is the phenomenon of *depressive realism* as noted by Taylor and Brown:

> Does there exist a group of individuals that is accepting of both the good and the bad aspects of themselves as many views of mental health maintain the normal person is? Suggestive evidence indicates that individuals who are low in self-esteem, moderately depressed, or both are more balanced in self-perceptions. (Taylor and Brown, 1988: 196)

Those who are neither depressed nor low in self-esteem are not necessarily self-deceiving, of course. But this at least suggests an incentive to do so. It should be emphasized that we are talking about moderate levels of both depression and cognitive distortion – those who are extremely depressed often have an unjustifiably negative conception of reality. Another issue is whether moderately depressed people are just generally better attuned to reality (whether it is self-interested or not), or if the biases we see with non-depressed people instead arise only with respect to personal matters. The former would indicate that a cold bias is at work, whereas the latter makes it more likely that it is a hot bias.

Many forms of self-enhancement are captured by the Better-Than-Average-Effect (BTAE). This psychological construct refers to our tendency to rate ourselves as better than the average peer for a host of positive attributes. The effect is "robust and pervasive" for psychologically normal and healthy people, extending along traits as diverse as: leadership, athleticism, sociability, material wealth, humanity, invulnerability, professional success, romantic success, happiness, and even immunity to the BTAE (Sedikides and Alicke, 2012: 307–308). The BTAE does not just exploit ambiguities in self-assessment, as it is displayed even by those who have good reason to have more modest rankings. A study showed that prisoners convicted of a range of offenses rated themselves above average for eight of nine social-moral traits when explicitly compared to non-prisoners. The one trait for which they did not display the effect? – law abiding (Sedikides et al., 2014). This effect is not only widespread, but it also appears to be effortless. Paulhus, Graf, and Van Selst (1989) found that positive self-presentation is even greater when the self-evaluation is performed under cognitive load. This suggests that the biases are automatic and unconscious, and that we might actually make efforts to lessen the phenomenon.

The most common psychological explanation for positive self-enhancement is that it is for the sake of improving affect, mood, or self-esteem. This is the first functional benefit of positive illusions discussed by Taylor and Brown (1988: 198), who conclude that these illusions promote happiness. Indeed, it has been shown that, cross-culturally, those who think well of themselves and are optimistic about the future report greater happiness and life satisfaction. Not only is happiness intrinsically good, it is also instrumental in producing a variety of other goods:

> Compared with unhappy people, happy people are more creative, sociable, and energetic, and more caring, helpful, and involved in community affairs ... They also live longer. (Marshall and Brown, 2008: 21–22)

It is normally granted that genuinely believed self-enhancement at least helps regulate mood in the short term, and the influences on life expectancy and interpersonal relations (a more disputed matter) reveal potential long-term benefits as well. In these psychological investigations, the self-enhancing tendencies that produce these benefits supposedly represent full-fledged beliefs. As we have discussed in detail, it is less clear that the philosopher's notion of self-deception involves genuine belief rather than a more tenuous state with correspondingly suspect benefits. Perhaps the phenomena that psychologists describe as self-enhancing or self-deceptive belief warrant a more subtle description also.

While self-enhancement for the sake of happiness is commonly referred to as a defense mechanism, self-deception can play either an offensive or a defensive role in promoting happiness. That is, it could preemptively promulgate an overly positive view even without any evidence or threat challenging one's value, or the self-deception could instead arise as a reaction to threatening information. While there is an across the board tendency to default to self-enhancement, experimental studies have supported the view that threats to self-esteem and other challenges make self-enhancement more likely (Roese and Olson, 2007).

234 FUNCTIONS AND COST-BENEFIT ANALYSIS

We have been discussing self-enhancement and optimism more as standing, general traits. Self-deception, in contrast, is often seen as situational and targeted. Whereas self-enhancement in general seems to be driven by deep drives shared by most of us, self-deception is more targeted because it is driven by psychological desires or emotions that are reactive to personal and contingent events occurring in their lives. The self-deception is tailored to matters that are especially important to the individual or are especially precarious for them (e.g., success at their particular career, having one's son be drug free). The self-deception might be derivative from more general self-enhancing and optimistic tendencies (distal explanation), but it is more episodic and psychologically driven. Self-enhancement in general is often not driven by desires that are present or easily accessible to consciousness, although this is more frequently the case for self-deception. As such, self-deception provides the pleasure or relief of desire satisfaction, much like we saw with the Johnston-Barnes theory that self-deception is for the sake of anxiety reduction.

Just because self-deceptive self-enhancement can improve affect, mood, and self-esteem, it does not follow that it has the function of so doing. It could be that this is just a fortunate by-product. There are various ways we could test the functional claim. For one, we could see if positive self-deception is sensitive to self-affirmation. That is, when one already feels good about oneself, does one self-enhance less? If so, it is more likely that the self-enhancement is to regulate affect, mood, and self-esteem. Remember that self-enhancement can also extend to the groups to which we belong. Sherman and Kim (2005) examined "group-serving judgments" by members of athletic teams. It was hypothesized that these group-favoring biases are also for the sake of boosting individual self-esteem. Sherman and Kim draw on self-affirmation theory: People are motivated to think of themselves as competent and valuable, and challenges to this can lead to self-deceptive enhancement. But the effects of this motive can be mitigated through an exercise of misdirection in which the person attends to their other valuable traits. Sherman and Kim conducted a field study in which they questioned athletes (volleyball and basketball players) immediately after their games and had them assign responsibility for their win/loss to self-factors, team factors, or external factors. Those who were non-affirmed displayed both self- and group-serving biases (e.g., those who won attributed their success to self and group factors; those who lost attributed their failure to external factors). However, there was very little difference between winners and losers who had been self-affirmed first – feeling good about themselves greatly mitigated and nearly eliminated the bias. These results also suggest therapeutic treatments if, indeed, the self-deception is something that should be corrected. We could also look for alternative explanations. If self-enhancement is sensitive to moderators and effects distinct from affect, mood, and self-esteem, then that lends some support to its serving a different function.

Thus far we have focused on positive illusions, but as we know there are negative illusions and self-deception as well. Negative self-deception can hurt self-esteem at least as much as positive self-deception can boost it. It is hard to see the jealous husband's unjustified belief in his wife's infidelity or the anorexic's belief that she is overweight as functioning for the sake of improving affect or self-esteem. They more plausibly function to motivate vigilance so as to deter or brace for unwelcome outcomes. But even here there is a role for ego protection: To overlook "failures" in these regards would be deeply damaging to their sense of self.

In addition to self-enhancement and optimism, Taylor and Brown (1988) single out illusions of control. People like to think that they have control over outcomes in their lives, and this is important to their self-esteem. Once again, those who are depressed are less likely to succumb to this bias (Taylor and Brown, 1988: 196). So, psychological health can incentivize self-deception about one's efficacy. The illusion of control can also aid goal pursuit. Those who think that they can succeed at a task are more likely to persevere, so positive self-deception might be adaptive for long-term tasks that have a reasonable chance of success (Marshall and Brown, 2008: 20–21). Unfortunately, the illusion of control can also have disastrous effects, as when someone thinks that he can control his physical health by thought alone or a gambler believes that she can influence a toss of the dice.

Goal pursuit is mediated by other forms of self-enhancement and self-esteem. It is intuitive that a person is more likely to pursue a task if they think that they are good at it, so it is logical that self-enhancement for a trait would tend to produce greater motivation within that domain (Taylor and Brown, 1988: 199). Yet, the evidence is not so clear. Robins and Beer (2001) focused on the longer term effects of positive illusions in a natural environment. They performed a longitudinal study that started with incoming college students self-assessing for academic ability. These assessments were then compared to their more objective incoming academic measurements (e.g., SAT scores and high school GPA) so as to detect for positive illusions. Robins and Beer found that the self-enhancers tended toward narcissism, and they self-attributed for success but externalized blame for failures. Over their college careers, these positive illusions negatively impacted both happiness and academic performance. Self-enhancers had declines in self-esteem over their college careers, did not receive higher grades compared to those who accurately self-assessed, and neither were they more likely to graduate college. These negative effects may be due to the mismatch between expectations and actual performance.

We might wonder if some negative self-deception could actually boost motivation by providing incentives to work harder and improve. If so, the negative self-deception would likely have to be moderate – extremely negative self-assessments or judgments of efficacy will tend to undermine goal achievement. We find examples in some cases of *learned helplessness* or *defeatism*. This is the converse of the illusion of control – the illusion of a lack of control over one's life. Sometimes this is not so much an illusion, however, as many fall into this condition because they have genuinely been rendered helpless or have sustained many setbacks, much like the unfortunate dogs in Seligman's (1972) original experiments. In these cases, the evidence might actually support their attitudes, so it is not accurate to describe it as self-deception. The sense of helplessness is also motivated, however, as it helps to protect the ego by lowering expectations and prepares the self for failure or unpleasant outcomes. In this regard, negative self-deception can have a similar function as self-handicapping. These extreme mindsets of causal inefficacy are not conducive to improving motivation. But it is possible that moderate levels of negatively skewed self-assessment could actually enhance motivation for some personality types, so long as the person still believes that they have control over the outcome. A lesson we have learned is that if self-deception is to enhance happiness or motivation, it is more likely at the moderate levels (be it positive or negative self-deception).

§7.3 Social benefits

Self-deception is not merely a private matter, and it could serve a social function. Not only can other people feed our self-deception (e.g., collective, imposed, baited, and enabled), but we can receive social goods and suffer harms by acting out of or displaying our self-deception to others. Certain types of self-deception – especially positive self-deception – might be initiated for this very reason. Regardless, social effects should be considered in any cost-benefit analysis.

Positive self-deception that results in self-enhancement can lead to some selfish behavior that benefits the person, at least in the short term. Vera

FUNCTIONS AND COST-BENEFIT ANALYSIS   237

Hoorens (2011) reviews many of the social benefits as well as the (likely more significant) costs. Those who self-enhance tend to "loaf" on group tasks, and they tend to have a sense of entitlement that leads them to take more than their fair share of common goods. This may be advantageous as a one-time occurrence, but such behavior harms the self-enhancer when iterated (at least with the same group members, and there are also reputation effects to consider). Self-enhancers may also also slack on their investments in intimate relationships, feeling that their enhanced worth justifies them spending less time on their partner and expecting more than their share of attention and care in return. A narcissistic sense of entitlement, often sustained by self-deception, also contributes to greater aggression and less willingness to forgive others when wronged. This closes off even more possibilities for mutually beneficial, cooperative interactions.

Self-deception influences how we present to others, especially when it concerns self-assessments of our intelligence, attractiveness, morality, etc. Beliefs, in general, tend to be transmitted to others once they are detected. Humans have a surprisingly high level of epistemic trust in one another, and people default to believing testimony – skepticism and distrust require effort (Gilbert, Krull, and Malone, 1990). The testimony need not be in the form of explicit avowals, as we have a universal ability to "mindread" (e.g., attribute beliefs to) one another. Self-enhancing beliefs could then benefit us by being transmitted to others, in turn causing them to behave in ways that benefit us beyond our merits (e.g., others are more willing to hire or date us because they too accept our overestimates). Indeed, experimental evidence has shown that people tend to trust the self-descriptions offered by others – e.g., if someone claims to be better than average in some regard (e.g., intelligence or athleticism), others typically accept that assessment (Hoorens, 2011: 249).

Social psychologists study the ways in which we manipulate self-presentation to our benefit through what is called *impression management*. Impression management refers to the goal-directed control of information to influence the impressions formed by an audience in a particular social environment; self-presentation is the special case in which this information is about the self. While this is sometimes defined as a conscious effort, I think it is better for our purposes not to insist on that requirement. For example, one could unconsciously regulate their body posture, voice pitch, candidness, and so on when at a job interview or on a date. The idea behind impression management is that information is tailored to a particular audience, with the information revealed in one situation often differing quite a bit from what is revealed in another. Much, but by no means all, impression management is misleading or even deceitful – he is a big tipper on that first dinner date, but that is not his common practice. Such impression management is supposed to differ from what these psychologists call self-deception in two important ways. First, impression management is specific to particular social environments, whereas self-deception is not supposed to be sensitive to social setting. Second, the regulations of impression management do not necessarily reflect the person's underlying beliefs or dispositions (Paulhus and Trapnell, 2008). For both of these reasons, impression management is described as an offensive tactic used to manipulate others, whereas self-deception is said to be a defensive mechanism. Impression management is offensive because it is aimed at others, but because it does not rise to the level of genuine belief it cannot be a personally comforting defensive measure. Since self-deception is said not to discriminate by social context and does demand genuine belief, it supposedly is not directed at manipulating others and can be self-comforting.

But impression management and self-deception need not be conceived as such disparate phenomena – the one an offensive tactic deployed for social purposes, the other a defensive tactic used to manipulate the self. Instead, the logic behind impression management can sometimes extend to self-deception. That is, beneficial social effects could be the reason why people sometimes are motivated to acquire evidentially unsupported beliefs. The idea here is not that self-deception is driven by a psychological goal (e.g., a conscious or even unconscious desire) to manipulate others. This is what is customary with impression management, as when the job candidate definitely intends to put on a good show during the job interview. But sometimes even impression management can occur without an intention to regulate information. For example, it seems a stretch to say that males who lower their voice before an attractive female are intending to mislead about their masculinity, or that a student who unconsciously improves her posture when meeting with her professor intends a respectful self-presentation. Nevertheless, the behaviors are strategic and sensitive to social setting. If a standing belief is valuable across a wide range of social contexts and is not particularly damaging to the person herself, then the value of social manipulation could also incentivize acquiring the belief for self-presentation purposes. It is not that the belief is strategically chosen by the person herself, but it could be a tactic that is "naturally selected" by biological evolution or individual learning within a lifetime (habituation). This is, in effect, the reasoning behind

Robert Trivers's theory that self-deception is an offensive tactic used for the sake of deceiving others.

Narcissistic self-enhancement, which holds across varied contexts and is genuinely believed, is a good candidate for an offensive strategy used for social manipulation. The genuinely believed self-enhancement might not be only, or even primarily, for the sake of self-esteem, but used also for self-presentation. While emphasizing its effects on happiness primarily, Taylor and Brown (1988) also claimed that self-enhancement improves social functioning and makes one more popular. Skeptical of these claims, Colvin, Block, and Funder (1995) conducted longitudinal and laboratory studies testing the social effects of self-enhancement. The longitudinal studies showed that those who self-enhanced at an earlier time were negatively evaluated when later assessed by strangers at five-year intervals:

> Men who self-enhanced were described as being guileful and deceitful, distrustful of people, and as having a brittle ego-defense system ...
>
> They [assessors] described self-enhancing men and women as concerned with their own adequacy, as self-pitying, self-defeating, as basically anxious, and as lacking a sense of personal meaning in life. In contrast, examiners described men and women who did not self-enhance as personally charming, socially poised, and sought by others for advice. (Colvin et al., 1995: 1154, 1156)

These were the long-term social outcomes of self-enhancement. A laboratory study revealed similarly negative social assessments for the self-enhancers over the short term, again with sex-based differences as to how they manifest socially undesirable behavior. These results have not gone undisputed, however. Taylor et al. (2003) conducted their own study of self-enhancers who were assessed for social qualities. They interpreted their results as contradicting the negative findings of Colvin et al. Specifically, they found that self-enhancers had friendships that seemed to be on par with those who did not self-enhance (Taylor et al, 2003: 172–173). Their results did not show that self-enhancement improves one's social life, as Taylor and Brown (1988) speculated. Rather, their results indicated that self-enhancers have equally good friendships. But this does not tell us how they are perceived by those who are not their friends.

The degree of self-enhancement is also critical, with extreme narcissism likely producing negative social outcomes. Indeed, the DSM-5 lists a host of negative social behaviors characteristic of narcissistic personality disorder: demands for admiration, a sense of entitlement, exploitative relationships, lacking empathy, envy, arrogance, invoking special privileges, poor mindreading of others, and impatience with others (American Psychiatric Association, 2013: 669–671). While these are the attributes of those who self-enhance to an extreme, it is not implausible that many of the same apply to a lesser degree to those displaying lower level, but still significant, self-enhancement.

We know that not all self-deception is self-enhancing; there is also negative self-deception. How are self-deprecating and other forms of negative self-deception received by others? Helweg-Larsen, Sadeghian, and Webb (2002) found that a social stigma attaches to those who are pessimistic and self-deprecating. For example, those who overestimate their risks in various domains (car accidents, STDs, heart disease) were judged to be less socially acceptable. This seemed to be mediated by a perception that such people are dysphoric (Helweg-Larsen et al., 2002: 102). So, the negative affect produced by negative self-deception also generates poor social outcomes. People tend to want not to spend time with those who are hopeless and sad (even though those are the kinds of people who might most benefit from companionship).

So far we have considered the social consequences of our partiality. But what about our irrationality or epistemic negligence? People can sometimes see through our self-deception, and in doing so they recognize that we allow our beliefs to be determined by our desires or emotions. This can cause them to take us less seriously, or even feel some anger or other negative emotion toward us for being the type of person who perpetuates falsehoods. That being said, people do tend to value confidence and decisiveness, with skepticism and doubt being disvalued (von Hippel and Trivers, 2011: 4–5). This is especially true when it comes to evaluating leaders or decision makers. Self-deceivers are often stubbornly confident and not appropriately skeptical (at least to appearances). Somewhat perversely, many people value this epistemic stubbornness in the face of evidence to the contrary as a sign of strength of will or character.

We should also consider views according to which the self-deceived are guilty of acting out of a fantasy or pretense rather than belief. Others, especially those who do not share the same motivations, are unlikely to indulge in the same fantasy. While they might excuse and tolerate some self-deceptive indulgences ("Who cares if she wants to pretend that he is being faithful to her? Let her have some peace of mind!"), for other matters, the escape from reality will be viewed critically ("He's living in a

FUNCTIONS AND COST-BENEFIT ANALYSIS 241

fantasy world, acting as if the stock market will continue to go up 20% a year. We can't trust him with our money").

We know that people sometimes fail to detect our self-deception because they participate in it with us. There is fascinating research showing that members of groups both inconsequential (e.g., fans of a sports team) and important (e.g., fellow citizens, members of the same religious community, or political activists) engage in collective self-enhancement and other forms of self-deception. They think their group is better than it is, and they are overly optimistic about their group's future. Perhaps nowhere is this more evident and personally important than in the family and with intimate relationships. Romantic couples are especially susceptible to one-party or joint self-deception about the prospects for their relationships, as long-term romantic success is very important to life satisfaction and romantic partners tend to strongly identify with one another. Sandra Murray and John Holmes (1997) conducted a longitudinal study testing whether romantic couples (dating or married) have positive illusions about their relationship and, if so, whether this proved to be beneficial for their relationships. The categories they investigated were modeled after Taylor and Brown's (1998) three individual biases: Do those in romantic relationships idealize their partner? Do they exaggerate how much control they jointly have over the success of their relationship? And do they have unrealistic optimism about the relationship's future? To try to ascertain this, partners and relationships were assessed in comparison to average partners or relationships. In all three areas, there were significant positive illusions. And there was a significant, albeit moderate, social interaction among these positive illusions:

> Men who admired their partners tended to have partners who idealized them; men's greater optimism predicted women's greater optimism; and stronger perceptions of control for men predicted stronger perceptions of control for women. (Murray and Holmes, 1997: 592)

Men in relationships were rewarded for their positive illusions by having it returned to them. But what effect did all these happy thoughts have on their relationship in reality? Positive appraisals correlated strongly with relationship satisfaction, trust, felt love, and relationship stability. Study participants were examined again four and 12 months later, and it was found that "relationship illusions" were better predictors of relationship stability (i.e., not breaking up) than were traditional indices such as satisfaction, trust, etc. Individuals also felt greater relationship satisfaction, trust, and love the more their partner idealized them. Positive relationship illusions lead to happy partners, which likely benefit the self as well.

Deception is prevalent in courtship and mating throughout the animal world, and people are no exception. Self-deception has a significant role to play even before a relationship starts. We already know that people overestimate their physical attractiveness, and men overestimate the sexual interest of their romantic prospects. These are beneficial biases to have if we take a biological perspective, in which there is a huge payoff for dating and mating with quality prospects. So long as suitors do not invest substantial resources in truly hopeless causes, there is strategic value in being skewed toward aiming high and taking chances. This biological logic has shaped our psychological preferences as well. There are sex-based differences in these regards, which can incentivize impression management and outright self-deception. For example, men tend to prefer youth and physical attractiveness while women tend to prefer social status and the ability to provide. Women then have an incentive to present as younger and more attractive, whereas men have an incentive to present as having a higher social and financial status.

We should anticipate impression management and self-deception in these regards, and the world of online dating confirms these suspicions. If the online participation is with the hopes of securing an in-person interaction, these misrepresentations should be relatively modest. Hancock and Toma (2009) studied the accuracy of photographs in online dating profiles to test for self-enhancement, hypothesizing subtle self-enhancement and that it would occur even more frequently with women (especially with respect to hair, skin, eyes, and other attributes known to be desirable to men). While it can be hard in these contexts to distinguish between intentional other-deception and self-deception, this study included both assessments by independent judges and self-assessments. The self-assessments, if taken at face value, could provide evidence that the daters are themselves deceived by their photographs. Independent judges (both male and female) judged that the men's photographs were significantly more accurate than the women's photographs, and trained raters found an average of three discrepancies per photograph of a woman compared to 1.33 for photographs of men. While male participants gave self-assessments of photograph accuracy in line with those of the independent judges, female participants did not. It is hard to sharply distinguish socially desirable responding from outright self-deception here, but the results suggest "that female daters did not view their photograph as inaccurate when independent judges did" (Hancock and Toma, 2009: 376–377, 382).

FUNCTIONS AND COST-BENEFIT ANALYSIS 243

Besides romantic relationships, we belong to a host of other partnerships and groups that foster collective self-deception. Prominent among these are one's country, religion, and economic class. As fellow citizens, congregants, or economic peers, we engage in self-deception that furthers solidarity and earns us credit from the group. There are strong social forces keeping us in many of these groups, and it is human nature to want to believe there really is value in our activities (e.g., cognitive dissonance). We do not want to believe that our country is perpetuating human rights violations; we do not want to believe that our church is protecting abusers; we do not want to believe that we are enjoying luxuries only because we have exploited others. There is often a strong social dynamic to the self-deception this induces. Our self-deception makes it easier for others to keep up the illusion, and they might consciously or unconsciously appreciate the work that we are doing on their behalf. It also earns us credit from our fellow group members. In particular, they will tend to trust us and see us as worthy of receiving goods due to our loyalty and willingness to reciprocate.

§7.4 Biological benefits

We previously discussed (§5.2) the most well-known and well-established biological account of self-deception, Robert Trivers's speculative proposal that we self-deceive in order to better deceive others. The primary aspect of his theory does not focus on direct biological benefits (e.g., health and survival), but rather claims indirect effects on reproductive success as mediated by social manipulation. The proposed role for self-deception here is subtle: It decreases cognitive load (among other cues for deception), and it mitigates retributive punishment. Still, he considers more direct effects on health and well-being as well.

Immunology and sex are about as close as you can get to survival and reproduction, and Trivers has fascinating examples of potential self-deception within each category. We are often very unaware of the influences on our behavior when it comes to sex. Men tend to find women more sexually desirable, and women are more sexual in their behavior, when they are ovulating. Trivers (2011: 103–105) discusses a study showing that strippers who are not on the pill earned 30% more in tips when ovulating. It is unlikely that the men who were tipping were aware of the biological factors driving their behavior. Unconscious motives and perceptions likely drive a lot of our behavior in sexual contexts, opening the door to many possibilities for self-deception. Trivers also notes that men with hostility toward homosexuals tend to self-deceive about their own homosexual desires. One study showed that those with such homophobic tendencies showed much greater arousal to male–male pornography (as measured by penile circumference) compared to non-homophobic heterosexuals (Trivers, 2011: 107). Even after successful sexual reproduction, our biases persist. For example, after a baby is born, the maternal family is skewed toward finding resemblances between the baby and the purported father (as compared to finding resemblances to the mother). Ostensibly, the rationale is so that he will be more inclined toward parental investment rather than opting out due to doubts concerning paternity (Trivers, 2011: 100–101). Strong unconscious biases are at work in these areas, leading us to acts of self-deception that might have been naturally selected for their positive effect on reproductive success.

It would not be surprising to discover strong enhancement biases within the family as well. The identification with one's children is perhaps even stronger than that with a romantic partner. Parents are, in a sense, literally partially identical to their children, as there is the strong biological bond of .5 genetic relatedness between parent and child. Those animals that preferentially favor and invest in their young will tend to have a greater genetic presence in future generations. This is true, at least, if that favoritism and investment improves the survival and reproduction chances of their offspring, as seems to be the case. So, there is a very straightforward biological reward for favoring one's offspring. If overestimating their value is a good means to furthering this goal, then it is reasonable that this tendency would be naturally selected so long as it is an available strategy that can be inherited. This can take many forms: overexaggerating a child's athleticism, intellect, physical attractiveness, originality, and so on. These should be easily recognizable candidates for self-deception, and it is commonplace for theorists to offer parental optimism as paradigm cases. There are obvious biological and cultural benefits to this optimism, since expectations contribute to actual outcomes: the child flourishes in socioeconomic terms by going to the best schools (which they clearly *deserve* to attend), they end up "marrying well," etc.

Self-deception can improve one's biological functioning by boosting immune system performance. This could be mediated by various psychological or social factors. Mood disorders (e.g., depression) and loss of sleep impair immune system functioning (Trivers, 2011: Chapter 6). If self-deception can sustain positive illusions that improve mood and one's ability to get a good night's sleep, then it can at least provide that health benefit. There is likely a

FUNCTIONS AND COST-BENEFIT ANALYSIS   245

social dynamic at work as well, with friendships and intimate relationships improving health outcomes. So, if positive self-deception can improve social relations, it indirectly provides health benefits, too. A general sense of positivity or optimism also improves one's health, perhaps in a mysteriously direct manner (much like the placebo effect). Trivers points out that more single-minded self-deception is especially powerful in this regard:

> Note that the positivity effect requires no suppression of negative information or affect. The bias occurs right away. People simply do not attend to the negative information, do not look at it, and do not remember it. Thus, the possible negative immune effects of affect suppression do not need to arise. This must be a general rule – the earlier during information processing that self-deception occurs, the less its negative downstream immunological effects. At the same time, there may be greater risk of disconnect from reality, since the truth may be minimally stored or not at all. (Trivers, 2011: 134–135)

In some cases, eliminating all unwelcome evidence might be biologically optimal but epistemically disastrous.

Other forms of self-deception actually harm the immune system, however. We know that theorists differ on whether self-deception requires a divided mind or at least the maintenance of dual representations, but some self-deception (e.g., "deeply conflicted") appears to be of this form. Such a psychic division can be especially taxing, impacting one's stress levels, ability to sleep, and immune system. Robert Trivers (2011: 128–130) reminds us that honest disclosures of one's health status tend to improve immune functioning. Duplicity and denial, in contrast, negatively impact the immune system's performance. Trivers (2011: 128) draws our attention to startling results that show that HIV-positive homosexual men who are in the closet "enjoyed 40 percent less time before they suffered from AIDS itself and 20 percent lower survival rate overall." What could explain this highly significant discrepancy? Trivers speculates that this is due to the great psychic efforts that are required to hide one's sexual identity from others. One does not have to self-deceive to be in the closet, of course. But it may be that the toll of dual-representation deception itself – whether other- or self-directed – harms the immune system. And there is also such a thing as being in the closet with respect to yourself, or, if not outright denying your own sexuality, having mixed or ambiguous thoughts about it that generate dual representations.

246 FUNCTIONS AND COST-BENEFIT ANALYSIS

The most important effect of positive self-deception might be on life expectancy itself. Matthias Bopp et al. (2012) followed up on over 8000 Swiss men and women over 30 years after they issued self-reports on this simple question concerning self-rated health (SRH): "How would you describe your state of health in general?" Of course, those who report that they are in good health often have very good reasons for saying so – in fact, there are multiple reasons why positivity here could track good health outcomes. But these researchers found some evidence that belief itself could be a contributing factor:

> We analysed to what extent the association between global SRH and all-cause mortality was influenced by socio-demographic, behavioural and clinical variables and examined the impact of the time passed between assessment and outcome. Even after full adjustment and considering maximum follow-up time, we found a strong and persistent "dose-dependent" relationship between SRH and all-cause mortality. (Bopp, et al., 2012: 7)

It is likely that positive thoughts improve life expectancy through various mediators. They will do so by improving mood, decreasing stress, increasing sociality, spurring activity and motivation, and so on.

The literature on self-enhancement and other positive illusions assumes that the people genuinely possess these beliefs. This might not be fully accurate in some cases – self-reports and other measures do not necessarily track genuine belief, or they do so imperfectly. We also know that it is even more contentious whether the positively self-deceived genuinely acquire the positive illusions. They might instead retain a grip on the truth or reside in some indeterminate doxastic middle ground. If self-deception often involves deep conflict, divided minds, or something other than belief (e.g., pretense), it is harder to assess the benefits that it bestows. A virtual belief or pretense might improve affect and motivation, but nagging doubts or unconscious true belief can undercut the effect. In fact, the psychic conflict could be positively harmful by increasing stress and cognitive load (think of the closeted homosexuals who are HIV-positive). Likewise, while we might avow a self-enhancing belief to others, we might not garner the full social benefits from this if they can see that we have some doubts and do not fully believe it. Given the subtlety of the phenomenon, it would be extremely difficult to ascertain the benefits of conflicted self-deception over outright delusion.

Summary

- By its nature, self-deception takes people away from the truth. It will then likely frustrate goal pursuit to at least some extent.
- Positive illusions are widespread, and they improve mood. Accurate self-perception is associated with negative affect (depression). Good mood and self-esteem tend to mitigate the illusions, suggesting that they are functional. It is unclear whether positive illusions boost motivation.
- Self-deception can become entrenched for the same general reasons underlying impression management. But there is mixed evidence as to whether self-enhancement improves social relations and social standing. Narcissistic self-enhancement, however, is socially damaging. Positive illusions about romantic relationships tend to make them stronger and benefit the self-deceived.
- Those who self-enhance have better dating and mating prospects. The tendency to self-enhance also extends to cover one's children. Positivity and optimism improve immune functioning and life expectancy, but conflicted self-deception is taxing and will harm immune functioning.

Recommended reading

McKay and Dennett (2009), along with all the accompanying commentaries, is a comprehensive analysis of the benefits (if any) of false beliefs.

To get a good sense of the back and forth regarding the value of positive illusions to mental health, read this series of papers: Taylor and Brown (1988), Colvin, Block, and Funder (1995), Robins and Beer (2001), and Taylor et al. (2003).

Robert Trivers (2011) is a wide-ranging, provocative, and entertaining read concerning the biological value of self-deception. Lockard and Paulhus (1988) is an older but still valuable collection of more academic papers on self-deception as a possible biological adaptation. Van Leeuwen (2007b) offers good, common-sensical critiques of adaptationist accounts, especially those offered by Trivers.

8

CONCLUSION

8.1 Future directions
8.2 Warning

The discussion of the Basic Problem (§2.1) showed us that there are *prima facie* difficulties with a single self taking real deceptive measures against itself and actually succeeding. Our rationality and our unity strongly resist such an effort. Half of this book (Chapters 3–5) has been devoted to exploring answers to this challenge. These answers deny that there is any such *effort* (deflationary), that there is a truly unified *self* (divided mind), or that the process ends in real *belief* (revisionary). We can plot several of the theorists we have discussed throughout this book under our headings of sacrificing deception, sacrificing the self, and sacrificing belief (see Table 8.1).

The details of any proposed answer to the Basic Problem can be charted by breaking self-deception into three major stages (initial conditions, deception, and outcomes) and raising 12 diagnostic questions within them (§2.6). We can also apply our inquiries into responsibility and cost-benefit analysis (Chapters 6 and 7) to the flowchart in Figure 8.1.

This is a map of where things stand today. Let us conclude with some thoughts about what we should look for in future research.

Table 8.1 Placement of theorists in response to the Basic Problem

Sacrificing deception	Sacrificing the self	Sacrificing belief
Mele's hot and cold biases	Davidson's or Pears' psychological partitions	Bach/Audi divisions between thought/avowal and belief
Johnston's tropisms	Bermudez's and Sorensen's temporal divisions	Schwitzgebel's "in-between" belief
Trivers's naturally selected biases	Freud's or Trivers's robust unconscious processing	Lazar's fantasy or Gendler's pretense account

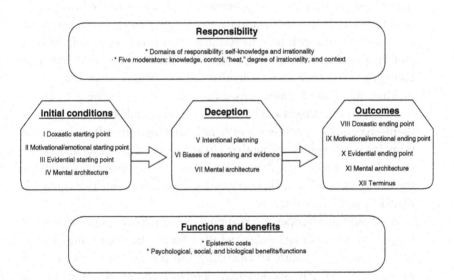

Figure 8.1 Conceptual map and assessments

§8.1 Future directions

Philosophers have pretty exhaustively mapped the theoretical problems of self-deception and the possible responses that one can give to them from the armchair. There is only so much that can be done with folk psychological theorizing in terms of beliefs, desires, and centers of agency. Future work will involve revisions and additions to folk psychology, as well as more empirically informed speculations. Rather than focusing on

250 CONCLUSION

analyzing self-deception and explaining how it is possible (a relatively *a priori* quest), upcoming research should continue or commence the task of explaining how it is psychologically implemented, identifying its common forms in real life, assessing it and recommending corrective measures (if necessary), and weighing its epistemic costs against various benefits. I foresee six promising areas of exploration in the short term:

1   *Further mapping the terrain of belief and rationality.* At their core, self-deception and philosophy itself are about reason and reflection. Philosophers should always have an interest in identifying irrationality and explaining its limits. Twentieth-Century philosophy of mind has established the orthodoxy that belief is governed, or at least strongly limited, by oftentimes holistic considerations of rationality and meaning. It is still coming to terms with how to reconcile that image of belief with the empirical discoveries of systematic irrationality. Perhaps many psychologists and other social scientists are too liberal when it comes to making belief attributions, especially when these attributions fail to cohere with the subject's behavior or evidence. Philosophers might see themselves as the gatekeepers of belief, offering reminders that deviations from rationality are neither cheap nor regular. Nevertheless, we should try to resolve the issue of how reasons responsiveness relates to the nature of belief. It is this very reasons responsiveness that is manipulated by self-deceivers.

　　We should also be open to expanding our conceptions. One of the challenges is to demystify rationality and allow for it to be empirically assessed. Self-deception is a failure of rationality, but this failure is not necessarily one of belief. Philosophers may develop accounts of rationality that extend to other psychological states that are operative in self-deception. We should expect a continued trend in the direction of showing how representational states besides belief can play guiding roles – rational, irrational, and arational – in our thought, affect, and behavior.

2   *More nuanced accounts of motives, especially the emotions.* Philosophers of mind and action are often boringly bland and abstract when specifying motives, relying on familiar standards like a generic "desire that not-p." (Guilty as charged.) The motives for self-deception can be given greater specificity so as to shed more light on its etiology and purposes. The philosophical literature probably does not do justice to the significant role played by the emotions, and non-specialists will likely be surprised by this relative neglect. Future work should examine the

extent to which emotions influence self-deceptive cognition, the epistemic consequences of such influence, and the extent to which we self-deceive to regulate our emotions. We can probably construct some rather specific desires (e.g., the desire that one's son is not using drugs) for any given instance of self-deception. But we should also investigate what we can think of as the secondary or background desires that shape many instances of self-deception. Prominent among these would be the desires for self-esteem and good social standing. Along these lines, we should also discern whether self-deceptive motivation can be broad and long lasting, such that it gives rise to a character type rather than merely a singular instance.

3   *Transition from conceptual work to proto-science.* After pressing up against the limits of conceptual spade work, we should welcome more proto-scientific speculations from philosophers. This should include: speculating about cognitive architecture (empirically informed, rather than purely *a priori* or metaphorical speculations as in the manner of Davidson); suggesting different forms of self-deceptive agency and ways to test for agential involvement; searching for distinctive motives, functions, and benefits; and proposing specific epistemic treatments to correct bias and deception.

4   *Interdisciplinary support.* Related to this transition to proto-science, philosophical treatments of self-deception will continue the trend toward greater interdisciplinary engagement. For a few decades now, philosophers studying self-deception have dipped their toes, if not more, into the psychological research on cognitive architecture (e.g., System 1 and System 2), heuristics and biases, positive illusions, social influences on belief, and the like. The resurgence of research on the unconscious should be of particular interest and have many potential applications. To a lesser extent, there has also been some engagement with biological theories of deception, self-deception, and error management. I hope and expect that this trend will continue.

I also encourage philosophers of self-deception to turn to a few other disciplines that have been largely untapped for philosophical insight: neuroscience, economics, and journalism/communication. Neuroscience offers hope for discovering neurophysiological bases for self-deceptive processes, which can help us identify drives and evidence of effort or agency. A neuroscientific approach also could shed light on how self-deception relates to others forms of psychic conflict (e.g., weakness of will), deception, biases, and the emotions. Economics offers experimental methods for testing and modeling self-deception, as well as pointing us to contexts in which it commonly occurs (e.g., advertising). Finally, journalism and communication theory provide insight into collective self-deception and how others impose, bait, and enable self-deception.

5   *Responsibility and correction.* There will be more work on our responsibility for self-deception and other forms of biased thought (e.g., implicit biases). The issues here are especially challenging because many of these biases and manipulations are unconscious and subpersonal. Responsibility for irrationality is a tricky matter regardless, as we tend not to want to blame people for their cognitive shortcomings. Yet, with self-deception it often seems as if they could and *should* know better. There is also work for practical or applied epistemology, recommending practices conducive to preventing or eliminating self-deception.

6   *"Real world" applications.* There are many opportunities to apply the philosophy of self-deception to "real world" issues of consequence. Responsibility for self-deception arises in the law when it comes to willful blindness, culpable ignorance, and neglect. These can be motivated, self-serving cognitive distortions for the sake of profit or conscience, but with potentially disastrous public consequences. Think, for example, of quality control managers who, due to corporate pressure, are incentivized to overlook manufacturer defects (say, in an automobile) that lead to customer injuries or even deaths. Self-deception also taints the accuracy of testimony (memory), as testimony is susceptible to self-serving biases and the desire to please others. In police and investigative contexts, it is not uncommon for there to be self-deception regarding the impartiality of one's inquiries. Officers can self-deceive about their reasons for pulling someone over, searching their car, or doubting their story. These are just a few salient applications.

Several subfields of philosophy have taken a "social turn" in recent years, and researchers on self-deception should consider following this trend. That is, they should explore how others influence our self-deception and how our self-deception influences others. The new media and new technology more generally make this especially timely. Today's information markets allow for an unprecedented level of biased information search due to selective information gathering and machine learning that indulgences these tendencies. As a consequence, we have seen widespread allegations of "fake news" and the spread of disreputable conspiracy theories largely through internet sources.

§8.2 Warning

I close with a warning directed not so much at academic research but everyday life. In the biological world, deception is a never ending struggle between deceivers and deception detectors. A toad "learns" to camouflage with its environment, but predatory birds counter with better vision or other means of toad detection; the toads come back with even better camouflage or other tactics. Deception is not static, because there are incentives to uncover it and natural selection is not stupid. The same is true of the human world. New tactics are constantly being discovered and resisted, such as email spam being met with email spam filters. Some times, however, favor the deceivers more than the deceived, as innovations can introduce novel ways to mislead or new strengths that people have not yet developed adequate protections against. We seem to be living in just such a time.

I have in mind the ways information is produced, distributed, and shared in the internet age. This has opened up not only a host of new ways to outright deceive others, but also new ways to induce people to deceive themselves. The low barrier to entry for producing and distributing online content (especially through social media) means that it is much easier to generate false or irrational content. Content providers have also become expert at drawing our attention to this content, tacitly or self-consciously picking up on our biases and desires to believe (in our cultural superiority, economic entitlement, or whatever). And then machine-learning algorithms reinforce our biased selection of information, drawing on our past preferences to selectively refer us to more information that fits with our preferred political beliefs, purchasing habits, and whatnot. A good magician knows that the audience wants to believe in something magical; faith healers and those pitching get-rich-quick schemes also know that people want to believe that they will get well or make a lot of money. Likewise, in information markets the consumer will do much of the heavy lifting themselves, given their natural biases and desires to believe. Because there is profit in accommodating those biases and strategic insight about how to get the most out of them (e.g., machine learning), we are entering a particularly bad era of initiated, baited, and enabled self-deception. The costs can be enormous. In an era in which psychologically and technologically sophisticiated advertisers and political propagandists have mastered the art of manipulation, the health of capitalism and democracy are put in serious jeopardy. Drastic efforts must be made to promote good epistemic values and practices in the face of this onslaught of deception.

GLOSSARY

agential involvement   The degree to which a person is involved in *doing* an action as opposed to merely having it happen to her.

baited self-deception   Self-deception in which a third party triggers someone with a pre-existing motive into self-deception.

belief   A representation of something as true by a person, where this representation is typically rational and action guiding. Belief should be distinguished from nearby phenomena like subdoxastic states, acceptance, imagination, and pretense.

bias   A systematic deviation from the standards of ideal reasoning (logical, causal, probabilistic, etc.). It is not simply an isolated mistake (performance error).

cognitive load   A task that draws on working memory and requires mental effort.

cold bias   A bias that exists merely as an acceptable imperfection given trade-offs elsewhere, as a functionally desirable distortion, or otherwise as a by-product. No desire, emotion, motivation, or incentive accounts for the deviation. These biases tend to be domain general.

collective self-deception   When several people are similarly self-deceived about the same topic, either as individuals or as a unified collective. The collectively self-deceived can encourage and otherwise further each other's self-deception.

GLOSSARY   255

confidence threshold   The evidential threshold for accepting or rejecting a hypothesis.

consciousness   One's awareness of one's own mental states, attitudes, or processes. Such awareness, typically, is reportable.

contradictory beliefs   Beliefs with contradictory content: believing that p and believing that not-p. This is to be distinguished from believing a contradiction: believing that (p and not-p). It also is to be distinguished from the logically impossible state of affairs of both believing that p and not believing that p.

deception   The spread of false belief or misinformation through bias, motive, or intention.

deep conflict   Widespread inconsistency in the manifestations or dispositions typical of belief, which makes it hard to determine what someone believes. Some theorists think that deep conflict is symptomatic of self-deception, whereas other do not.

deflationary accounts   Accounts of self-deception that downplay the degree of agential involvement. Such views deny intentionalism. They also tend to downplay the cognitive architecture required for self-deception (e.g., no dual belief or divided mind).

delusion   Strongly held irrational beliefs (or belief-like states) that are not properly amenable to the evidence. In addition to their extreme irrationality, delusions further differ from ordinary beliefs in that they often do not strongly guide action.

divided minds   The claim that the mind contains distinct partitions that can be used to execute and sustain self-deception. The most common such division is that between conscious and unconscious mental states/processes, but other kinds of functional unit could be posited as well.

doxastic voluntarism   The thesis that people have voluntary control over their beliefs. In its strong form, it holds that people can directly will to believe. In its worker form, it holds that people can voluntarily do things that indirectly cause belief.

dynamic problems Problems   concerning the process of self-deception as it unfolds across time. A particular worry is how one could possibly trick themselves into believing something that they antecedently have sufficient reason to deny.

enabled self-deception   Self-deception that is furthered by others, either explicitly or implicitly.

256 GLOSSARY

heuristic A cognitive shortcut used to reach a judgment.

hot bias A bias that exists due to a desire, emotion, motivation, or incentive. They are often specific to a particular topic.

imposed self-deception Self-deception in which the motivation is provided by a third party.

impression management The purposive regulation of information before a particular audience.

intention An intention is what one is trying to achieve by performing an action. Intentions tend to give rise to deliberation, effort, controlled action, and responsibility.

intentionalism The view that self-deception is always motivated by an intention to deceive oneself or acquire a particular belief.

mind-directed motive A motive to self-deceive that is directed at acquiring certain thoughts, rather than at the external world itself.

minimal conception of self-deception The idea that self-deception, at a minimum, requires a *motivated* misrepresentation of reality that is *irrational* given the evidence that is available to them.

mistakes (epistemic) Performance errors in reasoning, as distinguished from (systematic) biases.

motivationalism The view that self-deception always requires a motive, but not necessarily an intention aimed at deception or belief.

negative self-deception Self-deception that not-*p* in which the person desires that *p* or has some other positive attitude (e.g., hope) toward *p* or negative attitude (e.g., anxiety) toward not-*p*.

positive illusion Biased belief that is beneficial to the self.

positive self-deception Self-deception that not-*p* in which the person desires that not-*p* or has some other positive attitude (e.g., hope) toward not-*p* or negative attitude (e.g., anxiety) toward *p*.

pretense Acting as if something is true, but without actually believing it.

purposeful Something done so as to achieve a goal or gain an incentive, but not necessarily performed intentionally.

rationality The standards of proper reasoning, which includes logical deduction, induction, causal reasoning, and other forms of good judgment.

repression The mental activity described by Freud whereby certain unwelcome thoughts are kept out of the conscious mind by a censoring ego. This is seen as a defense mechanism.

GLOSSARY   257

self A person's identity over time, which includes (most, but perhaps not all of) their beliefs, desires, feelings, and other thoughts. The self can be both actor and patient, and it might play both roles in self-deception.

self-delusion When a person, such as a self-deceiver, succeeds at fully acquiring a false belief through their own agential involvement.

self-knowledge Awareness of one's own mind. It is common to view self-deception as a failure of self-knowledge – e.g., not knowing what one believes or feels.

signaling The designed (purposive, selected) communication of a message to an audience. This could be either honest or dishonest.

static problems Problems concerning the state of self-deception that arise at a given moment in time. In particular, they concern the apparently contradictory beliefs or motives that the self-deceiver simultaneously possesses.

subdoxastic A representation of the world that does not reach the level of full belief and resides at the subpersonal level.

tropism A purposeful, subintentional mechanism.

unconsciousness The lack of awareness of one's mental states, attitudes, or processes.

weakness of will Intentional action that goes against one's better judgment.

wishful thinking Thinking or believing that something is true merely because you want to believe so.

world-directed motive A motive to self-deceive that is directed at the external world being a certain way, rather than at thought itself.

BIBLIOGRAPHY

Allison, S., Goethals, G., and Messick, D. 1989. "On Being Better but not Smarter than Others: The Muhammed Ali Effect," *Social Cognition*, 7:3, 275–295.

Alston, William. 1988. "The Deontological Conception of Epistemic Justification," *Philosophical Perspectives*, 2, 257–299.

American Psychiatric Association. 2013. *Diagnostic and Statistical Manual of Mental Disorders*, 5th edn. (Arlington, VA: American Psychiatric Publishing).

Anderson, C.A. 2007. "Belief Perseverance," in *Encyclopedia of Social Psychology*, eds. R.F. Baumeister and K.D. Vohs (Thousand Oaks, CA: Sage).

Anscombe, G.E.M. 1957. *Intention* (Cambridge, MA: Harvard University Press).

Archer, S. 2013. "Nondoxasticism about Self-Deception," *dialectica*, 67:3, 265–282.

Artiga, M. and Paternotte, C. 2018. "Deception: A Functional Account," *Philosophical Studies*, 175:3, 579–600.

Audi, R. 1982. "Self-Deception, Action, and Will," *Erkenntnis*, 18:2, 133–158.

Audi, R. 1985. "Self-Deception and Rationality," in *Self-Deception and Self-Understanding*, ed. M. Martin (Lawrence, KS: University Press of Kansas).

Audi, R. 1988. "Self-Deception, Rationalization, and Reasons for Acting," in *Perspectives on Self-Deception*, eds. B. McLaughlin and A. Rorty (Berkeley, CA: University of California Press).

BIBLIOGRAPHY

Audi, R. 1997. "Self-Deception vs. Self-Caused Deception: A Comment on Professor Mele," *Behavioral and Brain Sciences*, 20:1, 104.

Bach, K. 1981. "An Analysis of Self-Deception," *Philosophy and Phenomenological Research*, 41:3, 351–370.

Bach, K. 1997. "Thinking and Believing in Self-Deception," *Behavioral and Brain Sciences*, 20:1, 105.

Bargh, J. and Morsella, E. 2008. "The Unconscious Mind," *Perspectives on Psychological Science*, 3:1, 73–79.

Barnes, A. 1997. *Seeing through Self-Deception* (Cambridge: Cambridge University Press).

Baron, M. 1988. "What is Wrong with Self-Deception?," in *Perspectives on Self-Deception*, eds. B. McLaughlin and A. Rorty (Berkeley, CA: University of California Press).

Bayne, T. and Pacherie, E. 2005. "In Defence of the Doxastic Conception of Delusions," *Mind and Language*, 20:2, 163–188.

Becker, E. 1973/1997. *The Denial of Death* (New York, NY: Simon & Schuster Inc.).

Bem, D. 1972. "Self-Perception Theory," in *Advances in Experimental Social Psychology, Vol. 6*, ed. L. Berkowitz (San Diego, CA: Academic Press).

Bermudez, J. 1997. "Defending Intentionalist Accounts of Self-Deception," *Behavioral and Brain Sciences*, 20:1, 107–108.

Bermudez, J. 2000. "Self-Deception, Intentions, and Contradictory Beliefs," *Analysis*, 60:4, 309–319.

Bopp, M., Braun, J., Gutzwiller, F., and Faeh, D. 2012. "Health Risk or Resource? Gradual and Independent Association between Self-Rated Health and Mortality Persists Over 30 Years," *PLoS One*, 7:2, e30795.

Borge, S. 2003. "The Myth of Self-Deception," *Southern Journal of Philosophy*, 41:1, 1–28.

Bortolotti, L. 2010. *Delusions and Other Irrational Beliefs* (New York, NY: Oxford University Press).

Bortolotti, L. 2015. *Irrationality* (Malden, MA: Polity Press).

Bratman, M. 1992. "Practical Reasoning and Acceptance in a Context," *Mind* 101:401, 1–16.

Bratman, M. 1999. *Faces of Intention* (New York, NY: Cambridge University Press).

Brownstein, M. 2017. "Implicit Bias," *The Stanford Encyclopedia of Philosophy*, Spring edn., ed. E. Zalta, https://plato.stanford.edu/entries/implicit-bias/

Butler, J. 1729/2017. *Fifteen Sermons and other Writings on Ethics*, ed. D. McNaughton (New York, NY: Oxford University Press).

260 BIBLIOGRAPHY

Cherniak, C. 1986. *Minimal Rationality* (Cambridge, MA: MIT Press).

Chignell, A. 2018. "The Ethics of Belief," *The Stanford Encyclopedia of Philosophy*, Spring edn., ed. E. Zalta, https://plato.stanford.edu/entries/ethics-belief/

Clifford, W.K. 1879. "The Ethics of Belief," in *Lectures and Essays, Vol. 2*, eds. L. Stephen and F. Pollock (London: Macmillan & Co.).

Clinton, B. 2004. *My Life* (New York, NY: Alfred A. Knopf).

Cohen, L.J. 1992. *An Essay on Belief and Acceptance* (New York, NY: Oxford University Press).

Colvin, R., Block, J., and Funder, D. 1995. "Overly Positive Self-Evaluations and Personality: Negative Implications for Mental Health," *Journal of Personality and Social Psychology*, 68:6, 1152–1162.

Currie, G. and Jureidini, J. 2001. "Delusion, Rationality, Empathy," *Philosophy, Psychiatry, and Psychology*, 8:2/3, 159–162.

Darwall, S. 1988. "Self-Deception, Autonomy, and Moral Constitution," in *Perspectives on Self-Deception*, eds. B. McLaughlin and A. Rorty (Berkeley, CA: University of California Press).

Davidson, D. 1980. *Essays On Actions and Events* (New York, NY: Oxford University Press).

Davidson, D. 1984. *Inquiries into Truth and Interpretation* (New York, NY: Oxford University Press).

Davidson, D. 2004. *Problems of Rationality* (New York, NY: Oxford University Press).

Demos, R. 1960. "Lying to Oneself," *Journal of Philosophy*, 57:18, 588–595.

Dennett, D. 1978. *Brainstorms* (Cambridge, MA: MIT Press).

Dennett, D. 1987. *The Intentional Stance* (Cambridge, MA: MIT Press).

Deweese-Boyd, I. 2017. "Self-Deception," *The Stanford Encyclopedia of Philosophy*, Fall edn., ed. E. Zalta, https://plato.stanford.edu/archives/ fall2017/ entries/self-deception/

Doody, P. 2017. "Is There Evidence of Robust, Unconscious Self-Deception? A Reply to Funkhouser and Barrett," *Philosophical Psychology*, 30:5, 657–676.

Dostoevsky, F. 2008. *Notes from the Underground and The Gambler* (New York, NY: Oxford University Press).

Dub, R. 2017. "Delusions, Acceptances, and Cognitive Feelings," *Philosophy and Phenomenological Research*, 94:1, 27–60.

Dunning, D., Heath, C., and Suls, J. 2004. "Flawed Self-Assessment: Implications for Health, Education, and the Workplace," *Psychological Science in the Public Interest*, 5:3, 69–106.

BIBLIOGRAPHY   261

Eidelman, S., Crandall, C.S., and Pattershall, J. 2009. "The Existence Bias," *Journal of Personality and Social Psychology*, 97:5, 765–775.

Epley, N. and Whitchurch, E. 2008. "Mirror, Mirror on the Wall: Enhancement in Self Recognition," *Personality and Social Psychology Bulletin*, 34:9, 1159–1170.

Fernandez, J. 2013. "Self-Deception and Self-Knowledge," *Philosophical Studies*, 162:2, 379–400.

Fingarette, H. 1969. *Self-Deception* (Berkeley, CA: University of California Press).

Fischer, J.M., and Ravizza, M. 1998. *Responsibility and Control: A Theory of Moral Responsibility* (New York, NY: Cambridge University Press).

Fraccaro, P., Jones, B., Vukovic, J., Smith, F., Watkins, C., Feinberg, D.,et al. 2011. "Experimental Evidence that Women Speak in a Higher Voice Pitch to Men They Find Attractive," *Journal of Evolutionary Psychology*, 9, 57–67.

Frankfurt, H. 1988. *The Importance of What We Care About* (New York, NY: Cambridge University Press).

Frankish, K. 2016. "Playing Double: Implicit Bias, Dual Levels, and Self-Control," in *Implicit Bias and Philosophy, Vol. 1*, eds. M. Brownstein and J. Saul (New York, NY: Oxford University Press).

Freud, S. 1927/1960. *The Ego and the Id*, trans. J. Riviere (New York, NY: W.W. Norton & Co.).

Freud, S. 1960. *The Psychopathology of Everyday Life*, trans. A. Tyson (New York, NY: W.W. Norton & Co.).

Freud, S. 1966. *Introductory Lectures on Psycho-Analysis*, trans. J. Strachey (New York, NY: W.W. Norton & Co.).

Friedrich, J. 1993. "Primary Error Detection and Minimization (PEDMIN) Strategies in Social Cognition: A Reinterpretation of Confirmation Bias Phenomena," *Psychological Review*, 100:2, 298–319.

Funkhouser, E. 2003. "Willing Belief and the Norm of Truth," *Philosophical Studies*, 115:2, 179–195.

Funkhouser, E. 2005. "Do the Self-Deceived Get What They Want?," *Pacific Philosophical Quarterly*, 86:3, 295–312.

Funkhouser, E. 2009. "Self-Deception and the Limits of Folk Psychology," *Social Theory and Practice*, 35:1, 1–13.

Funkhouser, E. 2016. "Is Self-Deception an Effective Non-Cooperative Strategy?" *Biology and Philosophy*, 32:2, 221–242.

Funkhouser, E. 2017. "Beliefs as Signals: A New Function for Belief," *Philosophical Psychology*, 30:6, 809–831.

Funkhouser, E. and Barrett, D. 2016. "Robust, Unconscious Self-Deception: Strategic and Flexible," *Philosophical Psychology*, 29:5, 1–15.

Funkhouser, E. and Barrett, D. 2017. "Reply to Doody," *Philosophical Psychology*, 30:5, 677–681.

Gendler, T. 2003. "On the Relation between Pretense and Belief," in *Imagination, Philosophy, and the Arts*, ed. D. Lopes and M. Kieran (New York, NY: Routledge).

Gendler, T. 2006. "Imaginative Contagion," *Metaphilosophy*, 37:2, 183–203.

Gendler, T. 2007. "Self-Deception as Pretense," *Philosophical Perspectives*, 21, 231–258.

Gendler, T. 2008. "Alief and Belief," *Journal of Philosophy*, 105:10, 634–663.

Gertler, B. 2011. *Self-Knowledge* (New York, NY: Routledge).

Gigerenzer, G., Todd, P., and the ABC Research Group. 1999. *Simple Heuristics That Make Us Smart* (New York, NY: Oxford University Press).

Gilbert, D., Krull, D., and Malone, P. 1990. "Unbelieving the Unbelievable: Some Problems in the Rejection of False Information," *Journal of Personality and Social Psychology*, 59:4, 601–613.

Gilovich, T. 1991. *How We Know What Isn't So: The Fallibility of Human Reason in Everyday Life* (New York, NY: Free Press).

Gilovich, T., Griffin, D., and Kahneman, D., eds. 2002. *Heuristics and Biases: The Psychology of Intuitive Judgment* (New York, NY: Cambridge University Press).

Grice, H.P. 1957. "Meaning," *The Philosophical Review*, 66, 377–388.

Gur, R. and Sackeim, H. 1979. "Self-Deception: A Concept in Search of a Phenomenon," *Journal of Personality and Social Psychology*, 37:2, 147–169.

Haight, M.R. 1980. *A Study of Self-Deception* (Hemel Hempstead: Harvester Press).

Hancock, J. and Toma, C. 2009. "Putting Your Best Face Forward: The Accuracy of Online Dating Photographs," *Journal of Communication*, 59, 367–386.

Haselton, M.G. 2007. "Error Management Theory," in *Encyclopedia of Social Psychology, Vol. 1*, ed. R.F. Baumeister and K.D. Vohs (London: Sage).

Haselton, M. and Buss, D. 2000. "Error Management Theory: A New Perspective on Biases in Cross-Sex Mind Reading," *Journal of Personality and Social Psychology*, 78:1, 81–91.

Hassin, R.R., Bargh, J.A., and Zimerman, S. 2009. "Automatic and Flexible: The Case of Nonconscious Goal Pursuit," *Social Cognition*, 27:1, 20–36.

Helweg-Larsen, M., Sadeghian, P., and Webb, M. 2002. "The Stigma of Being Pessimistically Biased," *Journal of Social and Clinical Psychology*, 21, 92–107.

Hemingway, E. 1952/2003. *The Old Man and the Sea* (New York, NY: Scribner).

Hewstone, M. 1990. "The 'Ultimate Attribution Error'? A Review of the Literature on Intergroup Causal Attribution," *European Journal of Social Psychology*, 20:4, 311–335.

Hieronymi, P. 2008. "Responsibility for Believing," *Synthese*, 161:3, 357–373.

Holton, R. 2001. "What is the Role of the Self in Self-Deception?", *Proceedings of the Aristotelian Society*, 101:1, 53–69.

Hoorens, V. 2011. "The Social Consequences of Self-Enhancement and Self-Protection," in *The Handbook of Self-Enhancement and Self-Protection*, eds. M. Alicke and C. Sedikides (New York, NY: Guilford Press).

Huang, J. and Bargh, J. 2014. "The Selfish Goal: Autonomously Operating Motivational Structures as the Proximate Cause of Human Judgment and Behavior," *Behavioral and Brain Sciences*, 37, 121–175.

Hughes, S., Farley, S., and Rhodes, B. 2010. "Vocal and Physiological Changes in Response to the Physical Attractiveness of Conversational Partners," *Journal of Nonverbal Behavior*, 34:3, 155–167.

Hume, D. 1739/1978. *A Treatise of Human Nature*, ed. L.A. Selby-Bigge (Oxford: Clarendon Press).

Hume, D. 1777/1975. *Enquiries Concerning Human Understanding and Concerning the Principles of Morals*, ed. L.A. Selby-Bigge (Oxford: Clarendon Press).

Jiang, Y., Costello, P., Fang, F., Huang, M., and He, S. 2006. "A Gender and Sexual Orientation-Dependent Spatial Attention Effect of Invisible Nudes," *Proceedings of the National Academy of Sciences*, 103:45, 17048–17052.

Johnston, M. 1988. "Self-Deception and the Nature of Mind," in *Perspectives on Self-Deception*, eds. B. McLaughlin and A. Rorty (Berkeley, CA: University of California Press).

Kahneman, D. 2011. *Thinking, Fast and Slow* (New York, NY: Farrar, Straus, & Giroux).

Kahneman, D., Slovic, P., and Tversky, A., eds. 1982. *Judgment Under Uncertainty: Heuristics and Biases* (New York, NY: Cambridge University Press).

Kahneman, D. and Tversky, A., eds. 2000. *Choices, Values, and Frames* (New York, NY: Cambridge University Press).

Kant, I. 1797/1996. *The Metaphysics of Morals*, ed. M. Gregor (New York, NY: Cambridge University Press).

Kipp, D. 1980. "On Self-Deception," *The Philosophical Quarterly*, 30:121, 305–317.

Krebs, D., Ward, J., and Racine, T. 1997. "The Many Faces of Self-Deception," *Behavioral and Brain Sciences*, 20:1, 119.

BIBLIOGRAPHY

Kunda, Z. 1990. "The Case for Motivated Reasoning," *Psychological Bulletin* 108:3, 480–498.

Langer, E. 1975. "The Illusion of Control," *Journal of Personality and Social Psychology*, 32:2, 311–328.

Lazar, A. 1999. "Deceiving Oneself or Self-Deceived? On the Formation of Beliefs 'Under the Influence'," *Mind*, 108:430, 265–290.

Leongomez, J.D., Binter, J., Kubicova, L., Stolarova, P., Klapilova, K., Havlicek, J. et al. (2014). "Vocal Modulation During Courtship Increases Proceptivity Even in Naive Listeners," *Evolution and Human Behavior*, 35:6, 489–496.

Levy, N. 2004. "Self-Deception and Moral Responsibility," *Ratio*, 17:3, 294–311.

Levy, N. 2014. *Consciousness and Moral Responsibility* (New York, NY: Oxford University Press).

Levy, N. 2015. "Neither Fish nor Fowl: Implicit Attitudes as Patchy Endorsements," *Nous*, 49:4, 800–823.

Lockard, J. and Paulhus, D. 1988. *Self-Deception: An Adapative Mechanism?* (Englewood Cliffs, NJ: Prentice Hall).

Longeway, J. 1990. "The Rationality of Escapism and Self-Deception," *Behavior and Philosophy*, 18:2, 1–20.

Lynch, K. 2012. "On the "Tension" Inherent in Self-Deception," *Philosophical Psychology*, 25:3, 433–450.

Lynch, K. 2016. "Willful Ignorance and Self-Deception," *Philosophical Studies*, 173:2, 505–523.

Machery, E. 2016. "De-Freuding Implicit Attitudes," in *Implicit Bias and Philosophy, Vol. 1*, eds. M. Brownstein and J. Saul (New York, NY: Oxford University Press).

Mandelbaum, E. 2014. "Thinking is Believing," *Inquiry*, 57:1, 55–96.

Mandelbaum, E. 2016. "Attitude, Inference, Association: On the Propositional Structure of Implicit Bias," *Nous*, 50:3, 629–658.

Marshall, M. and Brown, J. 2008. "On the Psychological Benefits of Self-Enhancement," in *Self-Criticism and Self-Enhancement: Theory, Research, and Clinical Implications*, ed. E. Chang (Washington, DC: American Psychological Association).

Martin, M. 1986. *Self-Deception and Morality* (Lawrence, KS: University Press of Kansas).

Mather, M., Shafir, E., and Johnson, M. 2000. "Misremembrance of Options Past: Source Monitoring and Choice," *Psychological Science*, 11:2, 132–138.

BIBLIOGRAPHY 265

McKay, R. and Dennett, D. 2009. "The Evolution of Misbelief," *Behavioral and Brain Sciences*, 32:6, 493–510.

McLaughlin, B. and Rorty, A.O. 1988. *Perspectives on Self-Deception* (Berkeley, CA: University of California Press).

Mele, A. 1987. *Irrationality: An Essay on Akrasia, Self-Deception, and Self-Control* (New York, NY: Oxford University Press).

Mele, A. 1997. "Real Self-Deception," *Behavioral and Brain Sciences*, 20, 91–136.

Mele, A. 2001. *Self-Deception Unmasked* (Princeton, NJ: Princeton University Press).

Mendoza, S., Gollwitzer, P., and Amodio, D. 2010. "Reducing the Expression of Implicit Stereotypes: Reflexive Control Through Implementation Intentions," *Personality and Social Psychology Bulletin*, 36:4, 512–523.

Mezulis, A., Abramson, L, Hyde, J, and Hankin, B. 2004. "Is There a Universal Positivity Bias in Attributions? A Meta-Analytic Review of Individual, Developmental, and Cultural Differences in the Self-Serving Attributional Bias," *Psychological Bulletin*, 130:5, 711–747.

Michel, C. and Newen, A. 2010. "Self-Deception as Pseudo-Rational Regulation of Belief," *Consciousness and Cognition*, 19, 731–744.

Mijovic-Prelec, D. and Prelec, D. 2010. "Self-Deception as Self-Signalling: A Model and Experimental Evidence," *Philosophical Transactions of the Royal Society B: Biological Sciences*, 365:1538, 227–240.

Murphy, R., Straebler, S., Cooper, Z., and Fairburn, C. G. 2010. "Cognitive Behavioral Therapy for Eating Disorders," *The Psychiatric Clinics of North America*, 33:3, 611–627.

Murray, S. and Holmes, J. 1997. "A Leap of Faith? Positive Illusions in Romantic Relationships," *Personality and Social Psychology Bulletin*, 23:6, 586–604.

Nelkin, D. 2002. "Self-Deception, Motivation, and the Desire to Believe," *Pacific Philosophical Quarterly*, 83:4, 384–406.

Nelkin, D. 2012. "Responsibility and Self-Deception: A Framework," *Humana Mente*, 5:20, 117–139.

Neu, J. 1988. "Divided Minds: Sartre's "Bad Faith" Critique of Freud," *The Review of Metaphysics*, 42:1, 79–101.

Nickerson, R. 1998. "Confirmation Bias: A Ubiquitous Phenomenon in Many Guises," *Review of General Psychology*, 2:2, 175–220.

Nisbett, R. and Ross, L. 1980. *Human Inference: Strategies and Shortcomings of Social Judgment* (Englewood Cliffs, NJ: Prentice Hall).

BIBLIOGRAPHY

Noordhof, P. 2009. "The Essential Instability of Self-Deception," *Social Theory and Practice*, 35:1, 45–71.

Pascal, B. 1995. *Pensées and Other Writings*, trans. H. Levi (New York, NY: Oxford University Press).

Paulhus, D. 1986. "Self-Deception and Impression Management in Test Responses," in *Personality Assessment via Questionnaires*, eds. A. Angleitner and J. Wiggins (Berlin: Springer).

Paulhus, D. 1991. "Measurement and Control of Response Bias," in *Measures of Personality and Social Psychological Attitudes*, eds. J. Robinson, P. Shaver, and L. Wrightsman (San Diego, CA: Academic Press).

Paulhus, D. 2002. "Socially Desirable Responding: The Evolution of a Construct," in *The Role of Constructs in Psychological and Educational Measurement*, eds. H.I. Braun, D.N. Jackson, and D.E. Wiley (Mahwah, NJ: Erlbaum).

Paulhus, D., Graf, P., and Van Selst, M. 1989. "Attentional Load Increases the Positivity of Self-Presentation," *Social Cognition*, 7:4, 389–400.

Paulhus, D. and Trapnell, P. 2008. "Self-Presentation of Personality: An Agency-Communion Framework," in *Handbook of Personality: Theory and Research*, 3rd edn., eds. O.P. John, R.W. Robins, and L.A. Pervin (New York, NY: Guilford Press).

Pears, D. 1984. *Motivated Irrationality* (New York, NY: Oxford University Press).

Pears, D. 1991. "Self-Deceptive Belief-Formation," *Synthese*, 89:3, 393–405.

Perring, C. 1997. "Direct, Fully Intentional Self-Deception is also Real," *Behavioral and Brain Sciences*, 20:1, 123–124.

Pinker, S. 2011. "Representations and Decision Rules in the Theory of Self-Deception," *Behavioral and Brain Sciences*, 34:1, 35–367.

Plato. 1997. *Plato: Collected Works*, ed. J. Cooper (Indianapolis, IN: Hackett Publishing Company).

Porcher, J.E. 2014. "Is Self-Deception Pretense?," *Manuscrito*, 37:2, 291–332.

Priest, G. 1995. *Beyond the Limits of Thought* (Cambridge: Cambridge University Press).

Quattrone, G. and Tversky, A. 1984. "Causal Versus Diagnostic Contingencies: On Self-Deception and on the Voter's Illusion," *Journal of Personality and Social Psychology*, 46:2, 237–248.

Quine, W.V.O. 1951. "Two Dogmas of Empiricism," *Philosophical Review*, 60, 20–43.

Robins, R. and Beer, J. 2001. "Positive Illusions about the Self: Short-Term Benefits and Long-Term Costs," *Journal of Personality and Social Psychology*, 80:2, 340–352.

Roese, N. and Olson, J. 2007. "Better, Stronger, Faster: Self-Serving Judgment, Affect Regulation, and the Optimal Vigilance Hypothesis," *Perspectives on Psychological Science*, 2:2, 124–140.

Rorty, A.O. 1988. "The Deceptive Self: Liars, Layers, and Lairs," in *Perspectives on Self-Deception*, eds. B. McLaughlin and A. Rorty (Berkeley, CA: University of California Press).

Rose, D., Buckwalter, W., and Turri, J. 2014. "When Words Speak Louder than Actions: Delusion, Belief, and the Power of Assertion," *Australasian Journal of Philosophy*, 92:4, 683–700.

Ross, L. 1977. "The Intuitive Psychologist and His Shortcomings: Distortions in the Attribution Process," *Advances in Experimental Social Psychology*, 10, 173–220.

Ruddick, W. 1988. "Social Self-Deceptions," in *Perspectives on Self-Deception*, eds. B. McLaughlin and A. Rorty (Berkeley, CA: University of California Press).

Sackeim, H. 1988. "Self-Deception: A Synthesis," in *Self-Deception: An Adaptive Mechanism?*, eds. J. Lockard and D. Paulhus (Englewood Cliffs, NJ: Prentice-Hall).

Samuelson, W. and Zeckhauser, R. 1988. "Status Quo Bias in Decision Making," *Journal of Risk and Uncertainty*, 1:1, 7–59.

Sartre, J.P. 1943/1956. *Being and Nothingness*, trs. H. Barnes (New York, NY: Washington Square Press).

Schiller, F. 1924. *Problems of Belief* (London: Hodder & Stoughton).

Schwitzgebel, E. 2001. "In-Between Believing," *The Philosophical Quarterly*, 51, 76–82.

Schwitzgegbel, E. 2002. "A Phenomenal, Dispositional Account of Belief," *Nous*, 36, 249–275.

Scott-Kakures, D. 2001. "High Anxiety: Barnes on What Moves the Unwelcome Believer," *Philosophical Psychology*, 14:3, 313–326.

Sedikides, C. and Alicke, M. 2012. "Self-Enhancement and Self-Protection Motives," in *The Oxford Handbook of Human Motivation*, ed. R. Ryan (New York, NY: Oxford University Press).

Sedikides, C., Meek, R., Alicke, M., and Taylor, S. 2014. "Behind Bars but above the Bar: Prisoners Consider Themselves More Prosocial than Nonprisoners," *British Journal of Social Psychology*, 53:2, 396–403.

Seligman, M. 1972. "Learned Helplessness," *Annual Review of Medicine*, 23:1, 407–412.

Shah, N. and Velleman, J.D. 2005. "Doxastic Deliberation," *The Philosophical Review*, 114:4, 497–534.

BIBLIOGRAPHY

Shakespeare, W. 2006. *Othello*, ed. M. Neill (New York, NY: Oxford University Press).

Sharot, T. 2011. "The Optimism Bias," *Current Biology*, 21:23, R941–945.

Sherman, D. and Kim, H. 2005. "Is There an 'I' in 'Team'? The Role of the Self in Group-Serving Judgments," *Journal of Personality and Social Psychology*, 88:1, 108–120.

Simon, H. 1982. *Models of Bounded Rationality* (Cambridge, MA: MIT Press).

Sloman, S.A. 1996. "The Empirical Case for Two Systems of Reasoning," *Psychological Bulletin*, 119:1, 3–22.

Smith, A. 1759/1982. *The Theory of Moral Sentiments*, eds. D.D. Raphael and A.L. Macfie (Indianapolis, IN: Liberty Fund).

Smith, D.L. 2014. "Self-Deception: A Teleofunctional Approach," *Philosophia*, 42, 181–199.

Snyder, M., Kleck, R., Strenta, A., and Mentzer, S. 1979. "Avoidance of the Handicapped: An Attributional Ambiguity Analysis," *Journal of Personality and Social Psychology*, 37, 2297–2306.

Soler, M. 2012. "Costly Signaling, Ritual and Cooperation: Evidence from Candomble, an Afro-Brazilian Religion," *Evolution and Human Behavior*, 33, 346–356.

Sorensen, R. 1985. "Self-Deception and Scattered Events," *Mind*, 94:373, 64–69.

Sperber, D. 2001. "An Evolutionary Perspective on Testimony and Argumentation," *Philosophical Topics*, 29:1–2, 401–413.

Stanovich, K.E. and West, R.F. 2000. "Individual Differences in Reasoning: Implications for the Rationality Debate," *Behavioral and Brain Sciences*, 23:645–726.

Steglich-Petersen, A. 2006. "No Norm Needed: On the Aim of Belief," *The Philosophical Quarterly*, 56:225, 499–516.

Stich, S. 1978. "Beliefs and Subdoxastic States," *Philosophy of Science*, 45:4, 499–518.

Stich, S. 1990. *The Fragmentation of Reason* (Cambridge, MA: MIT Press).

Sullivan-Bissett, E. 2017. "Biological Function and Epistemic Normativity," *Philosophical Explorations*, 20:S1, S94–S110.

Sullivan-Bissett, E. 2018. "Explaining Doxastic Transparency: Aim, Norm, or Function?," *Synthese*, 195, 3453–3476.

Sullivan-Bissett, E. 2019. "Biased by Our Imaginings," *Mind and Language*.

Tajfel, H. and Turner, J. 2004. "The Social Identity Theory of Intergroup Behavior," in *Political Psychology: Key Readings*, eds. J. Jost and J. Sidanius (New York, NY: Psychology Press).

Talbott, W. 1995. "Intentional Self-Deception in a Single Coherent Self," *Philosophy and Phenomenological Research*, 55:1, 27–74.

Taylor, S. and Brown, J. 1988. "Illusion and Well-Being: A Social Psychological Perspective on Mental Health," *Psychological Bulletin*, 103:2, 193–210.

Taylor, S., Lerner, J., Sherman, D., Sage, R., and McDowell, N. 2003. "Portrait of the Self-Enhancer: Well Adjusted and Well Liked or Maladjusted and Friendless?," *Journal of Personality and Social Psychology*, 84:1, 165–176.

Trivers, R. 1971. "The Evolution of Reciprocal Altruism," *The Quarterly Review of Biology*, 46:1, 35–57.

Trivers, R. 1976/2006. "Foreword," to *The Selfish Gene* by R. Dawkins (New York, NY: Oxford University Press).

Trivers, R. 2000/2002. "Self-Deception in Service of Deceit," reprinted in *Natural Selection and Social Theory* (New York, NY: Oxford University Press).

Trivers, R. 2011. *The Folly of Fools* (New York, NY: Basic Books).

Trope, Y. and Liberman, A. 1996. "Social Hypothesis Testing: Cognitive and Motivational Mechanisms," in *Social Psychology: Handbook of Basic Principles*, eds. E. Higgins and A. Kruglanski (New York, NY: Guilford Press).

Tversky, A. and Kahneman, D. 1974. "Judgment Under Uncertainty: Heuristics and Biases," *Science*, 185:4157, 1124–1131.

Uhlmann, E.L. and G.L. Cohen. 2005 "Constructed Criteria: Redefining Merit to Justify Discrimination," *Psychological Science*, 16:6, 474–480.

Valdesolo, P. and DeSteno, D. 2008. "The Duality of Virtue: Deconstructing the Moral Hypocrite," *Journal of Experimental Social Psychology*, 44, 1334–1338.

Van Leeuwen, D.S.N. 2007a. "The Product of Self-Deception," *Erkenntnis*, 67:3, 419–437.

Van Leeuwen, D.S.N. 2007b. "The Spandrels of Self-Deception: Prospects for a Biological Theory of a Mental Phenomenon," *Philosophical Psychology*, 20:3, 329–348.

Velleman, J.D. 2000. "On the Aim of Belief," in *The Possibility of Practical Reason* (New York, NY: Oxford University Press).

von Hippel, W. and Trivers, R. 2011. "The Evolution and Psychology of Self-Deception," *Behavioral and Brain Sciences*, 34:1, 1–16, 41–56.

Vrij, A. 2011. "Self-Deception, Lying, and the Ability to Deceive," *Behavioral and Brain Sciences*, 34:1, 40–41.

Wason, P.C. 1968. "Reasoning about a Rule," *Quarterly Journal of Experimental Psychology*, 20:3, 273–281.

Williams, B. 1973. "Deciding to Believe," in *Problems of the Self* (Cambridge: Cambridge University Press).

Wood, A. 1988. "Self-Deception and Bad Faith," in *Perspectives on Self-Deception*, eds. B. McLaughlin and A. Rorty (Berkeley, CA: University of California Press).

Zahavi, A. and Zahavi, A. 1997. *The Handicap Principle: A Missing Piece of Darwin's Puzzle* (New York, NY: Oxford University Press).

INDEX

Note: Page numbers followed by "n" denote endnotes.

acceptance 133–4n2, 179–81; *see also* belief

agency 55, 61; *see also* agential involvement in self-deception

agential involvement in self-deception 62–3, 116–19, 139–40, 143–4, 162, 207, 220–1; *see also* agency; robust self-deception

anxiety-based accounts 59–60, 129–32, 185–6, 215; *see also* emotions

Archer, S. 185–6

Audi, R. 73, 120, 124, 149–52, 168, 174–5, 209

Bach, K. 69, 72, 120, 168, 178–9, 218

bad faith 44–5, 78, 216

baited self-deception 27, 199, 253

Bargh, J. 148, 153–4

Barnes, A. 129–32, 217

Baron, M. 225

Barrett, D. 117, 154–5, 157

Basic Problem 26–31, 135, 248–9; *see also* Belief Problem; Deception Problem; Motivation/Intention Problem

Becker, E. 6, 222

belief 69, 104–5, 120, 123, 172–3, 181, 193; and accounts that eliminate belief 30, 149–52; contradictions 32–4; costs of false belief 4, 228–31; degrees of 122, 178; distortion 116–17, 161; doubt/suspicion 185–6, 213; doxastic voluntarism 35–6, 205–7; ethics of 203–9; false belief necessary for self-deception? 51–2; indeterminacy 176–8; sensitivity to rationality and evidence 35–8, 79, 125, 206, 250; *see also* acceptance, biases; dual belief; subdoxastic attitudes

Belief Problem 27, 30

Bermudez, J. 112–13, 163–6

biases: cold and hot biases 14–15, 53, 77, 89, 94–5, 207–8; confirmation bias 11–12, 59, 62, 89, 94–6, 155–6; examples 8–12, 116–17; memory search 156; moral hypocrisy 108–9; motivated irrationality 53–4, 59, 159; natural selection 192–3; self-enhancement 8, 125, 141, 162, 197, 218, 230–6, 239–42, 246; *see also* heuristics

biological accounts: Smith's teleofunctional theory 187–8; Trivers's other-deception theory 188–93; *see also* signaling accounts

biological benefits 243–6; and immunological 244–5; life expectancy 246; sexual 243–4

Bopp, M. 246

Borge, S. 30–1, 114

Bortolotti, L. 125

Bratman, M. 202n3

Brown, J. 231–3, 235, 239, 241

Buss, D. 100

Butler, J. 212–14, 219

character trait 225, 251

Clifford, W. K. 203–5, 223, 224

Clinton, B. 6–7

cognitive load 108–9, 143, 233

Cohen, L. J. 179–81

collective self-deception 200–1, 241–3

conceptual map 73–7, 248–9

consciousness *see* unconsciousness

cost-benefit analysis *see* biological benefits; psychological benefits; social benefits

Darwall, S. 215–16

Davidson, D. 36, 47–50, 55–7, 62–3, 77, 95, 136, 140, 159–60, 163

deception: animal 114–15, 187–8, 253; characterization 52, 63, 115–16; *see also* robust self-deception

Deception Problem 28–9

deflationary accounts: against robust deception 114–19; characterized 85–8; psychological case 94–101; *see also* agential involvement in self-deception; motivationalism

delusions 124–5; *see also* self-delusion

Dennett, D. 36–7, 228–9

Descartes, R. 45–6

DeSteno, D. 108–9, 143

divided minds 29–30, 40–4, 48–50; and functional unit accounts 158–63; intentionalism 144–7; temporally divided minds 163–6; unconsciousness accounts 147–58; *see also* doxastic conflict/tension; dual belief; robust self-deception

Doody, P. 158

doxastic conflict/tension 72, 119–28, 173; and deep conflict 122–3, 177–8, 181–4, 246; shallow conflict 121–2; *see also* divided minds; dual belief; robust self-deception dual belief: attempted empirical demonstrations 102–8; necessary for self-deception 63, 103, 163, 167–8; scattered event treatments 164–6; unnecessary for self-deception 88–9, 149, 167, 171, 217; *see also* divided minds; doxastic conflict/tension; robust self-deception

dual process psychology 15–16, 63–4, 108–10, 251

dynamic problems 34–40; and Mele's treatment 88, 92–3; robust unconscious accounts 153–8; *see also* robust self-deception

eating disorders 219–20

eliminating self-deception 219–21

emotions 58, 112, 128, 250–1; *see also* anxiety-based accounts

enabled self-deception 199–200, 253

escapism 123, 184–5

ethics of self-deception *see* belief, ethics of; responsibility for self-deception

evidence: avoidance 62, 70, 117–18, 150, 154–6, 183, 186; biased search 90; 156; *see also* belief, sensitivity to rationality and evidence

fantasy 182, 221, 240–1

fear 112, 185–6

Fernandez, J. 126, 218–19

Fingarette, H. 82n15

Freud, S. 42–7, 48–50, 58, 66, 73, 87, 95, 159, 232

Friedrich, J. 97–8

Funkhouser, E. 67–8, 70, 117, 121, 124, 126, 154–7, 178, 196

future work 249–52

Gendler, T. 37, 121, 124, 126–7, 181–5

Gur, R. 102–5, 144

Hancock, J. 242

Haselton, M. 99–110

heuristics 12–15, 19, 38; *see also* biases

Hieronymi, P. 206

Holmes, J. 241

Holton, R. 210–11

Hoorens, V. 236–7

Huang, J. 148

Hume, D. 37

hypothesis testing: asymmetric costs 97–100, 118; confidence thresholds 99, 111, 118; error management theory 99–100, 229; PEDMIN 97–101

imagination 79, 181–2, 184; *see also* pretense

implicit attitudes 208, 210–12, 226n3, 226n4

imposed self-deception 198–9

impression management 168, 237–8

intention: candidate intentions for self-deception 56–7; characterized 137–40; contrast with motivation 55, 57; contrast with purposiveness 62, 67–8, 167; deflationary accounts 86–8

intentionalism 47, 54–60; and arguments for 141–4; defined 55; divided minds 144–7; selectivity 113

INDEX

interpersonal deception: degrees of deception 61; as a model of self-deception 26–8; self-deception for the sake of interpersonal deception 188–92

Johnston, M. 59–60, 129–30, 162, 217

Kahneman, D. 12–15, 209
Kant, I. 215

Lazar, A. 58, 60, 65, 79, 83n22, 112, 115, 131, 182
Leontius 41–2
Levy, N. 208, 217–18
Liberman, A. 99
literary examples 5–7, 26–7, 182
Lynch, K. 122–3, 126–7, 178, 184–5

McKay, R. 228–9
Mele, A. 58, 66, 131, 139–40; and against dual belief 107–8, 163–4, 174; difficulties with negative self-deception 110–12; philosophical account of self-deception 88–93; psychological details 93–102; responsibility for self-deception 142–3, 217–18; see also deflationary accounts; doxastic conflict/tension; selectivity problem
metacognition 68, 128, 151; see also reflection; self-knowledge
Mijovic-Prelec, D. 193–5
Minimal Conception 51–4
misbeliefs 228–9
motivationalism: biological motives/purposes 186–90; candidate

motives for self-deception 57–8, 64–71; characterized 54–60; mind-directed motives (desire-to-believe) 66–71, 129, 142, 161; thematic motives/benefits for self-deception 230; world-directed motives 66; see also deflationary accounts
Motivation/Intention Problem 27–9
Murray, S. 241

narcissism 65, 104, 235–7, 239–40
negative self-deception: costs/benefits 235–6, 240; defined 64–5; emotions 132, 161, 186; hypothesis testing accounts 101, 111; intentionalist accounts 141–2; theoretically problematic 65–6, 110–12, 132
Nelkin, D. 66–8, 111, 116, 138
neutral (indifferent or ambivalent) self-deception 70
noble lies 221–2
Noordhof, P. 121, 124

Pascal's wager 6, 36, 117, 207
Paulhus, D. 168
Pears, D. 111, 136, 159–63, 166
philosophical approaches to self-deception 2–5, 251
Pinker, S. 167–8
Plato 40–2, 48–9, 221–2
positive illusions 231–5, 244–5; see also positive self-deception
positive self-deception: costs/benefits 232, 235–6, 245–6; defined 64–6; emotions 112, 186; unifying

with negative self-deception 111, 161; *see also* positive illusions

Prelec, D. 193–5

pretense 79, 181–5; *see also* imagination

process vs. state 71–3, 152, 163, 209

psychological benefits 231–6; and costs of negative self-deception 235–6; goal pursuit 235–6; happiness 233; self-esteem 232; testing for functions 234–5; *see also* positive illusions

psychological disorders 64–5

Quattrone, G. 105–7, 194

Quine, W. V. O. 20, 206

rationality/reason: practical rationality 55–6, 58–9, 138, 182, 184; rationalization 109, 155, 157, 198–9, 208, 213; responsibility for irrationality 216–22; self-deception as a failure of 17–18, 19–20, 48–50, 51–3; *see also* biases; heuristics

reasons for studying self-deception 17–22

reflection 1, 5, 16, 210, 213–14, 250; *see also* metacognition; self-knowledge

repression: Cohen's account 180; Freud's account 42–4, 232; Sartre's critique 45–7; tropistic accounts 60, 162

responsibility for self-deception: conscience 214–16; context relativity 222–5; control 142–3, 207–9; epistemic responsibility 216–22, 252; ethics of belief 204–6; self-knowledge failures 210–16; unconscious biases 208–9; *see also* belief, ethics of; self-knowledge

robust self-deception 117–19, 135–7, 141, 153–8, 162; *see also* agential involvement in self-deception; divided minds; doxastic conflict/tension; dual belief

Sackeim, H. 102–5, 144

Sartre, J. P. 44–7

Schiller, F. 222

Schwitzgebel, E. 176–8

Scott-Kakures, D. 132

selectivity problem 112–14, 141

self-deception skeptics 30–1

self-delusion 124–7, 150–1

self-knowledge: conscious awareness 148–51; responsibility 212–16, 218–19; self-deception as a failure of self-knowledge 5, 19, 151, 194–5, 210–12; self-perception theory 194; as valuable 5; *see also* metacognition; reflection; responsibility for self-deception

signaling accounts: honesty and handicaps 196–7; other-signaling 195–7, 224; self-signaling 193–5

Simon, H. 13, 38

Smith, A. 214

Smith, D. L. 187–8

social benefits 236–43; and costs 239–40; offensive social tactics 237–9; romantic relationships 241–2; spreading self-enhancement 237, 239; *see also* collective

276 INDEX

self-deception; impression
management; signaling accounts,
other-signaling
Sorensen, R. 164–6
static problems 31–4; and
contradictions 32–4; divided minds
144–5, 149–51, 163–6, 189; Mele's
treatment 88; *see also* belief
Stich, S. 173–4, 229
subdoxastic attitudes 173–5; *see also*
belief

Talbott, W. 145–7
Taylor, S. 231–3, 235, 239, 241
thoughts 178–9
Toma, C. 242
Trivers, R. 3, 143–4, 153, 157, 167,
188–92, 195–7, 198, 239, 243–5

Trope, Y. 99
Tversky, A. 12–13, 105–7, 194

unconsciousness 18, 20, 147–8; and
Freud's account 42–4; moderate
unconscious accounts 147–53;
robust unconscious accounts
153–8; unconscious belief 150–1;
unconscious desire 151, 157–8

Valdesolo, P. 108–9, 143
Van Leeuwen, N. 192
voice pitch modulation 158
von Hippel, W. 143–4, 153, 157, 167

weakness of will 48, 78
Williams, B. 35–6, 144
wishful thinking 47, 55–6, 79, 188